A RIBBON AND A STAR

Text by JOHN MONKS, JR.

Drawings by JOHN FALTER

A RIBBON
THE THIRD MARINES

AND A STAR
AT BOUGAINVILLE

ZENGER PUBLISHING CO., INC.
P.O. BOX 9883 • WASHINGTON, D.C. 20015

Copyright, 1945, by

Henry Holt and Company, Inc.

Reprinted 1979, with permission from Holt Rinehart & Winston

ALL RIGHTS RESERVED

Library of Congress Cataloging in Publication Data

Monks, John Cherry.
   A ribbon and a star.

   Reprint of the 1945 ed. published by H. Holt, New York.
   1. World War, 1939-1945--Campaigns--Solomon Islands--Bougainville Island. 2. World War, 1939-1945--Personal narratives, American. 3. Monks, John Cherry. 4. World War, 1939-1945--Regimental histories--United States--Marine Corps. 3d Regiment. 5. United States. Marine Corps. 3d Regiment--History. I. Falter, John Philip, 1910-   II. Title.
D767.98.M6   1979   940.54'26   79-19749
ISBN 0-89201-077-0

PRINTED IN THE UNITED STATES OF AMERICA

Acknowledgment

I ACKNOWLEDGE with pride and affection the efforts of every officer and man in the Third Marine Regiment who helped me to tell this story:

Major John Scott, Captain French Fogle, Captain Bert Simpson, Lieutenant Colonel Sidney McMath, Captain Steve Cibik, Captain Joe Nolan, Major Richard Moss, Warrant Officer George Cannon, Captain Don Baker, Major John Winford, Captain Jack Foley, Lieutenant Gibby Young, Lieutenant Tom Manion, and all the many others who so willingly co-operated, in order that, when their buddies returned to become a part of a new world which they tried to make better, they could be spared the thralldom of answering foolish questions. So that they could toss a copy of their story at the interlocutor and reply:

"Here, Mac, read it. I want a drink. You know any dames?"

And to my good friend, John Falter, who, notwithstanding his great and deserved success, will meet me at any time in any barroom and discuss for hours how we can steal six cents to buy a bag of nails to finish that tree hut.

JOHNNY MONKS

March 1945

A RIBBON AND A STAR

Chapter 1

THE FIRST LINE of boats sped past Torokina and Puruata Islands about one thousand yards offshore at Empress Augusta Bay, Bougainville, British Solomon Islands. Then came those telltale splashes.

"That ours?"

"Hope so!"

Four dive bombers swooped in low and deposited their explosive cargo, but too far inland to help the immediate problem substantially. Murderous fangs of machine-gun fire shot out from the two islands. The first wave of boats sped toward the shore. The second wave was close on its heels. The third wave, fully organized, unwound its rendezvousing circle and started in. The men who were to follow in succeeding boat trips stood by their respective cargo nets and watched the shore. Machine-gunners cast jerky professional glances at the islands, the cape, along the beach, back to the water around the boats. They knew where a trained specialist of the same profession had laid his guns; what kind of target a crowded landing boat made, ducks on a pond, plenty of time to work out ranges, interlocking bands of fire, smother an area with lead. They could almost see the smile on the little Jap's face as he squinted through the sights, caressed the trigger, and waited for that boat to plunge into his beaten zone. And they knew more clearly than anyone else that the little "Son of Heaven," for a while at least, was going to have his day in court. Then came the larger splashes.

In Boat 62, Lieutenants Kirk and Shelton crouched down behind the ramp. Following their example were two squads of Kirk's Platoon, a detachment from Headquarters Company of the First Battalion, and a demolition squad from C Company of the 19th Engineers. Thirty yards offshore. Stand by for a ram. Less than half a minute to go and the boat would plow up on the beach. The ramp would slam down, Kirk and Shelton would tear over the ramp, the men would follow. They'd fan out as they negotiated the last remaining enemy sucker-shot strip of beach and plunge behind some cover. The rest was their pidgin—they knew it by heart: mop up everything left, reorganize, locate the Company C.P., carry out their orders.

If something went wrong with the original plan, they'd ad lib another, but the mission would be accomplished. It was rugged but clearly defined: *Land! Destroy!*

Boat 62, one of the many and typical of all, was a boatload of experts: Kirk, Shelton, McNamara, McAllister, Bagley, Burns, D'Imperio, Smith, Snuffer, Lisecki, Morris, Crocker, Botkins, Birchfield, Masek, Hopkins, Dacey, Fulk, Pastrick, Chandler, Durling, Bailey, Hall, Newport, Johnston, Johnson, Lockhart, Constantino, and others; confident of their leaders, confident of their weapons, confident of themselves. B.A.R.s, Tommy-guns, rifles, carbines, hand grenades, and TNT in the hands of tough, aggressive, fast-thinking men. And now only twenty seconds to go—just twenty-more-luckyseconds. The muzzle velocity of a Japanese 75 mm. gun is 1200 feet per second, and twenty seconds is a long time.

Perhaps to cover up his nervousness, or perhaps to vent his relief at having passed through the hail of machine-gun fire unscarred, the seaman engineer in the boat turned to Sergeant McAllister, who was squatting in the stern, and muttered his pathetically ironic valedictory:

"That's the trouble with you Marines. All those fireworks and wasting all that ammunition—and you probably won't see any Japs for a week!"

The first shell hit the upper starboard corner of the ramp. Pieces of wood and steel flew into the air. The coxswain disappeared.

Lieutenant Kirk wheeled and shouted: "For God's sake, over the side!"

Two more shells followed in rapid succession. The third shell tore through the ramp, detonated against the bulkhead, and exploded in the center of the boat.

"After the first shell hit, the men in the forward part of the boat fell back toward the center as if a big wave had pushed them over," said Sergeant McAllister. "A shell fragment from the second hit me in the left thigh. The boat grounded, and I started over the side. It was an awful mess. Bloody men pulled themselves off the deck and forced themselves over the side. One man had part of his back blown off. Everyone kept hold of his rifle. Some of them only had a half a rifle. The water was up to my chin. As I hit the sand, I looked back and saw that Smith wasn't going to make it; he had a wound in his head. He was one of my boys. I went back, pulled him in, and dragged him behind a coconut log. Then a Jap ran out from one of the slit trenches. He bent over and armed a grenade—hit it against his knee. As he threw it, I hit the deck behind a ridge of sand. Couldn't have been over three inches high, but it was enough. Then I threw a grenade. It seemed to go off in the right place, but I threw another to make sure. I didn't see it kill the Jap, but Hopkins, who was over on my left, said the first one blew the Jap all to hell. Then I got the rest of my squad who were wounded behind the coconut log. All the time snipers were popping away at us. My foot started to hurt, and I pulled off my shoe. There was a big hole where my ankle used to be. I figured it was broken—hadn't noticed it before.

"McNamara said he was going to get the boat off the shore. The ramp was jammed, but that was the only way we could get the wounded back to the ship. I saw him crawl over the side into the boat; he had a bad wound in his hand. A sailor crawled in after him. They got the boat off the beach and started back toward the ship. NcNamara said he and D'Imperio, who was wounded, tried to plug up the big holes in the boat with some of the dead bodies. Then they put life jackets on all the other wounded. The boat

3

sank. Four or five of the wounded were picked up. The rest of my squad who were injured and myself were sent back to the ship three hours later. I checked up. There were twelve killed and fourteen wounded out of the whole boatload. Lieutenant Kirk and Lieutenant Shelton were both killed when the second shell hit."

Flares went up from the left and center sectors of the beach:

"*Landing successful.*"

So far, at least, the Second and Third Battalions were in the clear.

A radio message from the Second Battalion reported: "One man killed by sniper fire. Terrain to rear of beach bad. We are proceeding inland."

Marine and Seabee working parties were sweating in the holds of the transports out in the bay. Boatloads of supplies were racing toward the beach.

"*Condition Red! Enemy aircraft approaching!*"

The ships would have to make a dash for the open water. Suddenly everything seemed to stop. A few seconds for thinking. Then once more the pause before the execution of a prearranged plan exploded into the red heat of activity.

"*Man all sea details!*"

The transition was made with speed and efficiency. An untrained man thinks while he tries to perform; the veteran makes it two separate processes. There was no confusion. One operation momentarily ceased, then blended with the same intensity into another. There is no substitute for experience. Men who know their job tell other men what to do. Before the command is finished, trained men are in action. Not once. Every time. Only with dive bombers they do it faster. The small boats out in the bay dispersed and zigzagged crazily about in the water while the occupants watched the ships get under way. One of the transports had a pack howitzer dangling incongruously over its side. As the transports snaked away from the island, the bogeys swooped in low through the pass in the mountains and strafed the beach. Others glided out of the sun and dove toward the ships. The same destroyers that had previously been "snapping in" at the enemy shore installations were "firing for record" now. Three planes in quick succession burst into flames and spiraled into the sea. Marine fighter pilots with speed and deadly accuracy drove the attackers from the ships' area, then tailed the getaway boys and poured on the lead. Only a scant few escaped with the news that all was not well for Tojo's martyrs at Empress Augusta Bay.

The ships returned.

"Secure all sea details!"

"Unload ship!"

Again the transition. Again the same red-hot activity, more intense than ever. Time lost . . . couldn't be helped . . . tell the sun about it . . . today we need more daylight . . . tough job ahead . . . gotta work faster. They did.

Boatloads of wounded were hoisted aboard and hustled into ready and waiting sick bays. One boy, both legs blown off above the knees, lay on a stretcher grinning and smoking a cigarette.

"How do you feel, son?"

"Like a stuck pig, Doc—ha-ha-ha!"

Thirty minutes later he was dead. He was still grinning.

A message was received from the First Battalion: "Old Glory flies on Torokina."

Captain Gordon Warner had taken an American flag ashore with him, tied it to a coconut tree, and shouted in Japanese: "Come on, you slimy bastards! Come and get it!" Melodramatic, perhaps, but this was a melodramatic morning.

Another message from the First Battalion: "C Company totally lost. Fifty per cent of the Battalion wiped out."

A short time later another from the same unit: "All assault troops ashore. Contact not made between companies. Will give position as soon as possible. Need ammo of all calibers."

So far, the actual landing was two-thirds a success; that is, two-thirds of the beach area had been secured. The Second and Third Battalions had struck little or no resistance on the beach and were proceeding inland.

When the first waves from the Second and Third Battalions had hit the beach a few remaining snipers peppered away in one last token of welcome, then dove into the jungle and disappeared. After the men had cleared the beach, it took a while longer for each unit to make certain it was in its right spot. For each unit had orders to proceed inland on a definite compass azimuth, keeping contact at all times with the unit on its right and left. The men of the Third had trudged too many weary miles not to know that, when you start off on a compass course with the intention of ending up in the right place, you had better save yourself a million headaches by getting started right first. During this period of reorganization and establishing contact to the flanks, the first wave of Jap planes swooped in from the pass through the ridge and strafed the terrain to the rear of the beach. Again luck was with the Third Marines: the planes had swarmed in between waves, and there was no one on the beach.

They made four different runs along the entire length of the beachhead. Our own planes had their hands full protecting the transports. The strafing was intense, and the casualties would have been numerous if the Japs hadn't overestimated our speed in reorganizing and negotiating the jungle swamp. The bullets spattered harmlessly in the mud forty yards ahead of any of the troops.

The problem of landing in a succeeding wave is even tougher. You'd better find the right spot or you'll really be in business for yourself. Lieutenant Stets Holmes of G Company had the solution. He landed in the first wave, found that he was in the right place, then started into the jungle; but before leaving the beach he put up a sign that he and his Gunnery Sergeant had prepared the night before. Bert Simpson, his company commander, landed in the next wave five minutes later but was put ashore in the wrong place. Moving quickly down the beach, trying to estimate the distance from a landmark they had selected, he spotted a large white sign hanging on a bush at the edge of the jungle—and his troubles were over. For he read:

WELCOME TO BOUGAINVILLE.
WE WENT THIS WAY, BERT.
STETS

Men can be told innumerable times to crouch low in the landing boat and by no means to stick their heads above the gunwale. But curiosity is a powerful urge, and some of them just can't seem to resist the temptation to take a look at the shooting. But the referee of a fire fight is not immune, even though he feels down deep in his heart that these particular bullets haven't got his name on them. Some bullets never "get the word," and some very good gunners are lousy spellers. Stojek was crouching down low in one of the early wave landing boats. Maybe he was cramped and wanted to change his position, or maybe he thought he'd like to take a peek; anyhow, his head appeared for an instant above the boat's gunwale. A bullet tore through the front part of his helmet and grazed his forehead. That's all, brother—a hint's a hint. He plunged down into the bottom of the boat so fast he would have made an Arab blush with shame.

One of his buddies, seeing the incident, called after him, "Hey, Stojek, you can't see anything down there."

"*They* can't see *me* down here, either!" was his reply. True, that bullet which had missed by inches didn't have his name, but it sure had some big initials on it.

A company under the command of Bill Barnatt from the Third Raider Battalion had hit Puruata Island, the larger of the two islands in the bay, and the men were working their way through the heavy underbrush combing snipers out of trees and destroying pillboxes. No one had any idea of the strength of the force holding this defensive position, but the island was in a strategic spot and had to be neutralized. Not long after this rugged bunch of Raiders landed, the cross fire from the well-entrenched machine-gunners which had rained a gauntlet of fire out on the bay and along the beach subsided. Those same machine-gunners were now fighting for their own skins, and their price on the open market had fallen to an all-time low. They were trapped by a swarm of deadly hornets.

We were proud of these Raiders—who wouldn't be? But we were especially proud because many of their officers and men had come out of the Third Regiment when the Third Raiders had been organized on Samoa. And they really did a job. All that day, that night, and part of the next day they combed the island . . . fire power against fire power, speed and skill and perfect teamwork against prepared defensive positions.

One Raider flushed a Jap and fought a duel with him across the island. "Let him go," shouted the Raider to his buddies. "This son-of-a-bitch is mine!" The Jap would fire and retreat. The Raider would fire, weave off to one flank, and pursue. It was almost like a city gun-fight, like Cops and Robbers—except that, in the heavy underbrush, one adversary gets only a fleeting glimpse of the other, and fights by instinct and sound and sensing what the other man is going to do, snapshooting at an instantaneous target—where he was —then where he ought to be. Changing position, weaving back and forth through the brush, exposing himself just long enough to shoot, then working himself forward, keeping low, running as the Nip tries to get away, crawling into a position to fire as the Nip changes his tactics and tries to hide and ambush. . . . The Jap made the beach, threw down his rifle, and jumped into the water.

"I don't know where in the hell he thought he was going," the Raider said after it was all over. "I was too God-damn mad to shoot him. I threw down my gun and helmet, took a good run, and dove in after him. The little bastard was scared to death. I grabbed him by the neck and pulled him toward the beach. That was the hardest part—getting him back on solid ground. I couldn't get him up on the beach but went to work on him in the shallow water. Then I dragged him up on the sand and kicked his head apart. The slimy bastard. I'd been chasing him for over an hour."

By noon the next day the sound of firing on Puruata Island had ceased. There weren't any prisoners.

The Second Raider Battalion had landed to the left of the First Battalion. This was another hot spot with well-constructed bunkers. Lieutenant Colonel Joseph P. McCaffery, the Commanding Officer, had gone in with the first wave.

No better-known or more widely loved man ever wore a Marine Corps uniform than "Little Joe." He had been one of the finest quarterbacks on any Marine Corps football team. He had been with the Eighth Regiment in Samoa. When a battalion had lost its commander on Guadalcanal, "Little Joe," then a Major, had been there to take over and assume command. He had led them through the darkness and brought them safely out. He had been spot-promoted to a Lieutenant Colonel for his brilliant leadership. In the Munda-Rendova campaign he had made the long fifteen-mile trek through a mangrove swamp with the Raiders and wiped out a Japanese garrison, which had been caught completely by surprise. Back in New Zealand, he had flown out to take command of another new outfit, the Second Raiders. A great wit, a marvelous story-teller, a great companion, and an inspiring man, he was adored by all.

The Colonel and his party had cleared the beach and were moving along the edge of the swamp into position. Suddenly the advance was held up by machine-gun fire from a well-concealed bunker just off the beach.

"What's the trouble?" asked the Colonel.

"There's a machine-gun down there covering the beach," replied a Marine who had worked his way back to the group.

"Then we've got to knock it out. Got to keep moving. Let's go!"

The Colonel and his headquarters party started forward. A few moments later there was a burst of machine-gun fire; four rounds struck the Colonel in the chest. A corpsman went to work immediately, and the Battalion surgeon rushed to his aid. Everything was done to check the bleeding and get the Colonel into condition to be rushed back to the ship. Since a chest wound of this magnitude is always fatal, everyone near him worked frantically. The Colonel was carefully carried to a landing boat—still conscious, his pain

dulled by morphine. He gave his last instructions to his Executive Officer and turned over his command.

The landing boat raced back to the transport, and there the Colonel was rushed to the sick bay. Three doctors worked rapidly and with great care to replace the tremendous loss of blood. But four bullets through the lungs are just too many, and the Catholic Chaplain was summoned. Still conscious but rapidly growing weaker, the Colonel prayed with the good Father. When the last rites were finished, this great Marine smiled up at the Chaplain and whispered: "Well—it's been a short war. . . ."

That morning the Marine Corps suffered a great loss. "Little Joe"—brilliant officer, kind and loyal friend, magnificent, courageous hero, and, to all who ever met him, talked with him, fought with him, the most wonderful guy—"Little Joe" had died.

Chapter 2

THE RIGHT-HAND SECTOR of the beachhead, which included Point Torokina, had turned out to be the hot spot. This had been anticipated. Evidence of a few recently constructed installations and of a 200-foot trench extending generally east from the Point had shown clearly on aerial photographs. But even the best aerial photographs fail to reveal pillboxes, connecting trenches, and foxholes naturally camouflaged by the overhead cover of coconut trees and jungle growth. Naval gunfire and dive bombing had barely scarred the terrain. There was no longer any doubt as to the situation confronting the First Battalion. They had landed in the face of machine-gun, artillery, and mortar fire, and now had a knock-down-drag-out fight on their hands. How badly they had been hit, what strength remained, and how well this strength was under control was still unknown when Major Sidney McMath—"The Traveler"—Regimental Operations Officer, spark-plug, carburetor, and dynamo of the Third, rushed to this sector.

Another message arrived from the First Battalion:

"Bn C.O. and Bn 3 not yet seen on the beach. Believed lost. Co. C badly damaged. Mortar fire. Co. A meeting stiff opposition to left flank and left front. No reports from Co's C or B."

The Battalion commander, Major Mason, had been severely wounded. Major Steve Brody, Battalion Executive Officer, and Major Chuck Bailey, Battalion Operations Officer, were in command. B Company had landed on the left flank as planned and had proceeded inland. But A Company had been put ashore 150 yards too far to the left, and Company C and Headquarters Com-

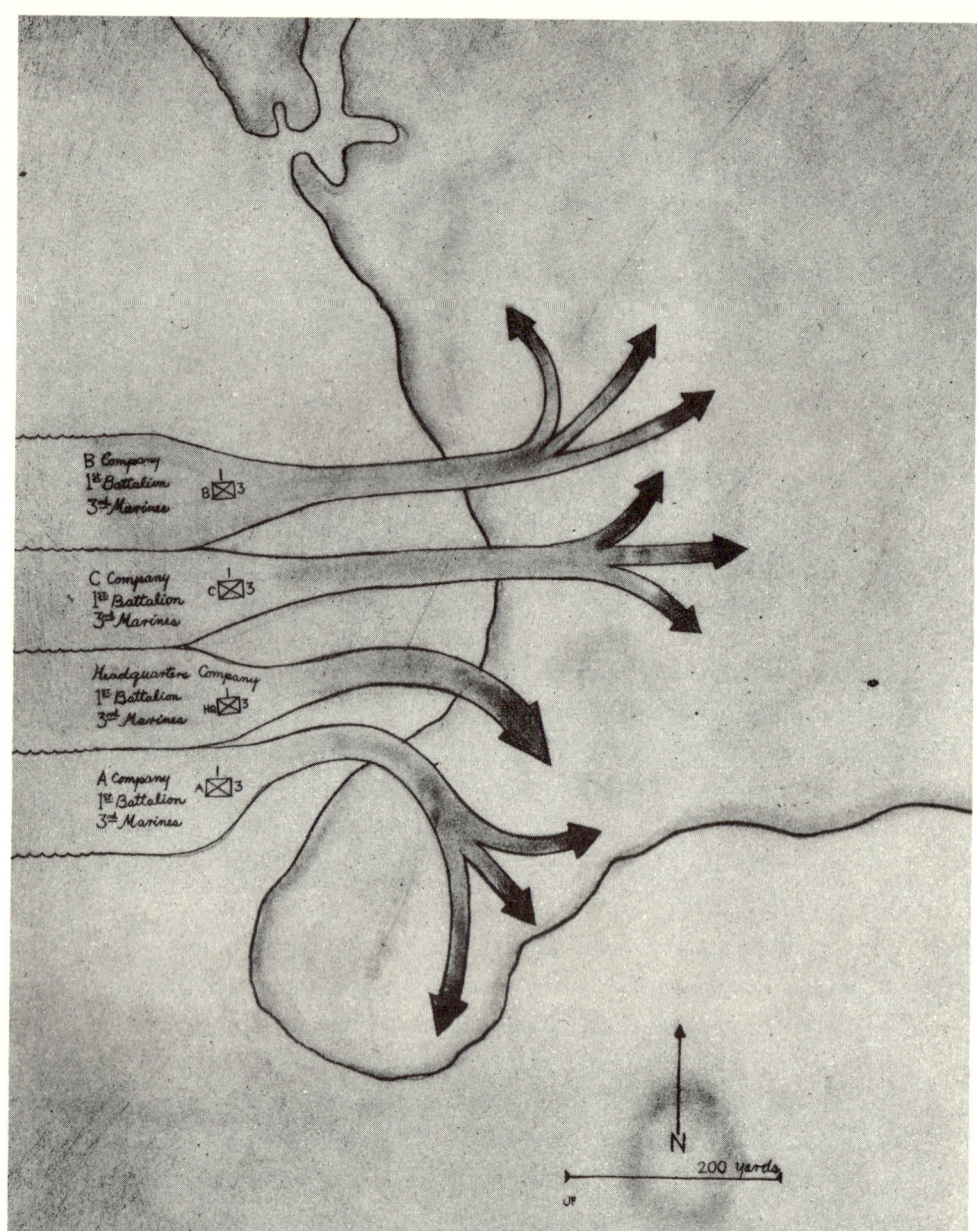

The original landing plan of 1st Battalion on Cape Torokina D day

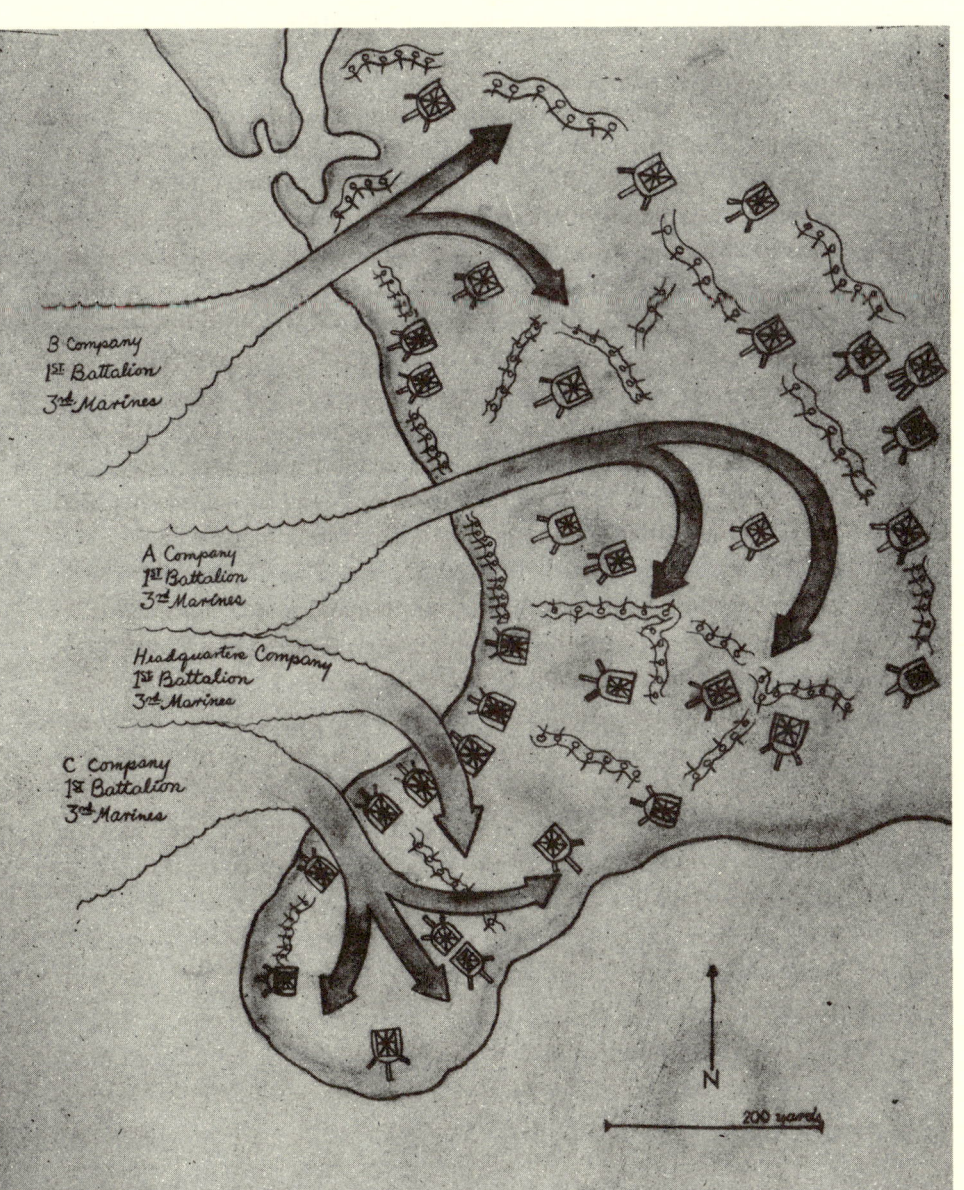

Actual landing of 1st Battalion on Cape Torokina D day

pany had landed about the same distance to the right of A Company. A Company had been originally ordered to sweep down to the right towards the Point. This now put C Company and Headquarters Company in the center of a hot spot. They faced the Jap's defenses on their direct front; their right flank was exposed to the Jap defenses on the Point; and, if A Company carried out its original assignment, their left flank was exposed to friendly fire. A Company organized its attack, but it wasn't going to "sweep" anywhere just yet. Companies just don't land, organize, and attack. It's not quite that simple, particularly when they land on a beach defended by well-built log bunkers, covered with sand, twenty feet from the water's edge, with some of their platoons landing at unscheduled places, and with company commanders, platoon leaders, and sergeants trying to tally their strength, establish liaison with their superiors, and fight for survival in the midst of a hornets' nest. The Jap defenses in this sector were well organized along both sides of the Point, extending along the shore to the right and left of the Point and in depth for 500 to 1000 yards inland. Not only did A Company face a complexity of bunkers interwoven by communications trenches to its now immediate front, but its flank was completely exposed to the fire of machine-guns and knee mortars from the bunkers and slit trenches to its left. Lieutenant Rouse was ordered to take his platoon and knock out this resistance on the left. The remainder of the company would have to do a handmade job on the bunkers ahead of them before they could continue with their mission.

The Jap 75 was still in action and taking its toll.

"We've got to knock out that big gun or it'll kill every Goddamn body," yelled Sergeant Owens.

He started off, followed by Willie Smith, Lucky Worbitz, and Weisner. Smith covered them with his B.A.R. (Browning automatic rifle), while the other two wormed their way through the fire toward the bunker. Inching his way along, Owens managed to get within ten feet of the bunker. He tossed a grenade; it landed just outside the entrance. A Jap dashed out, followed by three others.

Owens yelled, "There they go—let's get the bastards!"

He threw another grenade. This time it landed inside the bunker. Then Owens started after the fleeing Japs.

"As we got up, a shower of grenades came in on us," Worbitz said later. "I saw Owens go down. Another grenade landed right in the middle of us, and the concussion knocked me cold."

Smith had a leg full of shrapnel, but his B.A.R. had killed a Jap officer, in whose dispatch case was a complete sketch of the defenses of the Bay. Owens was dead, but his last grenade had done the job: there was a shell in the chamber of the 75, but none left to pull the lanyard. The remaining occupants of the bunker, lying near the gun, were all *good* Japs . . . very dead.

The heat was on. Individual jobs by individual groups. B.A.R. men would pin a bunker down by fire while two or three others would work their way through machine-gun and sniper fire towards the entrance in the rear of a bunker and knock it out with hand grenades. Two men crouching behind a log were frantically field-stripping two B.A.R.s in an effort to get one of them to work. Peep-sight Jones would crawl up to a bunker, thrust his carbine in through a firing slit, and yell, "Come out, you bastards, or stay inside! I'll get you either way."

Overholser took a bead on a pillbox, hoping to knock it out with an antitank grenade, and a Jap bullet passed through his launcher. Elza, the stowaway, kept shouting, "Reveille, you bastards! Rise and shine!" And then he'd squeeze one off on a fleeing Jap.

Over on the left flank, Rouse's platoon was operating on a series of pillboxes laid along both sides of the trail leading from the beach. Klemko stuttered to his squad leader, "Wh-wh-what's going on h-h-here? Wh-why d-d-don't you go up and find wh-wh-what the d-d-dope is?"

"Don't you know there's a war goin' on?" answered Buck, the assistant B.A.R. man.

And Whetford, whom everybody used to ride about his big nose ("You'll get hit in the beak, sure as hell. How could they

miss?"), was holding his nose, and blood oozed out between his fingers.

Sergeant McEvoy, tough and always ready for a scrap, was a fighting Irisher whom everybody loved, a real Marine, who worshiped his Corps. Left over in a cadre when the Fifth Marines shoved off, he had been with the Third since the day of its birth. He was an old-timer and a perfectionist. When things went wrong he would harp on the prowess of the men in the Fifth. But before the landing he finally conceded that the Third was a hot outfit and knew its job.

"The day before we landed we were sitting up on deck talking it over," Pappy Morris, a buddy of long standing, relates. "McEvoy talked about tomorrow as just another ball-game. After all the training we'd been through, he was anxious to get into battle. We kidded him about not being able to go in with the first wave and having to wait for the second, but he made a bet that he'd beat me in. We talked about how he'd act under fire. You didn't have to worry about McEvoy. He'd never even heard about being scared. At the same time he seemed to have a premonition. 'It'll be just my luck, after all this training, to get it in the first hour of the battle.' "

He went to church with another buddy, the day before we landed, and stayed for the Rosary. "This'll be my last chance," he told Thornton.

As platoon guide he was moving up with the reserve squad behind the two squads in assault. He crawled up to Lieutenant Rouse and begged not to be left back there. Couldn't he take somebody's place and get into the fight? Rouse told him he'd get his chance but right now he was needed where he was. As he started back, Sergeant Wilson was hit in the shoulder and had to be sent back to the aid station; and McEvoy jumped at the chance to take his place. Now Rouse really needed him up front. Three minutes later he threw a grenade; it did the job. Then he raised his head, slowly searching for another target, and a sniper shot him through the center of the forehead. The platoon had been ashore just about an hour.

Similar acts of heroism, skill, self-sacrifice, determination, and slaughter were going on throughout the entire sector—so many, in fact, that it is virtually impossible to record them. To tell a few at the risk of neglecting others is the best that anyone can do. Many a feat of bravery went totally unobserved. Often the smile of satisfaction on a sweating Marine's face would be the only living record of an act "beyond the line of duty." That same Marine, the night before, had lain on his bunk in the steaming hold of a transport, and he'd done a lot of thinking. From Boot camp to D-plus-one-day, he'd found the answer to many questions, but there still remained one unknown: how would he act under fire? On the morning of November 1, 1943, every man in and attached to the First Battalion, Third Marines, took the bath of lead and blood—and every one of them learned the answer.

Captain Shorty Vogel landed with what was left of his company about halfway down on the western side of the Point. The WELCOME mat was definitely not out on the doorstep. Lieutenant Mills, with the first platoon on the right, was in pretty good shape. Lieutenant Crosswell had scattered units from the second platoon. Lieutenant Harvey, after he had gathered together all the survivors from the boats that had been hit by the Jap fieldpiece, could account for fourteen or fifteen men. The mortar platoon was immediately transformed into a platoon of riflemen, and a short time later his Gunnery Sergeant with an unloading detail made up of riflemen, engineers, and Seabees, landed on the beach. Even to attempt to unload supplies under the hail of machine-gun, mortar, hand-grenade, and rifle fire on this section of the beach, the most heavily defended of the entire beachhead, would have been suicide. So this heterogeneous group, together with Gunner Slug Marvin, a Jap-hater of long standing, and his detail of engineers, were immediately commandeered for combat. Mills had in his platoon a number of green replacements. One or two of them kept raising their heads high above the ground in a most unmilitary manner, trying to locate the source of the Jap fire. McIntosh, still carrying bruises from hitting the deck in training, tired of this amateur display and appointed himself their Big Brother. "Listen, you damn fools," he barked; "there's people out there with firearms. They're going to kill you if you don't keep your God-damned heads down!"

Five hours later these same replacements—those who were still alive—were no longer green; in those five hours they had received many months' training.

Shorty Vogel, in addition to being a Company commander, had to be his own executive officer, signal officer, and runner; a spare officer, Lieutenant Shelton, assigned to him for just such an emergency, had been killed before landing. Head-up platoon leaders, smart noncoms, dynamic, brave, aggressive men in groups cut off from one another, maintained separate bases of fire, checked and changed directions when friendly units passed momentarily in front of them, and worked out their own rapid estimates of the situation. Outflanking pillbox after pillbox, they drove the Japs from their positions or trapped them inside, then blew the entombed to bits with hand grenades and TNT. They encircled fire lanes, tied down snipers from one flank, eradicated them with bursts of a B.A.R. from the other, completely disrupting the enemy's defense. And, once disrupted, he was never allowed to get set again and reorganize in supplementary positions. The few scattered Nips who remained tried to escape by dashing for the only remaining avenue of withdrawal, down the beach on the west side of the Cape.

While Shorty's men were ripping their way across the neck of the Cape, Major McMath had been given a picture of the new situation. In the Battalion C.P., twenty yards to the rear of the present front lines, Major McMath and Major Bailey quickly drew up a new but equally effective plan for resuming the advance to the day's final objective and for the defense against enemy counterattack, and orders were dispatched.

Shorty reorganized and pushed on down the coconut grove parallel to the beach, while B Company fought its way to the grove and cut off the Nip's retreat through the swamp on the left flank.

Captain Quillici, with what he had left of two platoons of A Company, pushed through to the beach west of the Cape. Lieutenant Rouse's platoon cleaned out the bunkers in its sector and then pushed through to rejoin A Company. A Company from the Third Raiders had hit the seaward end of the Cape and had tied down two large bunkers. Two half-tracks from the Regimental Weapons Company were dispatched to help destroy them. Both bunkers, filled with trapped Nips, were blown apart by the deadly fire of ten 75-mm. shells at a range of less than a hundred yards.

The events of the day are voluminous. Captain Big Tom Heaton took enough time out to show the hole in his helmet from a Jap bullet which spun him around but failed to penetrate past the inner lining. Captain Jake Mayer, operating with a crew of demolition men, tells how the drawl of a sharp-eyed private saved him from greeting his Maker: "You better roll over, Jake—you're in a fire lane."

Before the sentence was finished a burst of Japanese machine-gun fire ripped down the fire lane . . . but Jake was still rolling.

Tony Fabino of C Company came face to face with a Jap private who jumped out of a communication trench alongside one of the bunkers. The Emperor's terrified stooge jumped to his feet, dropped his rifle, and threw his hands in the air.

During a brief period of reorganization, a private called over to Shorty Vogel:

"Here's one, Shorty . . . he's only wounded."

Shorty, with about four thousand other things to think about at the moment, hurriedly replied, "O. K. . . . strip him and bring him in. We might need a prisoner."

By late afternoon the right flank of the beachhead was firmly in our hands. The two companies moving down the grove had cleaned out everything but an occasional sniper for a distance of 700 yards and were setting up a hasty defense. A Company was dug in in an organized beach defense. The Battalion C.P., functioning expertly behind the two forward companies, was in direct 'phone communication with the Regiment. E Company from the Second

Battalion, exhausted after a grueling day of unloading but answering the call with a dogged determination and willingness to support their buddies in the First Battalion in the event of a counterattack that night, were moving down the beach toward the Cape.

Chief Ballard, stripped to the waist, with his pistol belt draped on the bias over his bulging midriff, paced back and forth in the collecting station on the beach covering up the shock cases, feeding them hot coffee, and sorting out the wounded who were to be evacuated before the transports pulled away at dark from those less severely injured who were to be transferred to the field hospital. His fearless, life-saving band of corpsmen continued to administer morphine and blood plasma as they located the wounded and dragged them in.

Dr. Art Willets and Dr. Sam Elmore, the Battalion surgeons, had been working under fire since early morning. In the late afternoon, still kidding each other, Art would remind Sam of the delectable dishes Sam had left behind in Antoine's and Arnaud's in New Orleans. Sam would counter with the colorful description of a glass of Sparkling Burgundy or a beaker of rare prohibition corn.

Chaplain Father Kempker and Chaplain Glyn Jones had been on the Cape during all of the fighting, comforting the wounded, administering the last rites to the dying, and now, as evening drew near, in a small plot of ground, later to become a picturesque little cemetery of white crosses at one end of the fighter strip overlooking the sea, these two fine and highly respected officers were putting away to rest the brave and honored men of the Third Marines who had fallen and died alongside their buddies.

A drizzling rain developing into a typical tropical downpour set in towards the middle of the afternoon and, as evening approached, the men, weary and wet, set up their defensive positions, dug their foxholes in the mud, searched through their muddy dungarees for one remaining dry cigarette, then settled down to wait for what might come.

Just what had the First Battalion of the Third Marines accomplished? "Let's look at the record!"

They had landed on a heavily defended beach under fire. An amphibious operation on a hostile shore is a difficult military operation. It must be thoroughly planned, and then executed in strict adherence to the plan. The timing must be perfect. There are thousands of details, and each single detail is tremendously important. History is full of tragic examples of amphibious operations that have failed, and of others that have succeeded only at terrific cost. And unless one has at his command—as he never has— an inexhaustible supply of equally well-trained reserves ready for immediate commitment, a costly victory may ultimately develop into a costly failure. The element of control alone will put additional gray hairs on the head of the most seasoned commander. For, once that assault wave crosses the Line of Departure, there's no turning back. From the time the boats come within range until they hit the beach, until the men have dashed across that strip of sand and have established some sort of unit integrity, they are at the mercy of the shore gunners. And shore gunners have no mercy.

The early messages received from the First Battalion had revealed that they had suffered from the initial shock and confusion of "first blood." Every outfit does, and this one was no exception. But later messages indicated that it had quickly recovered from this shock, and subsequent events proved that it had successfully emerged from its initial confusion. Success became a reality because it had young, intelligent company commanders who lived up to the letter of the great responsibility of being a company commander in the Marine Corps; because it had platoon leaders who were able to act on their own initiative; because it had experienced noncommissioned officers, not of the "now in the old Marine Corps" school, but men who had worked diligently to "know the book" and then had adapted their knowledge to a particular kind of enemy and a particular type of terrain; and finally, but most important of all, because the First Battalion was made up of men thoroughly trained in the fundamentals of fighting as individuals and as a team. From the experience of this rugged training, they knew they were the best-schooled jungle-fighting regiment in the Corps. Their attitude toward the Jap as a fighting man was one of utter contempt; and, with an overwhelming desire to "close with the enemy," smoke him out, hack him to pieces, blot this miserable malignant parasite from the earth, they swarmed over, around, and behind him like a pack of vicious jackals.

Before dark they had cleaned out by hand nineteen Japanese bunkers and pillboxes, had killed over two hundred Japs and driven the rest out of their organized defenses, had captured all the enemy's supplies in this sector, had pushed through seven hundred yards to the first day's objective, and had reorganized for an enemy counterattack. The First Battalion—approximately one-third of the Third Combat Team, ably supported by units of the Second and Third Raider Battalions—had drawn first blood. It had had approximately fifty men killed or missing and twice as many wounded. Lieutenant Colonel Spike Mason had been wounded and evacuated during the early part of the fighting. His executive officer, Major Steve Brody, and Major Chuck Bailey, the Battalion's operation officer, had taken over. Experienced men had fought side by side in the toughest of all fighting—hand-to-hand combat, grenade against grenade, rifle against rifle, knife against knife. They had destroyed all enemy resistance and fought for every inch of the ground that was soon to become the site of important "military installations." It had been a cruel, tough day—a sad day. Good men—wonderful buddies—proud and honorable Americans, had lived and fought and died. But they had accomplished their objective.

Chapter 3

THE BOUGAINVILLE CAMPAIGN was a well-planned, daring operation—a real surprise job. During its conception the gentlemen of the upper deck took full advantage of two important battle factors: first, terrain; second, the Jap's ego, his propensity to underestimate the Marines' ability to acclimate themselves to the most torturous combat conditions, and equally to underestimate that magnificent combination of professional skill and love of achievement which characterizes the American Seabees.

Major General Barrett, the Corps commander, died during the final critical stage of the planning operation. Major General Vandegrift and his brilliant Chief of Staff, Colonel Gerald Thomas, were on their way back to the States to receive a grateful nation's highest honors. General Vandegrift and Colonel Thomas had planned and executed the successful Guadalcanal campaign. The Japs will never forget that licking. The General and the Colonel were flown immediately back to Corps Headquarters in the Pacific, rolled up their sleeves, and went to work. Certain factors in the situation that suddenly developed in the final days before the scheduled jump-off necessitated a replanning of the Bougainville operation. The Marine Corps' first team made the deadline. On D-day General Vandegrift was aboard one of the transports that sailed into Empress Augusta Bay, and remained in command until the success of the operation was assured.

Up to this time, our offensive strategy in the Pacific theater had been to land on an island held by the Japs, destroy the enemy, capture his airfield, reconstruct the area for a new Base, and de-

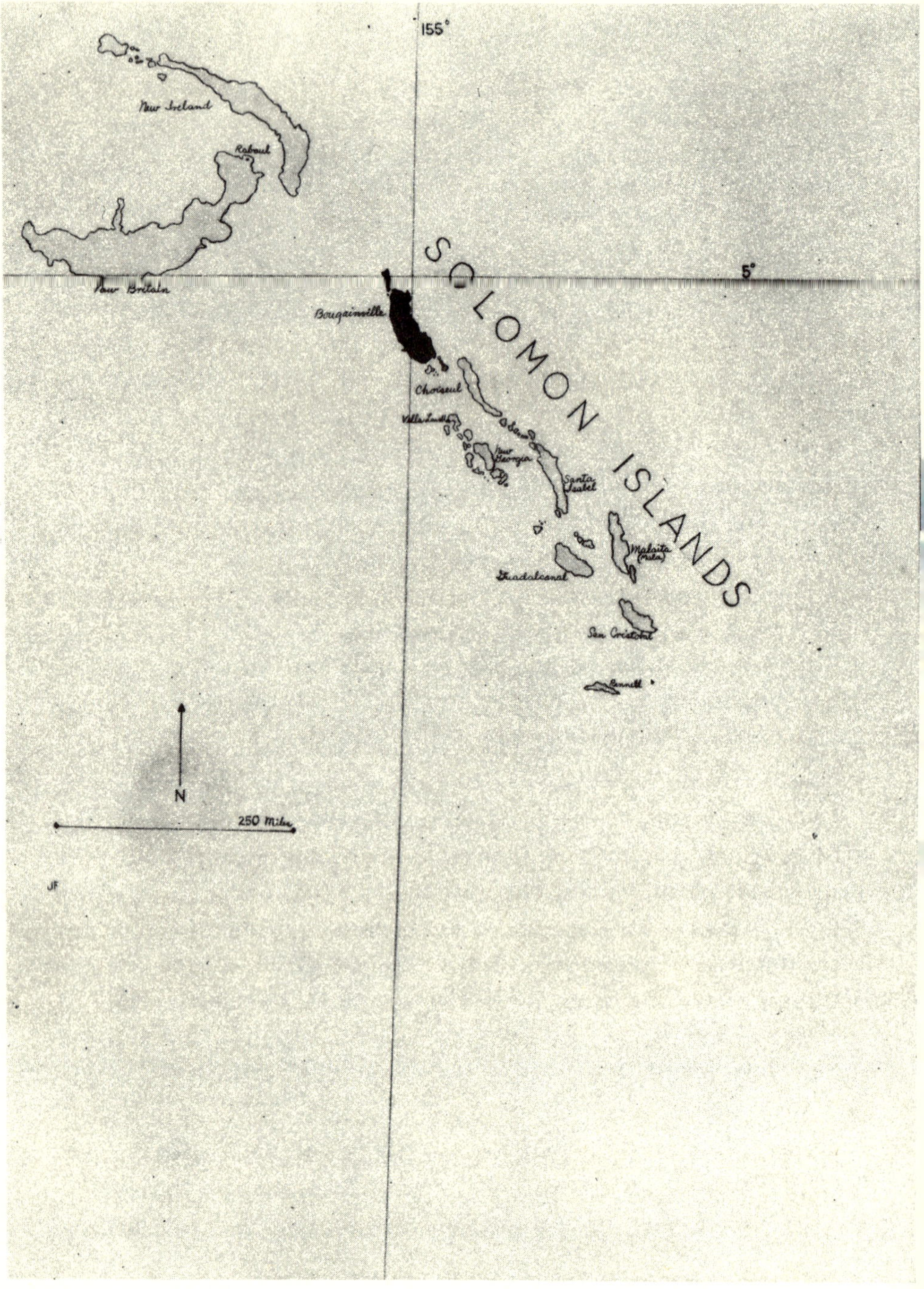

155°
New Ireland
Rabaul
New Britain
5°
SOLOMON ISLANDS
Bougainville
Choiseul
Santa Isabel
Malaita
Guadalcanal
San Cristobal
N
250 Miles
JF

fend it against counter air, amphibious, and land attack. The difficult and successful Guadalcanal, Russell Islands, Munda, and Vella Lavella campaigns had all followed this same general pattern. The Japs were overfamiliar with this type of operation and were reconstructing their shore, antiaircraft, and land defenses accordingly. Each succeeding campaign had met stronger defenses and greater opposition.

Rabaul, with its large harbor, was the Japanese key point of his Solomons defense area. Rabaul would event ally have to be knocked out, but Rabaul was a long way from our northernmost bases, and there were formidable steppingstones ahead, all of them being reinforced with additional airfields, shore guns, and land troops.

The island of Bougainville was one of these steppingstones. Its two main defensive strong points were the Kahili-Shortland area, with its large, well-constructed airfields and land force of approximately fifteen thousand troops, on the southeastern end of the island; and the Buka area with airfields and approximately twenty thousand troops, on the northwest end. Along the northern coast of Bougainville, most of which was rich, dry, cultivated land spotted with large coconut plantations, the Japs had additional garrisons of troops and good shore defenses at any logical landing spot. The Kieta and Numa Numa area, about halfway up the northern coast, contained one of these garrisons of about twenty-five hundred troops. An excellent vehicular road connecting the garrisons along this coast extended the full length of the island. Another road from the Kahili area extended along the southern coast for about thirty miles, supplying a garrison of nine thousand troops at the Buin and Gazelle Bay areas. Here the road terminated.

Typical of most of the islands in the Solomons group, Bougainville has a ridge running through the center for the entire length of the island. This ridge, with an active volcano in the central part of the island, rises in some spots to a height of ten thousand feet. Generally speaking, the terrain from the foot of the ridge to the sea and extending along the entire length of the southern coast is a

155°
5°
BUKAI IS.
Bukai Passage
BOUGAINVILLE
Numa Numa Harbor
Laruma River
Koromokina River
Cibike Ridge
Piva River
Torokina River
Volcano
Empress Augusta Bay
Cape Torokina
ISLAND
Gazelle Bay
Buin Area
Kahili Airdrome
N
20 Miles
JF

low, dense, jungle swamp. The area bordered by the Laruma River on the west and the Torokina River on the east overlooking Empress Augusta Bay was right in the center of this malarial wasteland.

Cape Torokina, jutting out into the bay, was populated by a garrison of approximately one thousand men. It could be supplied by boat from any of the other Jap bases—by carrying parties moving along the beach from Gazelle Bay, along the beach from Buka or along the Numa Numa trail. This trail extended from the Cape through the jungle to a wide gap in the ridge, then through the gap to the garrison and the good supply point at Numa Numa on the northern coast. The water in the bay is deep enough for transports and freighters. There is no protecting coral reef, but two islands, Torokina and Puruata, are situated strategically a thousand yards offshore. These two islands, together with the flanking protection of the Cape on the east side of the bay, provided excellent defensive hurdles against landing craft. The bay and surrounding area could be defended from the air by the Japs' fields at Kahili fifty-five miles to the east, from their fields at Buka sixty miles to the northwest, and from their main base at Rabaul only 210 air miles away. Our nearest land-based aircraft were at Munda, a distance of 180 air miles.

The Japs considered that it would be most illogical for us to attempt a landing in any force on either the Kahili or the Buka base, each of them over 70 miles away, a veritable nightmare. Even if it were possible to construct roads through the deep jungle swamp, it would take months of highly professional skill and arduous labor. Kahili and Buka were already heavily insured against overland attack, as well as against an assault from the sea. By the time a land force had beaten its brains out in the jungle, either or both of these bases could be reinforced to the point where such quixotism would result only in the wasteful expenditure of the limited trained troops in the Pacific.

The Japs were right in believing that an amphibious operation at Empress Augusta Bay for the purpose of future land operations against Kahili and Buka was illogical. They had allowed themselves to become accustomed to the general pattern of our previous island-to-island offensive tactics. But when they failed to accept the possibility that a landing might be effected to establish a beachhead for the construction of vital military installations that could be used to cut off their large base at Kahili, and in conjunction with future flanking moves to neutralize Buka and eventually Rabaul, they once more underestimated the imaginative minds of our expert Naval strategists, the striking, aggressive toughness of the United States Marines, and the brilliant engineering and construction power of the Seabees (United States Naval Construction Battalions). Underestimating the enemy is a grievous fault. . . .

In the first week of October, the D-day landing force of the Third Marine Division and some companies of a Raider regiment, plus two Seabee battalions and miscellaneous units attached to the Corps headquarters, embarked from a staging base and sailed south. For two and a half weeks we lay off an island and conducted full-scale dress rehearsals of the D-day operation. On two separate occasions all of the transports were unloaded, and then reloaded. Landing schedules were drawn up; the troops went over the side just as they had many times before; the transports were "strafed by 'enemy' aircraft"; all recently acquired weapons were tested and calibrated; and casualties were declared, and then evacuated from stations on the beach and hoisted back on the transports. Each unloading party and shore party tried to break all previous records. All the rough spots were smoothed out; no detail was overlooked. Every evening the ward rooms were jammed with the various staffs ironing out kinks, making changes wherever necessary in the D-day plans. Hour after hour they studied the aerial photographs of the enemy terrain, and all enemy information that had been assembled by the Naval and Marine Intelligence staffs was carefully digested. The dress rehearsal was completed, and the convoy moved on.

On D-minus-six-days, the Eighth Brigade Group (consisting of a division of New Zealand troops that had been training in New Caledonia) struck the Jap-held Treasury Island just south of and overlooking the heavily defended Kahili-Shortland Island area. The landing was successful. All enemy forces were destroyed and the island was made secure for an advance staging base and refuge for landing craft. While this was being effected, our task force—consisting of transports, freighters, and destroyers, and screened by still another task force of cruisers—headed for Kahili.

Here it was again—the same pattern: a direct assault on a Jap-held island in an attempt to capture the airport. This time Tojo was ready for us. He had beautiful airfields, which had been bombed continuously from Guadalcanal for the past five weeks but which after each pasting had been put back into partial operation. He had shore guns with a greater range than any of ours on a destroyer. He had shore defenses consisting of concrete bunkers constructed in depth, a garrison of well-trained troops, and a road over which additional troops could be rushed from Buka after being shuttled down from Formosa or the Philippines via Truk and Rabaul. What a set-up! This time he was really going to make us pay. Ten thousand troops already on their way to assault a base as formidable as Kahili—what a sucker shot! We were heading right toward the hornets' nest. But we weren't going to Kahili, Mr. Tojo. *Only you didn't know it.* On the night of October 31 we were off Shortland Island and heading straight in toward Kahili. A wag remarked, "If the Japs know it's Hallowe'en, we ought to be scaring hell out of them!" Then the convoy made a sudden turn, headed back out to sea, and was swallowed up in the pitch-black emptiness of the vast Pacific.

Every man from the Corps commander down to the least experienced private knew the big picture—knew that the two Regimental Combat Teams were going to land abreast, the Third Regiment on the right and the Ninth Regiment on the left. They knew that the ships they were on at that moment would pull away at dusk of D-day, and that none would return until D-plus-four-days. If something were to go wrong, they must be prepared to stretch rations, ammunition, and gas for ten days longer if necessary. The Guadalcanal campaign was not beyond the scope of memory.

The orders read that the remainder of the Division, which would include the Twenty-first Regiment, would arrive in a number of echelons: the first echelon on D-plus-four-days, the remaining echelons following at intervals of several days each.

The operation order had further revealed that the 27th Regiment of the Army was at its staging area and prepared to embark as a unit or by elements upon order; that a 155-mm. Artillery Battalion was prepared to land if necessary after D-plus-four-days; that the First Marine Parachute Regiment was standing by prepared to embark on short notice for immediate operations.

They knew that they would have fighter coverage and spotting planes during the daylight hours; that planes would be conducting striking missions on D-day at Kahili, Buka, and Rabaul, and that a task force would be employed at dawn of D-day off Buka on a diversion mission, shelling the coast and faking a landing. Every one of these items listed under the paragraph "Friendly Troops" in the operations order gave them additional confidence in the success of their mission.

They knew the little picture, too. Every scrap of information—from the distance they would proceed inland before reorganizing, to the number of hand grenades each man would carry with him—had been passed right on down the line. Regimental commanders had already met with their battalion commanders and issued their complete operation orders. Battalion commanders had gone over these many details and issued orders to their company commanders. Company commanders had had numerous sessions with their platoon leaders. These in turn had gone over every detail with their noncoms and squad leaders. And for the last two or three days small groups of men could be seen huddled in separate groups all over each transport as the squad leaders passed on the information to their own little families and acquainted the men with their own plans for executing their squad mission.

Not only must every man be familiar with every detail of the plan; he had to be familiar with alternative actions in the event that any part of the original plan didn't work. No answer to any question was left hanging in the air. D-day had been set, and was known: It was to be the next morning—November 1st.

In an operation such as this, a Combat Team consists of a regiment of Infantry with various units attached. The Third Combat Team was composed of the Third Regiment reinforced by the Third Battalion Twelfth Marines (pack howitzers), C Company Engineers from the Nineteenth, I Company Seabees from the Nineteenth, the third platoon of E Company from the Third Tank Battalion, and C Company of the First Medical Battalion. For the original landing on D-day there were additional attached units: the Second Battalion and Headquarters Company from the Second Raider Regiment, F Company (Pioneers) from the Nineteenth Marines, C Company of the Third Motor Transport Battalion, and sundry units attached primarily for transportation and debarkation. The Raiders and additional attached units reverted back to Division control a few days after the original landing. The commander of the Infantry Regiment is the Commanding Officer of the Combat Team. He's the boss. He co-ordinates the various units, and they in turn contribute to the team by supporting the Infantry Regiment in accordance with his command. The efficiency of a Combat Team is equal to the sum of the efficiency of all the units; each in its own important way helps toward the success of the operation. Every unit attached to the Third Marines was a crack outfit in itself, and each contributed immeasurably to the team's success. We were full of respect for each and every one of them—and they were proud and "glad to be with the Third." That's a tough team to beat.

"The 3rd C. T. [Combat Team], with the 2nd Raider Regiment (less Headquarters and 3 companies of the 3rd Raider Battalion) attached, will at H-hour, D-day, from Empress Augusta Bay, land four landing teams abreast, destroy Japanese forces encountered, and seize a beachhead 2250 yards in depth and secure that area for the construction of vital military installations."

Mission defined!

The designated sectors on the beach for each of the four landing teams were, briefly, as follows: The right flank, Cape Torokina, was assigned to the First Battalion, with most of the Regimental Weapons Company and a company from the Third Raiders attached; the Second Raider Battalion would be on their left; left of the Raiders, the Second Battalion of the Third Regiment; and, finally, the Third Battalion tying in with the left flank of the Second Battalion.

Land . . . destroy . . . seize and hold a beachhead.

The Third Marines had gone to war!

Just before darkness on the evening of October 31st, the final item of information was revealed:

"H-hour will be at 0715—chow starts at 0300."

Canteens were filled for the last time aboard ship. The men slipped out of their utility suits, took a last look at their arms, their packs, and their helmets, and then climbed into their hot canvas bunks.

"Good luck!"

"You too, Chicken!"

"It's goin' to be a damn short night."

In a small cabin aboard one transport, Captain Bert Simpson stood before Father Foley.

"I control the lives of two hundred men tomorrow, Father," Bert told him. "That's a big responsibility. I'd like to feel there was someone more powerful than I helping me to make the right decisions. I'm a Protestant, but there's no Protestant chaplain aboard. Would you give me your blessing?"

"Kneel down, son."

Bert knelt and prayed as Father Foley administered his blessing. After he had risen to his feet, Father Foley asked him, "What's the number of your debarkation net?"

"Number Four."

"Tell your men I'll be there. Just before they go over the side, tell anyone who wishes to look over to where I'm standing."

"Thank you. I'll tell them. Good night, Father."

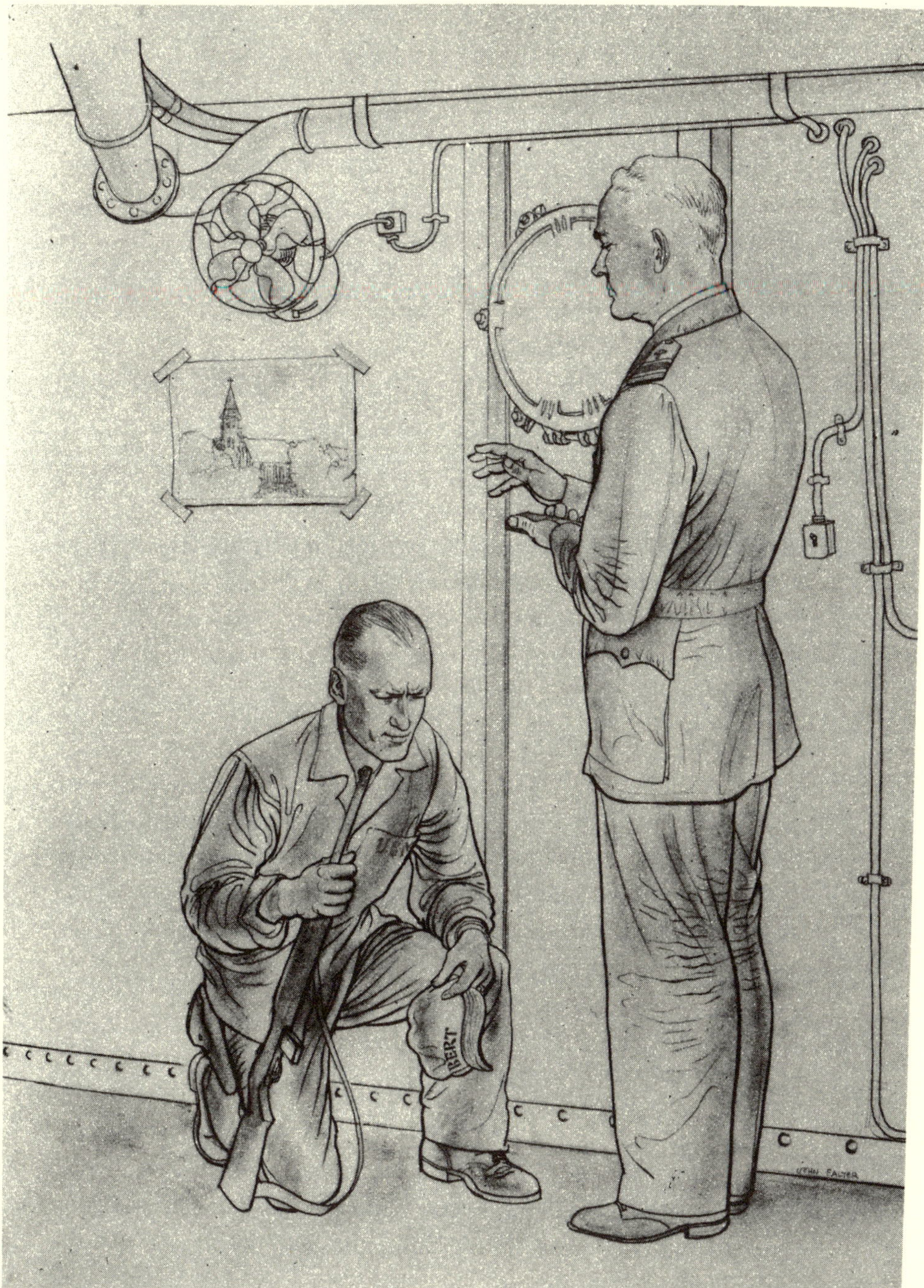
BERT

"Good night, Captain . . . and good luck!"

The next morning Father Foley was there, and each man in G Company of the Second Battalion, Third Marines, received his special blessing.

Looking back on that eventful morning of November 1, 1943, observers wondered at the seeming lack of excitement on board the transports. Lt. Frenchy Fogle of E Company, Second Battalion, who led an assault wave into the beach, paints the picture:

"Long before dawn, smothered activity filled the compartments of the transport. Troops ate chow uninterestedly and gave scant attention to their morning wash-ups and teeth-brushing. They were more particular in examining gear, in inspecting weapons, and in sticking with their squads. For this was not an ordinary day. This was to be a day of days—the day the highly trained but untested Third Marines were to get their first taste of battle.

"The test was to be of the most searching sort. A landing was to be made on an enemy-defended beach. The exact strength of the enemy was not known, but he *was* known to have defenses on the beach in such strength as to make a landing an extremely hazardous affair. Long, hard months had been spent in preparation for the main event. Eight and a half arduous months on Tutuila, American Samoa, had taken us well beyond initiation into the mysteries of the jungle and the black tropic nights; the seven weeks in New Zealand had not been all spent on wine, woman, and song; and two and a half months of additional hard work at the staging base had polished off the rough spots in what was already a disciplined and smart outfit. In addition, there had been weeks of practice landings in which no smallest detail was neglected.

"Many times during those months, it had seemed that all the training would be fruitless, that we would never actually reach the grand climax of real combat. Perhaps the big shots knew better all along, but the rank and file could not read their minds. And sometimes frustration and despair had covered us like a cloud. But that was all over now. Here—stark, grim, irrevocably present—was the moment every one of these Marines had dreamed of, the dream that had made him enlist in a fighting Marine Corps."

The men of F Company in the Second Battalion are still talking about Stinky Davis. Stinky had been with the company a long time and not a day passed that he didn't come up with some kind of grin. D-day was no exception. During the initial plunge, while shore gunners were ripping leaden death toward the rendezvousing landing boats, most of the men climbed down their debarkation net in awed silence. But not Stinky. As he threw his leg over and straddled the rail he looked back at the sea of silent faces. Then, imitating the ship's announcer who had barked messages over the public address system continuously during the entire trip, Stinky shouted: "Now hear this! *There will be no movies tonight!*"

Chapter 4

A FIELD MESSAGE received from the Second Battalion in the early stage of the action that first morning bristled with understatement: "Terrain to rear of beaches bad." Actually, the beach rose sharply for not more than ten yards and fell off into an almost impassable swamp. It was like running across thirty feet of the Sahara and suddenly dropping off into the Everglades.

Shore parties had gone in with the first wave and were operating under fire from the Cape and the two islands.

Even under the best conditions, the unloading phase of a landing operation is a hot, rugged chore. With a high surf pounding against a narrow strip of sand backed by a swamp of dense jungle undergrowth, with a set deadline of daylight hours, and under the scorching heat of a South Sea November sun, the job was an exhausting nightmare. Working parties were punching with every last ounce of blood to get ammunition, oil, supplies, vehicles, rations, and water out of the boats and above the high-water line. Shore-party commanders were frantically trying to find a few square feet of dump space and discovering nothing but swamp all along the beach. Seabees and Engineers were racking their brains and bodies in a desperate effort to construct any kind of road to high ground where vehicles could be parked, oil stored, and ammunition stacked. But there *wasn't* any high ground for thousands of yards—only a few scattered small islands of semi-inundated land surrounded by a sticky stinking mire. And hour after hour boats roared into the beach jammed with supplies.

Many of the landing boats had broached in the heavy surf and were strewn along the shoreline. Boxes piled up on boxes. Though everyone got in everyone else's way, still the boats were unloaded promptly. The transports and freighters would pull away at dusk and none would return for at least six days; every ration that remained on board would mean just one ration less for the hungry fighting men, and every round of ammunition left behind would be that much less firepower. The Third Regiment had hit its first great obstacle, and it was a serious one: the swamp. How would it be possible to construct roads through such impassable terrain? How replenish the unit of fire that the men carried with them, after it had been expended? How replenish chow, after the few rations every man carried in his pack had been consumed? These were serious logistical problems—but problems for the immediate future, not for now. GET . . . THOSE . . . BOATS . . . UNLOADED! Get every weapon ashore, every vehicle, every single item necessary for combat and existence. And they did. Every shore party on every one of the beaches hit its deadline.

Wherever one looked, men were fixing things. The youthful apprenticeship of tinkering—finding out what makes it run, making it run better, fooling around with old broken-down cars, building radios—all this was paying off in full. The man who had tinkered as a kid had now graduated and become a specialist in some department. A few had been professional mechanics on the outside, but most of them had mastered their specialty in the Corps: motor transport men, amphibian tractor drivers and mechanics, armorers, communication men. A truck would be stranded on the beach, the water covering part of its engine; and, wrench in hand, a Marine would be coaxing it back into running order. A tread was off a tractor, and four or five men with a makeshift rig would be sweating it back on. No room to do anything, but everything getting done.

The repair and supply section attached to the Regimental Communication Section was just one of the many little repair groups operating through confusion and rain and under fire. They had hit the beach in the late afternoon and gathered their gear together.

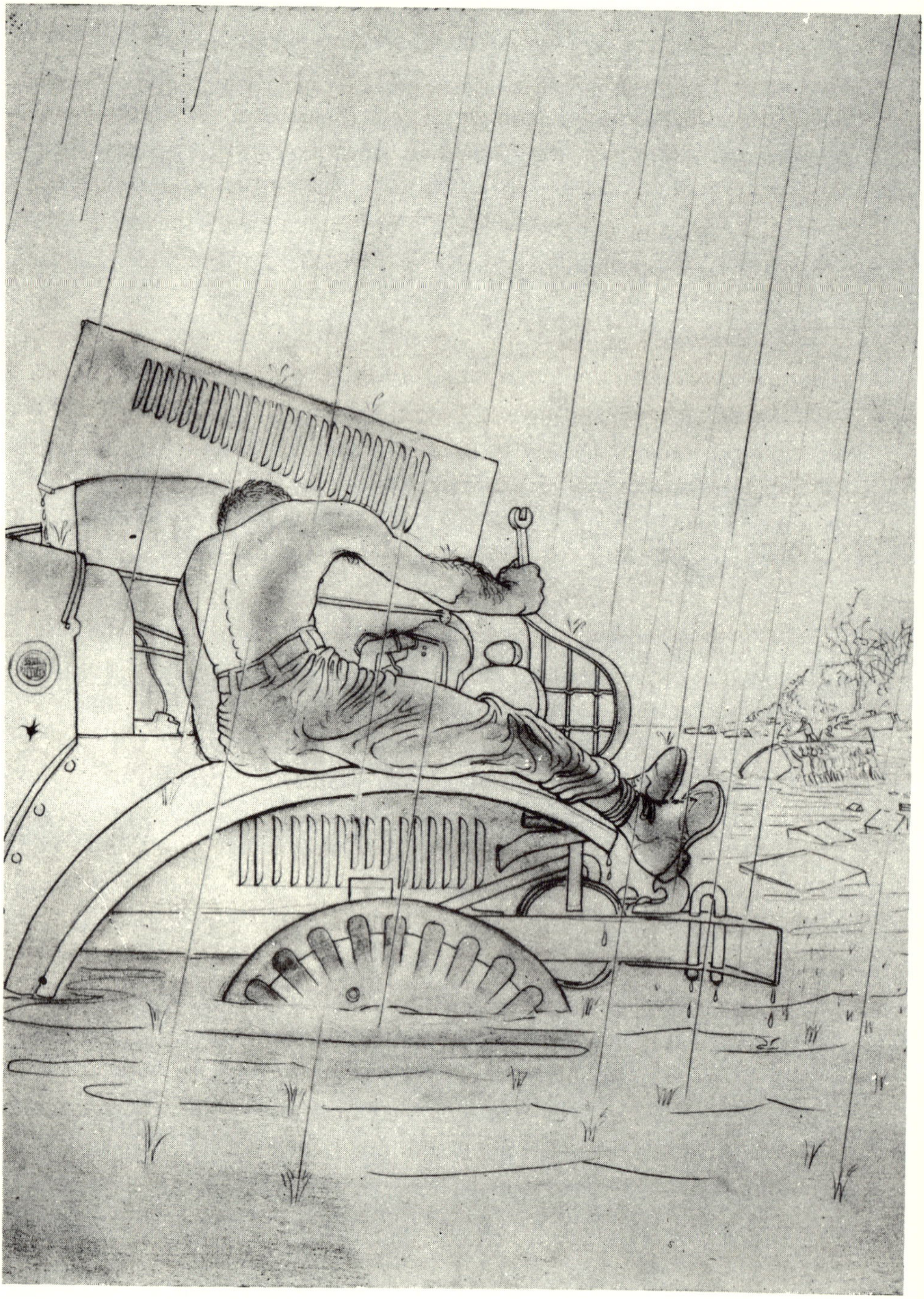

Located on a section of the beach twenty yards wide and backed up by a swampy lagoon, they were crowded in between stacks of quartermaster gear and beach defense emplacements. They rigged up a small canvas fly to keep out the rain and set up a workshop. Two watertight metal hand-cart bodies, with a kerosene flame underneath, served as hot lockers. They soon had their hands full. Wire had to be spooled from heavy drums onto lighter ones for wire-laying parties to carry through the swamp. One man answered the 'phone and took care of personal gear; this same man hunted up rations, cleaned weapons, dried clothes. One man—who freed six others for repair work. And there they stayed for the first five days, working from dawn until dark tearing down a piece of equipment, putting the various pieces in the hot lockers to be dried out as thoroughly as possible, then rebuilding it and rushing it back to the lines. Every radio and telephone was urgently needed. There were no replacements, and radios and telephones don't grow on trees. In those first five days, twelve radios, more than seventy-five field telephones, and countless other pieces of gear were brought in, repaired, and returned in working order.

Weaving their way through stacks of supplies, quartermasters strove to locate their equipment. Beach defense units threaded their way along the shore and selected positions where they could dig their foxholes, construct sandbagged emplacements, and lay their guns. This accomplished, they had to move stacks of equipment to insure a field of fire covering the bay and a designated sector in the sky.

Men from the Third Battalion, Twelfth Marines, the Artillery segment of the Third Combat Team, fought their way through the swamp, set up their pack howitzers on diminutive patches of solid ground, and stacked their shells in rubber boats. They felled trees, filled sandbags, and sweated their way back to their batteries in a desperate effort to be ready to support the Third Marines with fire.

Seabees dragged their heavy equipment across the beach on sledges pulled by tractors, had to coax their cargo to even a reasonable facsimile of the proper location for setting up and operating their equipment. Communicators with their heavy drums of wire were desperately striving to establish liaison between the various combat shore-party headquarters units and the Regimental Command Post. By nightfall they had laid one hundred miles of wire, and every unit was tied in. On the Cape, creeping and crawling through machine-gun and sniper fire, Ryan, Petriccione, Rogers, Thatcher, Zamillio, Zonker, Dunn, Zanner, Hogan, Howe, and Nick Casparre laid the wire that established 'phone communication with the First Battalion. And over this wire traveled the first artillery fire mission of the campaign. With this communication, I Battery, Third Battalion Twelfth, was able to lay down harassing fire in front of the First Battalion's front line throughout the first critical night. A beautiful lullaby when it's on your side.

Bolling and Dunne, two other men from Major Bob Walker's well-trained Regimental Communication Section, were laying a wire on a compass azimuth through the swamp to the Third Battalion. (Gunner Gannom, the handsome Major's able assistant, had been striving for months to discover one subject on which Bolling wasn't a vociferous authority; the degree of his familiarity with the subject bore no relation to his ability and willingness to talk. Aboard the transport, when he ran out of listeners—even in the middle of the night—he would corner sentries and talk to them.) Bolling is a small man just over the limit, and on this eventful day he was toting, in addition to his rifle and pack, a seventy-pound coil of wire. He would cautiously pick his way from one fallen log or shallow spot to another—then slip off into a quagmire up to his shoulders. Finally, he looped a length of wire under his arms and secured the other end to his teammate's belt. Now, unless they both fell in at the same time, he wouldn't drown. A few minutes after the team arrived back at the C.P., the entire Section had heard about his troubles and aired their comments. He stood the riding just long enough for his nimble brain to frame an answer: "Hell, it's not my fault if my mom didn't supply me with web feet!" The Section gave him 2.5 for effort, but he was still unbowed.

Before darkness fell on D-day at Empress Augusta Bay, the beachhead semicircle was 600 yards deep. All of the enemy had been destroyed and the area was firmly in our hands. The two ends of the semicircle cutting the shoreline on the two flanks of the beachhead were approximately 6000 yards apart. Looking inboard from the sea, the right flank of the beachhead, 775 yards east along the coast from Cape Torokina, was anchored down by the First Battalion of the Third Marines. A combat outpost from this same battalion had been established at the mouth of the Piva River 2000 yards farther east along the coast. The coast was a logical route of enemy approach, and the purpose of this outpost was to give warning and delay the enemy in case of an attack from this direction. The outer rim of the semicircle marked the limit of the beachhead—or, in other words, this was the front line; any territory beyond it was enemy territory, and in combat the assumption must be that it was occupied by enemy troops. True or false, this assumption did not overtax the imagination.

This outer semicircular line—the front line of the troops—was a long one and had to be held by two regiments and one battalion of Marine infantry troops. This necessitated putting every battalion on the line, and that's spreading the troops mighty thin. But it was a wide beachhead taken by two regiments, and two regiments would have to hold it. The left flank of the beachhead was being held by the Ninth Regiment. They had landed without opposition, but under very rough surf conditions that had caused the broaching of many boats; some of these had had to be abandoned and were being pounded to bits by the heavy seas. But the regiment had suffered few if any casualties and had proceeded to its first day's objective.

The Third Battalion of the Third Marines, on the right of the Ninth, had proceeded inland 600 yards through the swamp and had made contact and were tied in physically with the Ninth Regiment on their left and with the Second Battalion (which had also reached its objective) on their right. As darkness set in, both the Second Battalion of the Third Regiment and the Second Raider Battalion on their right were still trying to contact each other by patrols sent out from their flanks. It had taken all day to negotiate 600 yards of the waist-deep swamp and reach the line of the first day's objective.

By the time a defense had been set up on the line, a strong point established on the exposed right flank, and a series of small listening outposts set up out in the swamp in the gap between these two units, pitch darkness had completely enveloped the island. The Second Raider Battalion, holding the northeast sector of the beachhead line, were tied in with the First Battalion on their right flank. Patrols from each unit all along the line had been out as far as the limit of forward reconnaissance 2000 yards ahead of the front lines. Some of the patrols had returned, but some of them would be trapped by the swamp and the impracticability of trying to get back through the front lines after dark and would not return until the next day. All were in communication with their parent organizations and would be able to serve a warning function in case of attack that crucial night. Still another company from the Third Raider Battalion had moved up along the trail that started at the beach a thousand yards west of the Cape and wound its way through the jungle toward the northeast. This company had established a road block across the trail and was prepared to deny the use of the trail to the enemy. The Second Raider Battalion, holding that section of the outer perimeter through which the trail crossed at a point some 2000 yards behind the road block, was prepared on order to attack and delay the advance of Japanese forces from the northeast. This, generally speaking, was the way things stood on the night of D-day, November 1st.

Chapter 5

TO MOST PEOPLE in the world November 1st, 1943, was just another first of the month. But to the man in the Third Marines it was his first day of combat. When he returns, he may forget his sister's birthday, may overlook his own wedding anniversary, may fail to remember to pay his income tax—but he will never forget that first D-day. Or that first night, either.

The men had been up since 2:30 that morning. From H-hour until dark they had taken a physical beating. Fighting that swamp to the line of the first day's objective had been as exhausting as the fight for Cape Torokina. They had set up their defensive positions, dug their foxholes, cleaned their weapons, and wolfed their cold greasy rations in the rain. As night crept in around them, those not on the first watch took off their helmets, stuck their long-bladed knives into the side of their foxholes, wrapped themselves and their rifles in their ponchos, and snuggled down in four inches of water to try to get a few hours of rest. It would soon be their time to take the watch. They were tired.

And the men on watch were tired, too. But tired men can become dead men, for tired men grow careless. And they knew it. They strained to pierce the blank scrim of the jungle night, and listened intently to the million jungle noises—ground noises particularly, for they must learn to distinguish the sound of a lizard or a rat or a toad, or any one of the hundred little ground animals in the jungle, from the even belly-slide of a crawling Japanese jungle fighter. The men in the Third Marines were used to the jungle;

but every jungle is different, and for the first time after all their training they were playing for keeps.

By six o'clock that night it was dark and every officer and man on the line and in the many C.P.s was in his foxhole. For these were trained men and they knew the law of the jungle: each man must be in his foxhole at dark and there he must stay until dawn. Anyone *out* of a foxhole during the hours of darkness was a Jap. Sudden death for the careless. From seven o'clock in the evening till dawn, with only centipedes and lizards and scorpions and mosquitoes begging to get acquainted—wet, cold, exhausted, but unable to sleep—you lay there and shivered and thought and hated and prayed. But you stayed there. You didn't cough, you didn't snore, you changed your position with the least amount of noise. For it was still great to be alive.

Not a light could be seen anywhere in the area, pitch-black darkness all along the beach, blacker still in the jungle. Though none were visible from the outside, lights were being used—flashlights mostly, under ponchos, inside blackout tents. Back at the Division C.P., the Regimental C.P., and the headquarters of the lower echelons, commanding officers and members of their staff worked over maps, written messages, and orders; and switchboard operators, already under ground, shunted messages to their important destinations.

There was another light, too—a very important one, shedding rays of mercy and hope: the light of Hippocrates. C Medical Company had landed early that morning. Doctor Glystine (the company's commanding officer) and Dr. Leo Koscinski had worked their way through the swamp searching for an island of dry land. They found a spot less than 200 yards in the rear of the front lines. With the help of two corpsmen they dug a hole ten feet square and three feet deep and covered it with canvas. Now, stripped to the waist, sweat pouring from their bodies, they crouched near a stretcher. A corpsman held a flashlight. Leo was administering the anesthetic. Dr. Sheppard, a Mayo-trained surgeon, was removing a bullet from the body of a wounded Marine. He had been hit by a sniper late in the afternoon, too late to be evacuated. The ships had gone. Four buddies had fought the swamp and carried him to Bougainville's first hospital.

Major Steve Brody, acting Commander of the First Battalion, knelt in his foxhole and listened. His battalion C.P. was up forward near the front lines. He could hear the sound of men picking their way through the underbrush up ahead. Other men heard the sound, too—felt for their knives and waited. They knew what to expect. They knew there were Japs out in front of them. The operation order had accounted for at least a battalion less than twelve miles down the coast. An attack that night would be expected anywhere in the northeast sector, along the coast or through the swamp from the east. The sounds came closer. Steve waited. Those sounds could mean only one thing: a Jap patrol. The Japs would know this terrain well, but they wouldn't know the location of the Battalion's front lines or the position of the automatic weapons. They were out there to find out. Maybe a trigger-happy Marine gunner would open up, blaze away at a sound or a shadowy form, and reveal his position. That's what the Japs wanted. But the men in this outfit weren't raw recruits. They had had fire discipline shoved down their throats for months. They had patience and knowledge and self-control. Steve lay there and smiled. He was their commanding officer. They were his men. He was proud.

In about an hour the sound in the underbrush ceased. Some of the patrol might have crawled through the lines, might even be behind them. Let 'em crawl. They wouldn't see a thing in that darkness. There wasn't a human sound anywhere along the lines. Another hour went by. Nothing happened. Steve drove his knife into the bottom of his foxhole. It was a good knife; his brother had sent it to him in New Zealand. "Hope it comes in handy," he had written. The rain was letting up a bit but it was pretty cold. "Guess I'd better try to get some rest. Might even be able to sleep a little if I could get a little warmer," thought Steve. He reached over and straightened out his poncho, pulled the other half over him and looked up at the sky. A few stars were trying to come out, but it was still pretty cloudy. That was a break.

"The enemy will most certainly attack our beachhead with all the aircraft he has available. Air attacks can be expected at any time, day or night." Last night those had been just words in an operations order.

Planes were probably already warming up at Buka and Rabaul. Steve thought about his former battalion commander, whom he had relieved. "Guess Spike was hurt pretty bad . . . they got him back to the ship . . . hope he'll make it O.K. . . . great guy, Spike. Well, no one let him down. That'll make him feel good . . . tell him all about it when I see him again." He closed his eyes—the first time in sixteen hours. It felt good. . . .

"Jesus Christ— *Uhh*— Grab that son— Sam!"

Something had happened. *Damn*—a Jap had fallen into the foxhole of one of the men in the C.P. The Jap jumped out and started to run, tripped and fell on top of Dr. Sam Elmore, lying in a foxhole near by. Before Sam could recover from his surprise, the Jap was out of the hole. Steve, in a hole next to Sam, threw off his poncho with one hand and grabbed his knife with the other. He saw and smelled the Jap in the same moment—no mistaking that smell.

"*Watch* it, Steve—*Jap!*" Sam yelled.

The Jap plunged in again on top of Steve, and Steve was over him like a tent.

Sam crawled quickly over the edge of his foxhole and slid into Steve's. "Got him, Steve? You got him?"

Steve grunted as he hacked away with his knife. The Jap was screaming and crying at the same time. "No kill . . . no kill! I'm too . . . young . . . to . . . die!" wailed the Jap in high-pitched, terrified English.

"You're old enough," said Steve as he drove his knife into the Jap's back. They lifted up the bloody mess and dumped it out of the foxhole.

I Battery sounded off in the distance. A few seconds later they heard the shells pass over their heads, exploding a thousand yards in front of the lines. Japs were still dying.

On another section of the beach, a loading officer lay in a Japanese slit trench alongside one of the sand-covered Jap bunkers. He had had a busy day. His unloading party of Marines and Seabees had handled cargo from two transports and one freighter. The surf up on the left flank had been too high for unloading on that section of the beach, and all of that additional cargo had been shunted down to his area. The supplies had been stacked above the high-water line, but dispersion had been impossible. Every inch of dry land and some of the swamp had been utilized. Ammunition, chow, and gasoline had been separated from one another, but each of the dumps was piled high. They had finished the last boatload at 5:30 in the afternoon. There was just enough light left to dig foxholes. The officer found his pack, grabbed a shovel, and started inland. He hadn't eaten since early morning, but there wasn't time now.

"The Jap will really work the beach over tonight," he thought. "If he hits that ammo dump, they won't even find our dog tags. Better obey the rules and dig a hole in the swamp. Going to be awful wet, though."

He found a spot about a hundred yards inland, cleared away the wall of thick vines, and started to dig. It was an exhausting job. Before he had finished a third of it his muscles refused to work. His head felt as if someone were beating on it with an ax. He leaned against a tree and vomited. Then he tried to dig some more, but the maze of vine roots was too tough; he didn't have enough strength to cut through them. Every time he lifted his shovel, the roots would grab it and the dirt would be spilled back in the hole. The brush was thick, and it was now dark in the jungle.

"The hell with it!" He picked up his pack and shovel and went back to the beach.

The damp sand was soft. He had scooped out a hollow for his hips and it felt wonderful. He didn't even mind the lingering

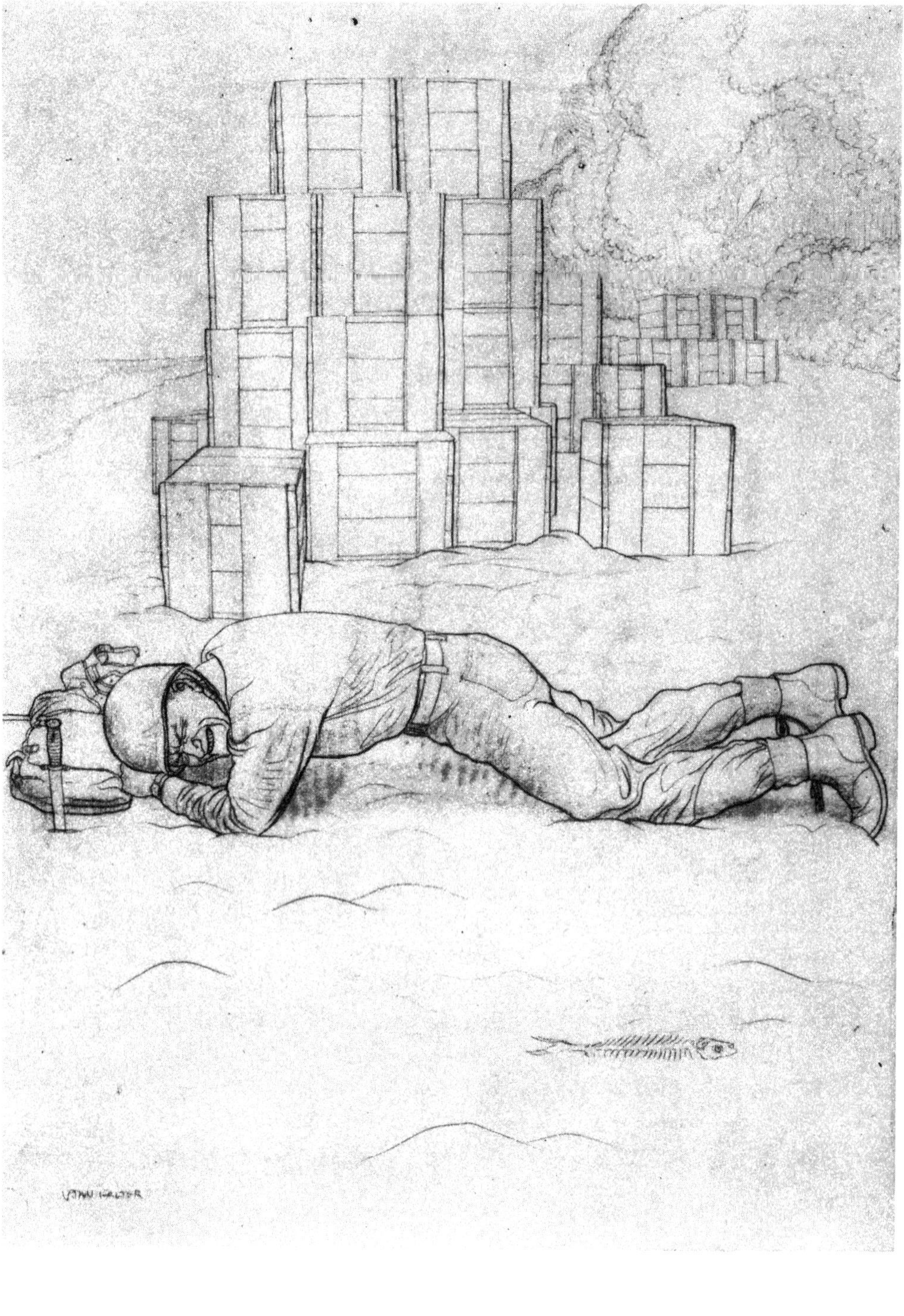

stench of Japs emanating from the bunker. The ammunition dump with canister upon canister of high explosive mortar shells was less than thirty yards away. It was dangerous and stupid . . . but it was comfortable. "What the hell! Maybe they won't hit the dump. This is war. Gotta take some chances," he rationalized.

Five feet away, the shore-party commander was talking in a projected whisper over a field 'phone. "Condition Red," he whispered.

A few minutes later, the loading officer heard the drone of Jap planes. They had to be Jap we didn't have any night fighters in the area. He had been bombed many times on Guadalcanal and he could recognize that pulsating hum of unsynchronized Jap motors anywhere. For a long time the planes circled the bay and beachhead area. Then, one by one, they would dive, drop a stick of bombs, and circle again.

"I wish those bastards would run out of gas," he said to the Commander.

"They've got plenty of gas."

"Did you ever sleep in a subway station, Commander?"

"Once."

"Wasn't it peaceful?"

Most of the bombs had dropped up at the other end of the beach; nothing had been hit. Now they circled closer.

"Why didn't I finish that foxhole back in the jungle and get off this damn beach?" the loading officer asked himself. "Too tired. Screw it . . . all a matter of luck, anyhow." Then he addressed his thoughts to the Jap flyers. "Drop your God-damned bombs and go home. You bother me. I want to get some sleep. Unh-hunh—must have heard me." One of the planes off to the left had gone into his dive. The screaming motor came closer and closer. The officer rolled over, humped his belly off the ground, and rested his weight on his knees and elbows. It was a good position; too bad it had to be wasted on such an enterprise. *Wish . . . uh wish . . . uh wish . . . uh wish . . . uh wish . . .*

"Here they come!"

Raah voomb! . . . Uh wish . . . uh wish . . . uh wish . . .

uh wish . . . Raah voomb! . . . Uh wish . . . uh wish . . . Raah voomb! Raah voomb!

One of the bombs landed close to the beach, the rest of them back in the swamp. The officer rolled over on his back and let out a sigh of relief. All of a sudden courageous, he called after the departing planes: "You couldn't hit the broad side of a bull's ass with a spade, you slant-eyed bastard! Go home and lie your head off! 'Flames could be seen for fifty miles'—and you didn't hit a God-damned thing!" The plane droned off in the distance.

"Have to go back when it's light and see whether a bomb fell near that foxhole I was digging," thought the officer. He did, early the next morning. No bomb crater anywhere near, but—lying right on the surface of the ground not five feet from where he had finished digging—was a Japanese land mine.

Later that night it started to rain again. When it rains in the tropics, it never kids around about it—it's always real heart-and-soul stuff. A machine-gunner in one of the many emplacements along the beach leaned up against the sandbags and cursed his luck.

"It is estimated that the enemy can attack our forces in the Cape Torokina area with two battalions coming from the Buin-South Augusta Bay area by sea on the night of D-day." That order had stressed the imminence of enemy action during the first night. Well, this would be the perfect night to hit us: tired troops, defenses only partially organized, bad visibility.

The machine-gunner had just relieved his assistant and had taken over the watch. Of all the lousy nights he had spent in the South Pacific, this one took the ribbon. "The poorhouse wasn't tough enough—they had to put a hill in front of it." A landing boat could be up on shore before you could even see it. Even the dark forms of the two islands silhouetted against a lighter background could no longer be seen. He looked at his watch. It was almost midnight; plenty of darkness left. Then in the distance far out to sea he saw flashes followed by a deep bass rumble. Lightning, maybe. There had been a thunderstorm that afternoon. The flashes came pretty close together. The phone rang softly. He reached over and answered it.

"Condition Black—enemy landing expected. You may expect shelling from enemy ships followed by counter invasion."

That wasn't lightning. "Let 'em come," he thought. He could feel a twinge of excitement, but it was a good excitement—not fright, not the fear of the unknown or of being unsure of oneself. He knew what was expected of him, what to do, and how he'd do it. "I'm the best God-damned machine-gunner in the Marine Corps. We've got 40 and 20 millimeters, 37's, and half-tracks all along the beach—that's before they ever get to the machine-guns. I'll keep this son-of-a-bitch firing till I burn out the barrel. And we've got two dozen hand grenades. Between the two of us, that's a lot of Japs," he thought. He could still see the flashes. The rain was letting up a little. Things were looking better. He smiled and reached over to wake his buddy. The rest of the night the two stood watch at the same time, talking their way through a dozen invasions after which it would take at least three days to bury the Jap dead.

The flashes and the rumbling lasted for over an hour. Then it was black again.

"Hope the Navy hasn't let us down," said the gunner.

"The Navy stinks," his buddy replied.

"I don't mean the Navy on transports. I mean the shooting Navy."

"I wouldn't know. I was never sea-goin'."

The Navy didn't let them down. A strong task force had put out from Rabaul and was headed for Empress Augusta Bay. The Navy was waiting with a reception committee far offshore. Four Japanese cruisers went to the bottom. The Japanese task force returned to Rabaul. The sea off the south coast of Bougainville no longer belonged to the Mikado.

Chapter 6

DAWN BROKE at about 5:30. Morning was never more welcome. No one had slept, muscles were stiff from the day before, bones ached from lying on stones in soaking wet dungarees—but it was light and you could see what you were doing. In a little while the sun would be up. It would be hot and you could dry out. We had been bombed on and off all during the night but with no casualties. The expected enemy naval shelling had not materialized. The company of Raiders at the road block up the trail had been hit by a strong combat patrol. Four of five men had knife wounds, but still more Jap dead had to be buried. I Battery had laid down harassing fire in front of the First Battalion, thwarting any attack from the east. Snipers had pinged away during the night at the Raiders on the island, but these Nips were only tapping out their swan song.

The earliest action of D-plus-one-day occurred at daybreak. One of the men on the Cape started to leave his foxhole and was greeted by a Jap, stark naked, walking down the trail a few yards from him; he had probably swum over from the smaller island. The two saw each other at the same time. As the Marine reached for his rifle, the Jap darted into the underbrush out of sight. A small patrol was quickly organized and overtook him about a hundred yards away. He had an M-1 rifle which he must have picked up on the beach. He didn't want to be taken prisoner, so one of the more obliging members of the patrol, with the aid of a Tommygun, helped him to die for the Emperor.

It didn't take anyone very long to test the fuel possibilities of the waxed cover of a K-ration box. One box torn into small pieces provided enough heat for a canteen cup of coffee. Many had already learned that a hand-grenade canister made an excellent waterproof cigarette case that would hold about three packs of cigarettes, so there were smokes with the coffee. Some of the men on the Cape were even luckier. The Japs have an excellent canned heat that they carry with their field ration. Four or five boxes of these cans had been found in the rustic Japanese storehouse. We never have been able to understand why our rations were not equipped with some type of canned heat such as Sterno. The little white heat tabs that are furnished are about as effective as a large fish fork in a soup storm.

The men on the beach were faring best. They had regular little stoves. All along the beach small groups of men were brewing coffee over small cans that had had holes punched in the sides, half filled with sand and then soaked with gasoline. Gasoline is used to clean a machine-gun. Most of it. A guy's got to have his coffee.

Daylight ushered in a certain freshness. Everyone anticipated a tough day ahead, but the strain of that first night had been relieved. There were enough hints of combat about as a reminder of more to come. Unburied Jap bodies furnished the olfactory evidence, and the sound of the higher-pitched rapid fire of a Jap machine-gun intermingled with the sound of our own weapons on Puruata Island was convincing proof that the Raiders weren't holding an early morning skeet shoot. But it was light—a man could see what he was doing, could clean his weapon, relieve his bowels, wash his face, and talk out loud.

Now it was 7 A.M. It had been light for an hour and a half. Commander Bruce, commanding officer of the medical battalion, trudged along up the beach in the direction of the Division C.P. He had been one of New York City's prominent eye specialists before he had joined the Navy and was assigned to the Marines. Now he was an expert on every branch of field medicine, from diagnosing and treating rare tropical diseases to methods of evacuating wounded from the swamp to the field hospitals, to the beach, to a ship. He knew men and he knew them well, all of them—Marines, corpsmen, doctors, and officers. He understood the problems of the military as well as the medical, and he knew how to solve them and make the two separate departments dovetail. A big man with a boyish face smiling its love of humanity, he has a rapid-thinking brain, a witty tongue, and a feeling for the incongruous. Everyone knew him and was anxious to hear the latest scuttlebutt rendered in his inimitable style. But today he had to supervise the installation of three medical company field hospitals and had time only for a greeting and a few short plants for future reference. Bull-session time would soon come again and he would have some juicy contributions. Commander Bruce had a great imagination and he knew how to tell a story.

"Hiya, Brucie, where have you been?" called an officer on the beach.

"Morning, Hank. Been down on the Cape. Went down to give the boys a hand. Willets and Sam pretty busy. Got right in between the fire of two machine-guns. Should have seen me hit the deck!"

"It was pretty hot down there all right," Hank answered.

"Damn near had my butt shot off," grinned the Commander. "How's it going?"

"Pretty good. Lousy beach. Heard Steve stabbed a Jap." Hank wanted to hear the story.

"Yeah—cut him to ribbons. Big fella. I damn near had my butt shot off. Tell you all about it later." The Commander started up the beach.

"S'long, Brucie. Take it easy!"

The Commander raised his hand—then stopped, turned, and with the old mischievous twinkle in his eye called back, "Did you hear about the woman sniper?"

"Heard something about it," lied Hank. He'd heard about the woman sniper ever since he'd been in the Pacific; so had the Commander. "Did they really find one?"

"Tell you all about it when I see you." The Commander grinned and puffed on up the beach. Too bad there wasn't more time. In every campaign there had always been a "woman sniper." Sometimes she had been found chained to a tree—sometimes she had been a Chinese woman—sometimes she had been a Japanese, but dressed exactly like a soldier. No one had ever actually seen her, but everybody knew someone who had. Now Hank knew there hadn't been one on the Cape, but Brucie's story would still be a good one.

A number of stories have sprung up from the island campaigns. Some are pure fabrication, many actually happened, and those of the "didn't happen but could have" variety are so probable that it doesn't really matter. One of the last variety is about a Marine Sergeant who was a machine-gun section leader. His section was attached to a combat patrol which had been beating the bush all day long without running into even a rumor of a Jap. Now a machine-gun is not something you can take or leave alone. You're either not interested, or you're a confirmed fanatic. You have to be. In weight alone, there is a considerable difference between an M-1 rifle and the gun with its tripod and ammunition supply, even in easy going country. In the jungle it is comparable to the difference between pickabacking your neighbor's six-year-old son and the kid who has just become eligible to join the Boy Scouts. This Marine Sergeant, off to one flank, was separated from the rest of his section by heavy underbrush. Nearing the crest of a hill, he halted, cautiously crept along the top, and looked down on a small valley on the other side. The vision before him made his mouth water. Less than 300 yards in front of him stood a whole Jap company lined up for chow. He had dreamed about a target like this for fifteen years. The Sergeant was an expert, and he knew in an instant where to lay his guns and the range and the number of bursts it would take to massacre everyone in the Nip company. He turned toward the underbrush where he knew the rest of the section would be and called excitedly: "Charlie—bring the guns over and lay them on the left."

A voice answered from the brush: "No—be better keep them on the right."

There wasn't even a field of fire on the right. His squad leader must be crazy. Now more excited than ever and growing madder by the second, he shouted his order again:

"Goddammit, Charlie—Japs! Bring those guns over here on the double and lay them on the left."

Same voice, same answer: "No—be better . . . keep them on the right."

Now there comes an end to every sergeant's patience. There are periods in his life when he even forgets the Golden Rule. This one sprang to his feet and tore through the underbrush. Here was one corporal who had disobeyed his last order. By God, he'd beat him down to parade rest. . . . But as soon as he had cleared the bush his eyes fell upon a diminutive, toothy, English-speaking Jap squatting in a clearing. Still white with rage, he dashed up to the Jap and shook a finger in his face and barked: "Listen, you little son-of-a-bitch. You run your outfit and I'll run mine!"

E Company was trudging its weary way back from the Cape. Imagine yourself rising at 2:30 in the morning, unloading a transport all that day, hiking 3000 yards through loose sand with nothing on your stomach since early morning, digging foxholes at the end of the journey, being bombed all night as you waited in reserve to be thrown against a land attack or a counterinvasion, cleaning out left-over snipers the next morning, then—after a quick meal of a can of cold C ration and a lukewarm cup of coffee—hiking back along that same stretch of loose sand to join your outfit, which by this time will be over 800 yards away in the swampy jungle. Then grab the next Marine you see with a Pacific ribbon on his blouse, take him into the nearest good bar, and buy him a drink. Marines hate to drink alone . . . and it'll make you feel better.

Captain George Coupe and Lieutenant Dick Maxwell were at the head of the column. Here was another crack company of the Third Marines. Coupe had been with the company since it had been formed over eighteen months before, and he knew the age, life history, and fighting potential of every one of his men. Maxie—an end from the famous Georgia football team of 1930, expert swimmer, fine baseball player, great boxer in and out of barrooms—was also one of the best instructors the men had ever known. He had taught every officer and noncom in the Third Marines when they had done their stretch in a rugged jungle school at Samoa. There wasn't a subject in the manual at which Max wasn't an expert, and at one time or another he taught them all: the compass, map-reading, scouting and patrolling, demolitions, hand grenades, Molotov cocktails, barbed-wire defenses, bayonet, knife-fighting, judo, gas, camouflage, every weapon. He stood six feet two and had a forearm as large as the average man's leg. A deep scar from a Kansas City gangster's knife slash crossed his face from the corner of one eye to his ear. He had the charm of a matinee idol, a quiet, kind Southern drawl, and the straight right of a Jack Dempsey.

Max had come up from the ranks, had been commissioned, was finally given a platoon of his own just before the Third had shoved off from Samoa, and now was second in command of a rifle company. To every officer in the regiment he was a true buddy; to every enlisted man, a rugged hero. It was difficult to conceive of any living thing big enough to beat him—and there wasn't, not in the South Pacific. But there was something small enough: a little mosquito—and he contracted filariasis. He had lain on his bunk for three weeks before we shoved off from our staging area, refusing to turn in. "If I went home without killing a Jap, my daddy wouldn't let me in the house," Maxie told us. He was carried on the transport. He skipped the landing operations, and the three weeks' rest aboard the ship had reduced his swelling and given him back his strength. So he said. He knew how much his being with them meant to the men. He wouldn't go near a doctor. But that day of unloading and the succeeding exertion had brought the trouble back. The company had halted and was taking a ten-minute break. Maxie limped away from the company out of earshot of the men and flopped down under a tree.

"What's the matter, Maxie?" an officer asked him. "You look like a death's head at the feast."

"Can't keep anything on my stomach."

"Mumu?" asked the officer, using the native name for the first stage of filariasis.

"Yeah. Thought I'd licked it."

"Hurt pretty bad?"

"Like I'd been kicked in a football game and hadn't worn a jock." Pain was written all over Maxie's face. He was really suffering.

"You'd better turn in, Maxie—you'll never lick it on your feet."

"I can't let George down."

"You *are* letting him down. Give him a chance, Maxie. He's got to break somebody else in. How long do you think you'll last? About two more days. Then they'll carry you in."

"I know. . . ." Tears were forming in the tough guy's eyes. He wiped his face on the sleeve of his dungaree.

"On your feet!" shouted Coupe.

Maxie pulled his body off the sand. "On your feet!" he barked. "There's a lot of water and chow waiting up ahead." He limped to the head of the weary column. The company started down the beach.

Three days later, Maxie collapsed in the field hospital. They evacuated him by stretcher. An arm, a leg, and his testicles were twice normal size. It was not only filariasis—soon, in hospital, he was in the first stages of elephantiasis, and further stages were to follow. Before Pearl Harbor we hadn't paid much attention to tropical diseases. But then, before Pearl Harbor, there were a lot of things we hadn't paid much attention to.

On another part of the beach a canvas fly had been rigged underneath a tree on the edge of the jungle, in the bivouac area of a Seabee working party. Inside the tent a piece of white target cloth had been thrown over a large wooden crate. On the top of this counter there was a half bottle of methiolate, a couple of bandages, and a bottle of C.C. pills. Though inadequately equipped, one might suspect that this tent was some kind of temporary first-aid shelter or sick bay, but a sign over the entrance removed all speculation. It read:

BOUGAINVILLE'S LEADING DRUGGIST

Work had been resumed in earnest. Bougainville's first highway had already been started, although at the moment it rated slightly less than a short dotted line on any road map. But when the Seabees go to work, a start is a promise. Groups of these beavers were cutting logs and brush and hauling them to the trail leading off the beach just west of the Cape to the northeast. A power shovel was operating on the beach filling trucks with sand. The trucks would deposit their load over the recently laid logs on the trail; then a bulldozer, that beloved prince of all invasion equipment, would smooth it out. Another bulldozer, hauling three wooden sledges of equipment, would follow immediately. In this way, an impassable swampy lagoon between the beach and an island of dry land would have been bridged and another dump for valuable equipment established. More logs, more sand, and the road would grow a few yards longer. Finally, a short stretch of the road would be solid enough for trucks to pass. More supplies would be dispersed, and equipment for another field hospital would be hauled up to a group of corpsmen busy clearing away the undergrowth on a small patch island of solid land, digging dugouts, and pitching tents.

Farther along on the other side of the trail a Marine fighter control group were clearing the ground and digging in their installations. A little farther on, a motor park was being established. Dry land at a premium, and every inch of it being utilized for bivouac and operational areas. Get off the beach, disperse, become operative. The road would be torn up and a truck would mire down. A bulldozer would come to the rescue; the truck would be hauled out. Then more logs, a deeper drainage ditch along the side, more sand, more work for the bulldozer—then another line of overloaded trucks and sledges would crawl farther up the trail.

In the midst of this activity a sniper's bullet would ricochet off the side of a truck. Sniper patrols would soon spot the source of this temporary aggravation, and a few of the younger Seabees to relieve the monotony would sneak off with the patrols. A tall tree would be spotted, surrounded by the patrol, and another foolish Nip would have committed suicide. But the work went feverishly on. No one even bothered to take cover. Everyone was too busy.

Farther west along the beach, Marine Engineers and Amphibian Tractor men were pushing a cat trail through the swamp to the Second Battalion's front lines. Still farther along Lieutenant Joe Gehring and his I Company Seabees were constructing a road to the Third Battalion. No outfit can advance too far beyond the base of its supplies. D-plus-two-days called for the further advance of 600 yards. Every yard of advance by the troops meant one more yard of swamp separating them from the beach . . . and the beach was the only base of supplies. Ammunition must be brought up, and men must eat. It would be weeks before roads over which even the lightest of vehicles might travel could be constructed through this thick jungle swamp, a great portion of which was below sea level.

How could this very important supply nightmare be licked without delaying the advance? But it *was* licked: by Marines and Seabees, by bush knives and axes, by hours of sweating toil, and by a special type of transportation, the only vehicle that could negotiate the swamp—the amphibian tractor. Until D-day almost everyone, except a few broad-minded souls and the specialists themselves, despised these awkward, wallowing, noisy monsters. Every ship loading officer cursed them to the skies. All his vehicle problems would be solved—and then he would be given a consignment of amphibian tractors to load. There would be only one boom on the ship large enough to lift them; then either the hatch under the boom would be too small or the clearance of the upper 'tween decks too low. They would end up in the bottom of the hold, loaded in the tank lighters, or else on the only open fresh-air space for the troops on the deck. They were the cause of more arguments with the ship's cargo officer, more readjustments in loading plans, more bad feelings all around, than any other single item of cargo. In a noncombat movement from one place in the Pacific to another, we would try to get the use of them to facilitate the movement of cargo from the ship to the beach, and permission would always be refused: "The life of a tractor is limited . . . can't waste them . . . got to save them for combat."

"What good will they be in combat? They're only made of aluminum. A machine gun'll cut them to ribbons," we'd answer.

"They can go places where other vehicles can't go. We've got machine-guns too. What do you think we'll be doing while they're trying to cut us to ribbons?" from the tractor Marine.

"Treading water and hollering for a Higgins boat to save your butt—or getting in everybody's way on the beach."

"Yeah? It's a damn fine piece of machinery!"

"So is the Twentieth Century Limited, and it doesn't make as much noise."

"These tractors will come in handy."

"Let me know. I'll get a rhyming dictionary and write a poem about 'em."

But after D-day on Bougainville we wanted to bite our tongues off. No one worked harder or longer than the amphibian tractor crews. The tractors were used to haul supplies from one part of the beach to another, to crush through the thick undergrowth, bowl over trees and make trails, haul ammunition, chow, gear and medical supplies, and evacuate the wounded. Not once but all through the campaign the amphibian tractor bridged the vital gap between life and death, available rations and gnawing hunger, victory and defeat. They roamed their triumphant way all over the beachhead. They ruined roads, tore down communication lines, revealed our combat positions to the enemy—but everywhere they were welcome.

Major Grant Crane, Major Whitman, Captain McDonald, Captain John Winford, Quartermaster Clerk Bill Pollack, Lieutenant Breen, Gunner Greer, Lieutenant Duke Shananan, and all the quartermaster and supply units, men and officers, on the beach worked like Trojans to sort out supplies, obtain the transportation, and find the means of getting chow, medical supplies, and ammunition through the swamp and up to the troops. They knew these supplies were the life blood of the Regiment. They had to keep the ticker pumping. And when the fighting men of the Regiment needed that chow, when the doctors needed medical supplies, when units of fire had to be replenished, these officers and their men had them there.

"Condition Red."

The bogeys were at it again. Work ceased. Everyone ducked for his foxhole. Two of the planes came in low to strafe the beach and were greeted by an overture of machine-gun fire. It felt good to let it go—the barrels had been cooling for a long time and trigger fingers needed exercise. But the gunners on this second day on the beach failed to take the proper leads. The planes climbed swiftly back into the sky preparing to make another run. This time they would be able to do a better job. They had the limits of the working section of the beach clearly marked. They could take their time in judging the distance, peel off, dive at one end, and rake the beach unmolested. So they thought. . . .

But high in the sky, circling around and around on station, were six Marine fighters. They had been there at daylight, they would stay there for the limit of their gas time, then be relieved by another six from our air base at Munda. These in turn would be relieved by another six, and so on all during the daylight hours. They were our daylight fighter coverage. And so just at the moment when the Jap falcon began to drool at the mouth, the Marine flyers roared from their high perch and dove at their unsuspecting prey. It was a beautiful sight—these roaring silver streaks flashing through the sky and spitting leaden death at the bogeys. It was more beautiful still to watch the columns of smoke spiral downward from the sky and pierce their watery graveyard in a splash of flame. The Marine flyers rolled in salute to their grateful buddies on the ground, and then soared back into their commanding haven high in the sky. More raids followed intermittently all during the day, but the Nip soon got the word: the daylight air above Empress Augusta Bay also belonged to the United States Marines.

Up on the lines, a muddy, wet Marine pulled himself to his feet, stretched the kinks from his stiff body, and took a look around. Streaks of daylight were beginning to filter through and around the large banyan trees in the jungle. His buddy was still curled up in his poncho. He kicked the protruding bulge halfheartedly. His buddy opened his eyes.

"Hey, eight-ball. Get your ass out of the sack."
"What for?" his buddy yawned.
"Time to go to the office."
"What time is it?"
"Five-thirty."
"Too friggin' early."
"Get any sleep?"
"What sleep?" He threw back his poncho, climbed out of his muddy foxhole, pulled back the operating handle of his rifle, ejecting the round from the chamber, pressed the clip release, caught the clip of cartridges, picked up the ejected round from where it had fallen on the deck, wiped off the mud, put it back in the clip, tapped the noses of the rounds in the clip against the sole of one of his boondockers, and laid the clip on the top of his pack. Then he held the receiver of his rifle toward the light, inserted his forefinger in it to reflect the light, and looked down the barrel. "Who can sleep with a snoring bastard like you around?"

"You never talked like that when we were first married, you sourpuss eight-ball." The first Marine had already disassembled his piece and was brushing off the grit that had gathered on the bolt with a cut-down paintbrush. A small bottle labeled "Mosquito Repellent," which now contained oil, half of an old skivvy shirt, a cut-down toothbrush, a thong with a small weight on the end of it, and a half-dozen gun patches, lay strewn out on half of the poncho;

the various parts of the field-stripped rifle lay together on the other half.

The second Marine pulled his poncho out of his hole and spread it out on the ground. Then he went over to his pack, stuck the clip in his belt, opened his pack, pulled out his cleaning kit and a can of ration, left the can sitting on the outside of his pack, went back to the poncho, and started to strip his rifle. When both had finished they walked off a short distance in the jungle away from the rest of the troops. Both carried their rifles, and one of them carried an entrenching shovel; one would cover for the other, who in turn would indulge in the early-morning luxury common to all mankind.

All along the line the men were climbing out of their holes, shaking off the mud, opening their packs. Each greeted the welcome morning in much the same way and each, without even thinking about it—before any part of his toilet was attended to, before he washed his face from the cleaner water drained into his helmet from one of the large cupped jungle leaves, before he brushed his teeth—he instinctively field-stripped and thoroughly cleaned his rifle. In less than an hour after he had rolled out of his sack he had his rifle in shape for immediate action, had smoked a cigarette, had changed his socks (he still had a clean pair this first morning), had cleaned himself up as well as possible, had moved his bowels, eaten his ration (some trying to heat a canteen cup of coffee, others sparingly drinking part of the remaining water in their canteens), had folded his poncho and put it back in his pack, and was fastening the straps when the word starting the day's action passed down the line: "Prepare to move out!" In less than five minutes he would be starting through the jungle. Before he had gone ten feet and shot his second azimuth with his compass, he would be up to his knees in mud; but for a moment—a precious, luxurious moment—before the beginning of another long, arduous, steaming-hot hike through the thick wall of vines and tangled bush, he was clean—at least a little cleaner, a trifle fresher, a bit more comfortable than he had been for hours.

Then came the bogeys. Word down the line:
"Condition Red!"
"Enemy planes!"
"Get . . . in . . . your . . . foxholes!"

Not back in those stinking, slimy, muddy foxholes? The planes could be heard circling over the area, but none seemed at the moment to be directly overhead. Maybe just squat near the hole . . . right on the edge . . . you can hear a bomb fall . . . still time enough to tumble in that mud. Now the planes seemed closer, but they couldn't be seen through the thick jungle ceiling. They wouldn't be able to spot us either, but they knew we were somewhere within a perimeter off the beach; if they could estimate the size of the perimeter, they would know the position of our front lines. A bomb anywhere along that irregular line was bound to hit someone. *Wish . . . uh wish . . . uh wish . . . uh wish . . . uh wish . . .*

"Here they come! Hit . . . the . . . deck!"

Two men made a dive for the same foxhole. One of them made it.

"Hey, Mac—that's my foxhole!" yelled the unlucky one.

"Semper Fidelis, Mac," from the man who had gotten there first. Which, translated literally, means "Always Faithful"; but it is commonly used by Marines, as occasion demands, for "Frig you, Mac—I got mine," or "Pull up the ladder, Mac—I'm aboard."

No one needed any further coaxing to "hit the deck"! That familiar, unmistakable sound of a bomb falling through the air meant "positively."

Everyone had plunged back into the mud and was lying on his elbows and knees waiting for the ground to tremble, for the sound of splintering trees, the roar of the explosion, and the shove of high-explosive concussion. They closed their eyes, gritted their teeth, held their breath. *Uh wish . . . uh wish . . . uh wish . . . uh wish . . .* No bomb takes that long to fall. The sound continued; then it got louder; then it was a different sound. It belonged to the jungle. A string of pornographic oaths—unprintable but in keeping with the highest traditions of a Marine's vocabulary—was justifiably hurled from every hole. A new, eagle-sized type of jungle bird, flying low and flapping its wings loudly, gunned its way through the bush. . . .

The men lay in their holes cursing Bougainville's wild life, and the mud, and the swamp, and the war, and Fate. The water once again seeped through their utility clothes, making them thoroughly miserable. Then the raid was over. Word was passed again.

"Condition green. Moving out."

The men moved to their respective places in their squads and platoons. Squad leaders shot an azimuth with their compasses, scouts moved out, the men took the necessary interval for dispersion—though close enough to remain at all times in sight contact with one another; then they started to cut their way through the jungle swamp towards the second day's objective 600 yards farther from the beach.

As a company moves forward in combat formation, it lays its combat communication wire connecting it with the Battalion C.P. Whenever a phase line is reached (a phase line being an imaginary line on a map of the terrain so many yards or at such-and-such a time interval from the starting point or last phase line), the order to halt is issued and passed to the front of the formation by means of arm and hand signals. All orders are issued in this manner in the jungle when contact with the enemy is imminent. Then the men halt, take cover, and remain silently alert. A 'phone is tapped in on the combat wire, and each company commander re-establishes contact with his battalion commander. On the move the companies will be out of 'phone communication until it reaches a phase line. When this is reached, the company commander checks in: "Buck calling Joe."

"What's the situation, Buck?"

And the company commander makes his report and receives any change in orders.

All during this second day, at every phase line, the battalion commander tried to talk his company commander into an optimistic report of dry land, rising ground, the end of the swamp.

"How's the terrain, Buck?"

"Swamp."

"How about over on your right?"

"Swamp."

"Does it look like there might be dry land up ahead?"

"Swamp."

"There must be *some* dry ground up there?"

"Swamp."

"O.K.—move out at 1320."

The company commander laid the 'phone down and whispered his orders to the platoon runners, and they started off toward their platoon leaders. Then after a few moments of relaxation, the company commander checked his direction of march, glanced at his watch, and at 1320 signaled to move out. The word had passed from platoons to squads, and the men, already on their feet, pushed off through the bush toward the next phase line.

By midafternoon the battalions had reached the line of the second day's objective. Again defenses were set up. Sketches of the terrain and their defensive positions were drawn and dispatched to their battalion C.P.s; carrying parties were sent back through the swamp to the terminus of the axis of supply for water, rations, and ammunition; communication lines to the battalion C.P. were tied in by lateral lines connecting each company; and foxholes for the night had already been started.

Again the men dug through the mud. Even those who were fortunate enough to be located on a small island of dry terrain found water at the eight-inch level. Some of the men had made up their minds that they were going to get one good night's rest, flooded foxholes notwithstanding. They constructed small shelters out of saplings and broad jungle leaves on the edge of their holes. Here they would sleep until enemy planes overhead would force them to roll over the edge of their foxholes onto the water-covered decks below the dangerous surface of the ground. Then, as on the preceding day, at three o'clock, the sluice gates in the sky opened up, a torrential downpour tearing through their leaf-covered shelters and flooding the foxholes and machine-gun emplacements. The dream of a warmer and more comfortable night faded with the last rays of daylight.

While the Second and Third Battalions were moving up to the new line and the First Battalion was consolidating its position east of the Cape, the Regimental C.P. had moved farther inland and was being dug in behind the right flank of the Third Battalion. By late afternoon communication lines had been laid to the Battalions; strength and unit reports from these units had been 'phoned in to the Adjutant; overlays of the Battalions' positions had been brought in by runner and were being plotted on the situation map; requests for supplies had been made to the Quartermaster; the Operation Officer had been out all day checking positions and trying to close the gap between the right flank of the Second Battalion and the Second Raiders, and was now getting the reports from the battalion operation officers. The Regimental Commander had been brought up to date by the reports from these various members of his staff, had made his report to the Division Commander, had received his orders from the same source together with all the latest enemy information which Division Headquarters was able to supply, and was now able to issue his orders for that night and the next day's advance.

A patrol on the way to the small native village up the trail to the northeast had located a platoon of Japs. Information from the one wounded Jap prisoner taken on D-day had substantiated the prior-to-landing reports of a Jap battalion fifteen miles down the coast to the east and two battalions ten miles farther down. They were equipped with enough barges to attack from the sea that night.

The First Battalion had had only sniper action during the day, and the Second and Third Battalions had met no enemy resistance. The beachhead at Empress Augusta Bay was now 1200 yards in depth. Each unit along the perimeter line was set up for hasty defense. All units attached to the Regiment were in direct telephonic communication with Regimental Headquarters and with each other.

The Jap bombers returned shortly after dark and pasted the beach and beachhead area all during the night. But expansion had increased the space between jungle targets, and the work of beach crews had broken down the heaping piles of supplies into smaller, better-dispersed, camouflaged dumps. The cold rain and droning planes were a ceaseless exasperation to the weary men. It was another miserable, sleepless night. But the skies were dark, the targets small, and the Japs' aim poor. No damage occurred and no casualties were inflicted. D-plus-one-day had been operationally smooth and thoroughly successful.

Two down, many more to go—but we were getting stronger all the time. The Jap was wasting valuable time. He shouldn't have done that.

Chapter 7

DOWN ON THE BEACH on the morning of the third day, Lieutenant Powell and Lieutenant Rivers, two Seabee officers of Commander Brockenbrough's Seventy-fifth Battalion, were lining up an engineering survey party. Brock had been the shore party Commander for this particular section of the beach. He had been pushing his men hard for three days, and everyone in his outfit had done a terrific job. On D-day, when cargo-laden boats would pull into the beach at any spot they could find, Brock would run from one working party to another and yell: "I know that boat doesn't belong on this beach, but—Goddammit, men, this is war!" A burst of machine-gun fire raking the trees above his head would punctuate his declamation. And the men, who had already unloaded twice as many boats as any other working party on the beach, would give him a weary grin, take a deep breath, and pitch into the latest arrival. The second day's work on the beach had been just as rugged. On the third morning they were beginning to see a patch of blue sky ahead. It doesn't take long to get a bellyful of beach work, laboring under combat pressure, even when sheer, urgent necessity is providing the impetus. And so, when the time came for them to revert back to Corps control, when they faced an even bigger job—but the job they had come to do—they were happy.

Rivers, the engineer, and Powell, in charge of construction, gathered their gangs together and started toward the Cape. They were off to make a preliminary survey of the coconut grove and swamp. This, on the third day, was the start toward the construction of "important military installations." They knew what the Marines had been through in taking that ground, and the number of good men who had been killed and wounded. But they also knew that the Cape and the land around it would stay firmly in our hands. They knew, too, that their own mission called for ingenuity, backbreaking labor, and speed. Now they were on their way to find out how it could be done. Not *if*, but *how*—how they could build an airfield.

When Powell and Rivers returned that evening they had seen the worst and knew most of the answers.

"What do you think, Rivers?" a Marine officer asked him.

"We can build it."

"How long will it take?"

"Depends on the material we have to work with. Looks like there's coral under the mud layer, and we can get some coral from the point of the Cape. The land isn't too bad in the grove, but the grove doesn't extend very far. The rest is all swamp."

"How the hell are you going to build an airfield in a swamp?" The officer was groping for good news.

"Dig a ditch," said Powell. That was his department.

"You mean drain it—that's a big swamp."

"We'll have to dig a big ditch."

Commander Brockenbrough came up and started to discuss immediate plans. He had been a successful construction engineer for years. The Battalion had just come from the States, and this was his first assignment of the war. It was a tough one, but he knew he had a crack battalion. Brock was out for a record. He worked out with Powell immediate plans for clearing part of the area. Most of their equipment and the rest of their men would arrive in later echelons, but they would start with what they had.

The Marine officer listened to the plans. There's something hopeful and refreshing about creating and building things after one's whole being for a long time has been steeped in killing and destruction. Brock left to carry out another assignment on the beach.

He was a man who had been busy all his life—he liked it that way, was used to it.

The Marine turned again to Rivers. "I don't know a damn thing about it, but it's hard to believe you can build an airfield in a swamp."

"You can build anything anywhere," said Powell—Vanderbilt footballer, road-gang foreman, construction engineer, builder of roads and dams and airfields.

"I guess you're right, with the proper equipment," the Marine agreed. "But it's going to take a long time."

"Not if the gold braid leave us alone," Rivers answered.

"How long, with a break on everything?"

Rivers thought for a moment. Then he answered confidently, "Three weeks."

"That I gotta see."

"You'll see," said Powell.

On the fourth day of the Bougainville Invasion the beachhead was in a more stable condition. Action east of the Cape had ceased and the defenses there were strong. There had been no action anywhere along the front except for strong enemy patrols hitting the Raiders every night at the road block out in front of the northeast section of the perimeter.

All artillery batteries of the Third Battalion, Twelfth Marines, had been surveyed in and were able to support the Third Regiment with harassing fire in front of the lines during the day or night, and to support the Third offensively in a co-ordinated attack.

On this day a shift of units occurred. A battalion of the Ninth Marines which had been holding the left flank of the perimeter since D-day relieved the First Battalion of the Third Marines, taking over the Third's positions on the right flank. The First Battalion pulled out, made the shift with the usual trials and tribulations to the left center sector, and went into regimental reserve behind the Third Battalion. The First Battalion needed a breathing spell and a chance to lick its wounds. It had lost officers, men, and equipment; it had to reorganize and to replace equipment, and—above all—it needed hot chow and rest.

The men of the First Battalion had already received one welcome shot in the arm when on the second day Major·General Hal Turnage, Commanding General of the Third Division, had gone to the Cape and spoken to them.. He told them what they had done, how well they had done it, and how very proud he was of each and every one of them. Marines get used to pep talks. They are a courteous audience to any and all superiors—they are too well disciplined to be otherwise; but try to tell what they're thinking! That morning you could feel it. They all knew that the General was their big boss and that they were an integral part of his command. The old-timers remembered that he had been the Commandant of the Post at New River when the Third Regiment was organized. And when a field General whom all respect leaves his Division C.P. and makes a special visit to a hot spot, snipers notwithstanding, to tell them in person what a damn fine job they have done, they are not only respectfully, but also emotionally, appreciative.

The long shift from the right flank was wearying but not without compensation. The men were back with the Regiment, no longer stuck out on the wing. They knew they had brought honor to their regiment. "You'll get your chance," was the answer to all praise. Then, just to keep the other two battalions straight on how they felt about their own outfit, they would add: "If you run into any trouble, let us know and we'll help you out." For "the battalion in reserve" is not "the battalion on vacation," as the phrase might seem to imply. It is the battalion sitting on the powder keg with that meat cleaver of old man Damocles dangling over its head. The front lines were spread mighty thin, there were gaps in the line, stretches of swamp where it was physically impossible to set up defense positions; but the present front line, now over 1500 yards off the beach, was a stark reminder that the swamp, though rugged, was still not impassable. The Jap has a propensity for attacking in the strangest places. There are always logical avenues of approach and attack, but late rule books don't compel the enemy to be logical. *We* certainly hadn't been. The battalion in reserve is the one that can be and often must be rushed to a break-through on the line, on a flank or on the beach. The men of the First Battalion were glad of this chance to catch their breath, but they had no illusions about being "on liberty." They ate, slept, and reorganized in the rain and mud.

Accompanying this move, Major Moss, Commander of the Regimental Weapons Company, was ordered to make a readjustment of his platoons. His forces, consisting of 37-mm. guns and 75-mm. half-tracks, were distributed from the right flank of the Third Marine sector of the beach to and including part of the Ninth Marine sector on the left flank. He established an observation post on the beach from which he was able to observe the entire bay area between Cape Torokina on the right of the beachhead and the point of land jutting out into the bay west of the left flank of the beachhead.

In spite of the continuous forward movement of the front lines, the Seabees and Marine Engineers had managed to push amphibian tractor trails up to the Second and Third Battalions. The men were still living on canned rations. On the fourth day the cooks were able to obtain enough facilities and supplies to give the men in the lines their first hot coffee. This was really a treat and made the day a memorable one.

Active patrolling continued, but no daytime contact with any Japs had yet been made by either the Second or the Third Battalion. New defenses were set up at the end of each day's move. Bombing every night had been the principal Jap protest. The enemy was out there some place. It was evident that he didn't know where we were—not yet; but he would certainly take steps to find out. If he could discover the strength of our forces, and if he could bring up sufficient strength to oppose them, he might attack at any time.

In the early part of the war the Japs laid great stress on night attacks. Widely publicized, they were intended to terrorize the opponent, but they proved to be very costly to the attacker and were never successful against Marines. Most attacks follow a general pattern and at night the plan must be simple. It should also be a surprise. But it is very difficult to move units of any size noiselessly through the jungle in the dark. Control between attacking units is hard enough in the daytime; in the dark it's a nightmare. And trained, alert troops quickly recover from the initial shock of surprise. So the Japs, not being blessed with better eyes than anyone else, discontinued their widely heralded night-attack policy, resorting to it only when they were able to preface their attacks by extensive daylight reconnaissance. They will, however, indulge extensively in night patrolling, varying their tactics by trying either to slip silently through the lines and search out positions or to create an obvious disturbance out in front of the lines. They resort to many corny tricks, such as crawling up close to the lines and calling out names in English, shouting insults, firing their weapons —anything that will cause the defender to open fire and reveal his position. The amount of information the enemy is able to obtain depends on the will power and fire discipline of the defender. Lieutenant Frenchy Fogle, executive officer and second in command of E Company, thus describes the actions of a Jap night patrol up on the lines:

"On the third night our battalion frontage was limited by the fact that our lines had to bend back for flank protection. On the right, E Company had two platoons in line with the third extended back at right angles to the front in an attempt to close the right flank. Men were in two- and three-man foxholes. Four machine-guns of the attached H Company machine-gun platoon were in line, and three machine-guns of the Company Weapons platoon were placed on the flank. All in all, the position seemed as secure as possible under the circumstances.

"Captain George Coupe, commander of E Company, issued orders that the men were to fire at night only in case of an attack in some force, and everyone crossed his fingers and crawled into his foxhole.

"That night a few straggling Nips came out of the swamp and started nosing about the positions. One stumbled into a foxhole, apparently by mistake, and was set upon by two Marines. In the pitch blackness he managed to extricate himself and ran down the line in sheer fright. There he fell into another hole. The confused performance was repeated, and he dropped into still a third before he was able to get away with only a few knife wounds. Scattered shots were fired at other snoopers, but on the whole the night was relatively uneventful.

"On the following night the Nips returned. They seemed to like what they had found the night before, for when darkness fell they again came back from their swamp hideout and started fooling around the right flank. Their numbers were small—only twelve or fifteen in the bunch; but they acted with no apparent concern for danger. They located our open right flank, came up within ten feet of our positions, and in plain sight deployed along our line and infiltrated through the foxholes until they were in rear of the line. Our men had been absolutely forbidden to fire, and so they allowed all this to go on, only clenching their knives and rifles a bit tighter and waiting for the Nips to come within arm's reach. But it was the Japs themselves who broke the silence by setting off a string of firecrackers which they had carefully laid among our foxholes. Apparently they had American weapons, too, which they fired to add to the confusion. Our men couldn't resist firing in reply, and at times during the next hour and a half the sound of firing became quite heavy. Then there were only occasional shots till a dawn that took a hundred years in coming. Never was a night so long as that one. Came the light of a miserable day, and we counted two dead Marines—one a machine-gun squad leader, and both of them as good Marines as you could find anywhere. We could ill afford to lose them.

"The next night the Japs came back again. This time they seemed more curious than belligerent. They crept quietly in and around our right flank positions. The night passed, however, without a shot being fired, and although the men looked haggard

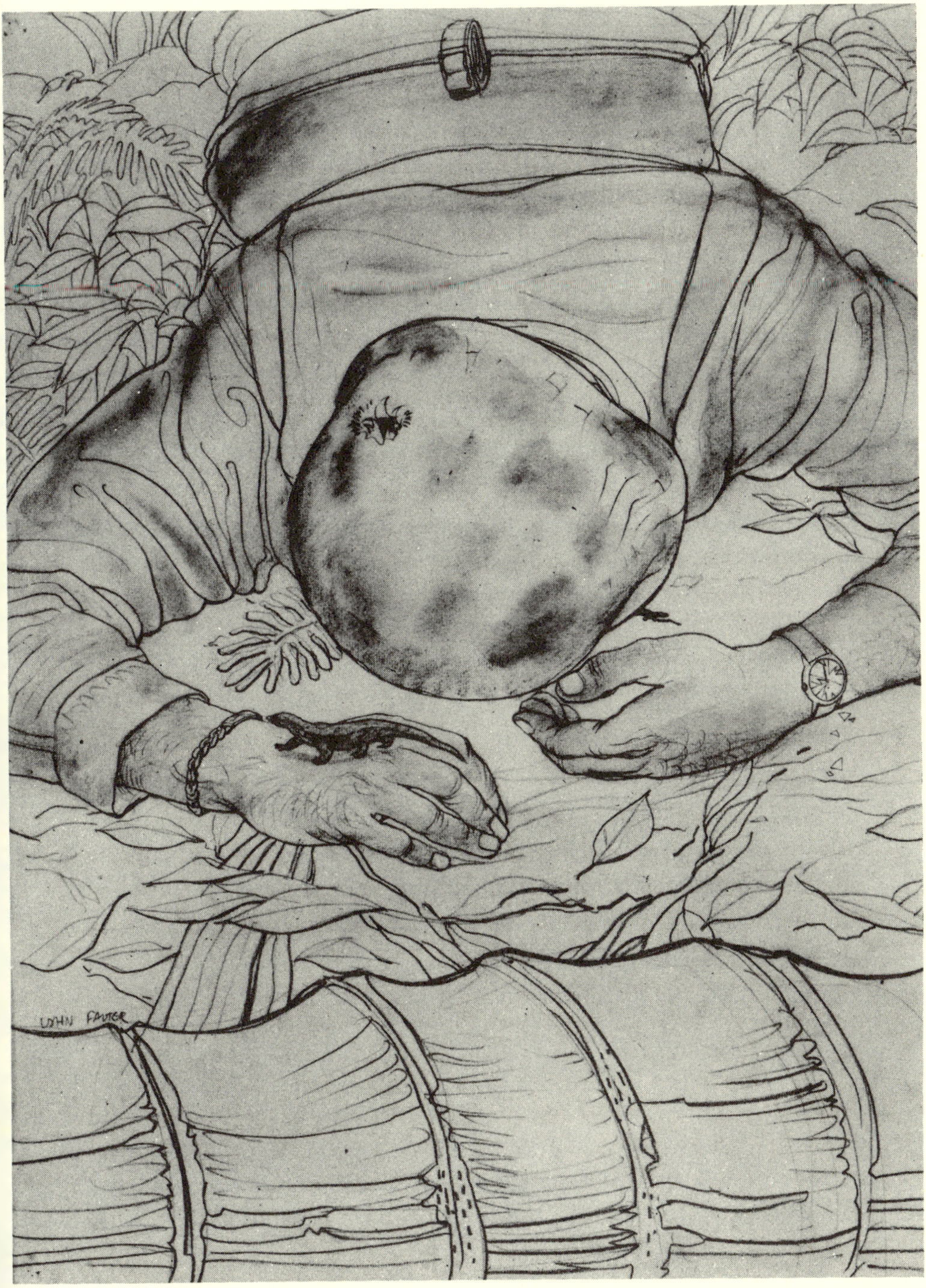

enough, they were pleased by their fire discipline. That seemed to be the answer to a lot of problems."

This is an example of learning the hard way. All these men, with the exception of a few recently acquired replacements, were well-trained jungle fighters. They had been schooled in Japanese trickery; they had been through many night problems, some resembling very closely this Japanese night raid; they had been warned repeatedly and knew what to expect. But the difference between an opening night and the best dress rehearsal is an emotional difference. The best training problem can never duplicate an actual combat situation, for it is utterly impossible to simulate danger. Men acquire knowledge, become skilled in their profession, and develop their reflexes through good training. But only through actual combat experience do they learn emotional control. As in any other form of endeavor, it is true that experience is the best teacher. The tragedy lies in the fact that in actual combat one is not allowed many mistakes.

Dawn may not be "the very witching time of night," but up on the front lines it is certainly the time most likely for Hell to "breathe out contagion to this world." It is an excellent time for enemy patrols to be scouting information. It is often the H-hour of an enemy attack. It is also the time when men, weary of the long mysterious stretch of a dark watch, tend to let down their guard, and when other men, waking from a troubled sleep, are lethargic, still sleepy, temporarily lost. Their reactions are slower at dawn than at any other time of day, and they take longer to spring into immediate action. Men are cautioned to be especially alert at this time of day. Anything can happen.

At dawn of the fifth morning in the swamp, a Marine by the name of Harry was awakened by his foxhole bunky. His bunky, having seen that he was awake, had left the hole. Harry rubbed the sand from his eyes, put on his helmet, and—as he wiped the mud off his knife and replaced it in his sheath—he tried to pick up the remaining threads of that sizzling-sirloin-steak dream. He shot a blank stare out into the jungle. It was sure a beautiful-look-

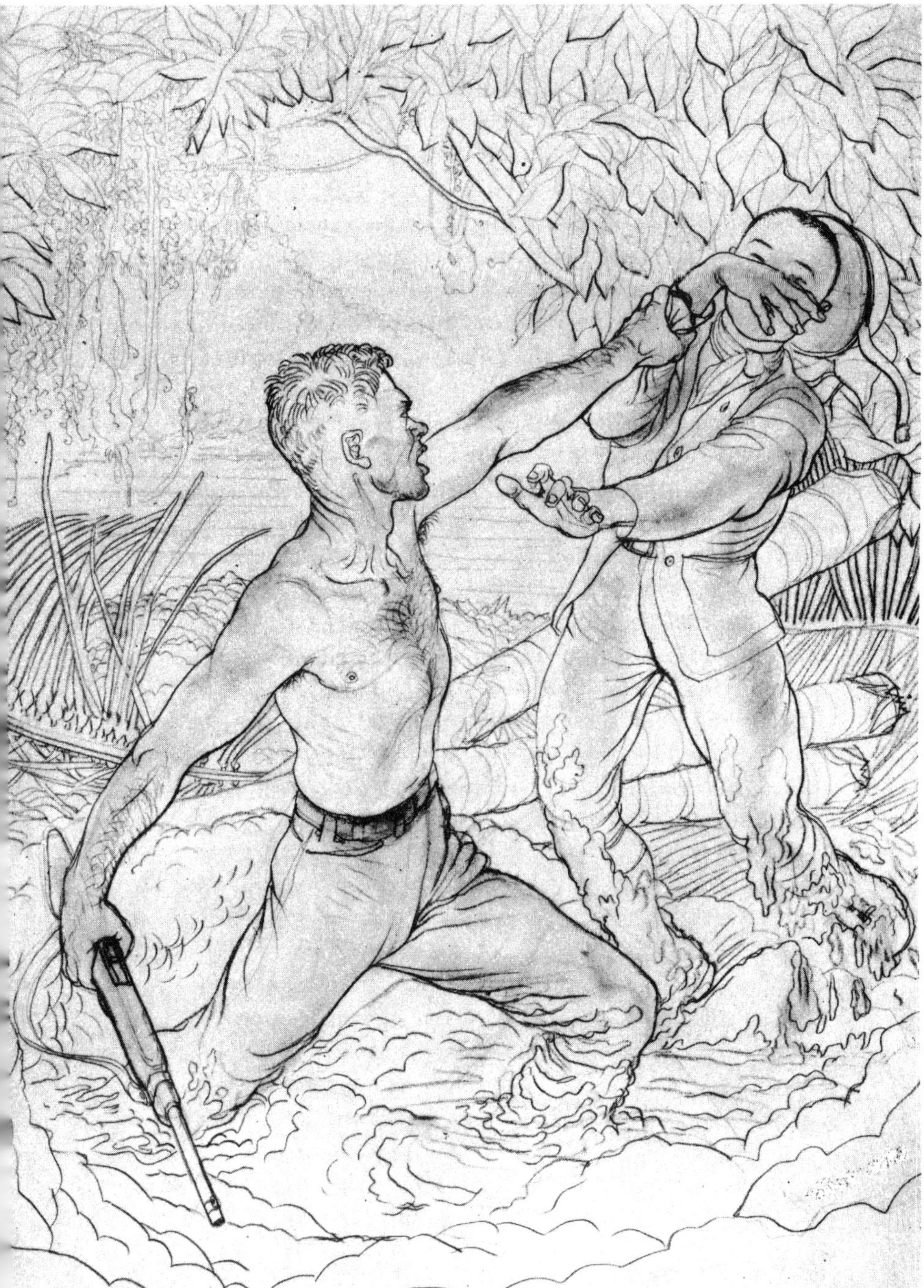

ing steak . . . ought to tell that guy walking toward the foxhole about it . . . sure was a beautiful steak . . . that's a funny-looking Marine . . . no . . . couldn't be . . . that guy walking toward the foxhole was a Jap! The Jap, less than ten feet away, caught Harry's double-take, saw him grab his carbine and jump to his feet. Too late to get away, the Jap charged. Harry swung into position and pulled the trigger. The carbine wouldn't fire. With a million thumbs in his way, Harry struggled desperately to release his safety catch and push the clip release. As the carbine clip fell to the deck, the Jap plunged in on top of him. Now Harry—typical American boy, victor and loser in a hundred brawls, and recently trained knife fighter—might be expected to sidestep the Jap's rush, whip out his knife, and bury it in the Jap's body while screaming the Rebel yell. But this was dawn. Two buddies, rushing to his aid, arrived in time to find Harry holding his carbine away from the Jap with his right hand, shoving the Jap away from himself with his left, and shouting loudly: "Get away! Get away from me! I haven't done anything to you." Then a latent barroom technique smoldering in Harry's drowsy brain suddenly burst into conscious flame, and a few seconds later an elbow, a butt of his head, a well-aimed knee, and some help from his buddies saved his life. But to regain his prestige as Harry, the quick-witted, calm, rugged, hand-to-hand jungle fighter . . . that took a bit longer. Harry had no love for the jungle night, but he hated the dawn.

Chapter 8

ON THE MORNING of November 6 the first ships since D-day arrived at Empress Augusta Bay. A welcome sight. They brought additional ammunition, chow, fuel, supplies, and equipment. They also brought troops of the second echelon attached to the First Marine Amphibious Corps, the Third Marine Division, the First Battalion of the Twenty-first Marines, the second echelon of Seabees, advance liaison units of the 148th Army Regiment, and the second echelon of the Marine defense battalion. There was also one other very important passenger, a Brigadier General of the United States Marine Corps.

A landing boat sped through the shallow water and scraped up on shore. A middle-aged Marine officer, small in stature, wearing combat utility clothes, helmet, and combat pack, carrying a carbine and with dispatch case slung over his shoulder, trotted over the lowered ramp and leaped ashore.

An Army Major and a Captain who had arrived a few moments earlier were standing on the beach talking when the General disembarked. At this moment a jeep laden with supplies and driven by a sweating young Third Marine sped past the group of officers. The jeep driver, recognizing the General, burst into a grin from ear to ear. Waving one arm so strenuously that he nearly fell out of the jeep, he shouted as he shot past, "Hi—Speed!" The Army officers looked up, astonished. The General, beaming a smile of recognition, kindness, and love, turned toward the officers and, gesturing toward the vanishing jeep, commented with dignity and pride, "That's one of my boys!"

The sixth day of the invasion of Bougainville was a happy day for the Third Marines. Brigadier General O. R. Cauldwell had come to be with his boys.

"Speed's here"—"Speed's with us"—"Speed got here this morning." These phrases rang the gong of confidence in the soul of every Third Marine as the word spread along the beach and on up to the little but important fighting man in the front-line foxhole. The news passed from private to private, from noncom to officer, and it had a wonderful sound. For up until six weeks ago Speed had been their Colonel, their skipper. In keeping with his promotion to General he had been transferred to the next higher echelon and had become Chief of Infantry, Assistant Division Commander of the Third Marine Division. Every man in the Third Regiment understood the importance of that promotion, and every man was proud. But in their hearts Speed would always belong to them. He was their General. He had been and would always be the living spirit of their regiment. The men knew Speed would always be a Third Marine.

The Third Marines—the Third Marine Regiment—had been formed at the Marine Base at New River, N. C., in the late spring of 1942. Colonel O. R. Cauldwell was appointed Regimental Commander. Small cadres from the First and Second Divisions had been left over to form a nucleus for this new regiment. But by and large the great majority of its officers and men were the greenest of the green. Junior officers recently graduated from the Marine Officers School at Quantico and Reserve Officers recently called back into active service made up the leadership personnel. The men came from Navy yards in various parts of the East, and others were raw recruits just out of Boot Camp at Paris Island. Many of the men came from the brig. The Colonel, a professional Marine with an outstanding record of the First World War and subsequent service, had been given the assignment to form and equip the regiment, and have it in shape to sail for a destination in the Pacific that same summer. In August, the Third Regiment sailed for American Samoa. It relieved an older regiment of Marines for offensive duty elsewhere and took over the assignment of defending Tutuila (Samoa), which at that time lay astride our main sea lanes en route to New Zealand and Australia. A few of the men suspected that this newly formed regiment was not quite ready for combat, though by the time we arrived at our first South Pacific destination most men in this still motley crew were mentally prepared to destroy regiments of Japs. Yet those same men had never seen even a coconut tree, much less the jungle. But we didn't realize how well one man understood us. We knew little or nothing about his thorough schooling, his reputation as an Infantry specialist, his great ability to train and develop combat troop leaders and fighting men. That one man was our skipper, Colonel Speed Cauldwell.

Adequate defenses were established all over the island. But it was not to be a case of sitting and waiting for the Japs to invade. Defense was a primary mission. It would be accomplished. But this was only one of the Colonel's objectives. We were going to work. Officers were to be trained in a new type of modern jungle warfare. They were to be retrained in the handling of men, for to the vast majority this was their first command. Major Sidney McMath, an instructor from the Marine Officers School at Quantico, had joined the Colonel at New River. In less than a week after our arrival on Samoa this important officer was nominated by the Colonel to supervise the training of Third Marine Officers, noncoms, and officer candidates from the ranks at a school previously established and still ably commanded by Brigadier General Henry L. Larson, Commanding General of the Second Marine Brigade, and supervised by Colonel Victor Bleasdale. The school had been formed for the purpose of adapting the recent lessons being learned by Marines now fighting the Jap on Guadalcanal to a new outfit's repertoire. Two weeks after our arrival on this South Pacific island we "went to the salt mines."

First the officers and noncoms learned how to do it themselves; then they taught their men. Only then were we able to train as an outfit, as a jungle-fighting regimental combat machine. Weeks and even months were spent on the training of the individual. "This is for the men. This is their only pay-off. We not only have to train them how to fight—we've got to bring them back. You'll get your fun when we get into company, battalion, and regimental problems," Speed would tell his officers. His frequent visits to the various defensive Bays, his personal demonstrations, his demand that every officer follow to the semicolon the regimental training orders and schedules, brought many a worried frown to the brow of a company commander and platoon leader. And every officer was held accountable. There was no excuse for failing to adhere to the least, minute detail. "Any officer who fails to give his men the proper training is a no-good eight-ball. He's not thinking about sparing his men. He's just lazy. That's a no-good eight-ball excuse. He has no feeling for the private. That officer will get his men killed. I'll eight-ball that no-good lazy guy back to the States." The wrath of an inexhaustible disciplinarian would descend on an erring officer, and he was through. Some lost their commands; some took a trip home; others were transferred to other outfits; none were given the chance to jeopardize the lives of the enlisted men.

Over seven weeks were spent on the proper way for a man to take cover, hit the deck, creep and crawl. Weeks were consumed on specially constructed musketry courses adapted to the jungle. Additional weeks of rugged training on combat courses designed from the ever increasing flow of intelligence reports sent in from the Pacific combat theater, Guadalcanal. Every conceivable type of tree and ground sniper was duplicated. Targets representing Japanese strong points, ambushes, and patrols were erected. Men ran these courses firing live ammunition, throwing live hand grenades, improvising and throwing home-made Molotov cocktails. Slit-trenches, emplacements, and foxholes were dug, and then filled in again. The hills and jungles of Samoa absorbed many a unit of fire, but none was wasted. Night compass problems sometimes lasted from dark until daylight the next morning. Men got lost in the jungle, and stayed lost until a patrol could go out and find them the next day—

because they had decided that "the compass must be wrong, I'll trust my own judgment." Equal accent was placed on the man's familiarity with all of his weapons. One Company Weapons platoon boasted that every man could strip and assemble every infantry weapon in the Marine Corps blindfolded in three minutes.

An emergency would occur somewhere in the Pacific and the Regiment would be stripped of many of its finest men. Replacements would arrive from the States. Basic individual training would start all over again and continue until these new men were as good as the old. The Regiment would be further whittled down by sickness. More new green replacements. More individual training. Many were the days that started at reveille with bayonet, knife, and hand-to-hand fighting. Stress was laid on sanitation, personal cleanliness, and the living and eating facilities, though material was hard to obtain. Parade-ground inspections and formal guard mounts were out. Every hour of working time was spent toward the Colonel's primary objective: to prepare the Regiment for combat.

The only recreation facilities available were moving pictures, shown in the evenings, when it usually poured rain. A limited ration of beer; mail from home or from one's girl, or soft ball—there was no one place level or clear enough on the entire island for a hard-ball game. Nowhere was there a U.S.O. club or a Red Cross Hut. The men worked hard and made their own fun or wrote letters in their free time. Sack drill naturally took precedence over athletics. Training in the tropics is a rugged routine. Months of company, battalion, and regimental problems in the jungle followed the individual training. Some of these problems lasted thirty-six hours in a stretch.

Then came word that we were moving out in three weeks, slated for action in the Gilberts. We must be ready. So now we had specialized training in landing operations for a month off a neighboring island, with special schools for loading transports and moving equipment. It meant camouflaging every piece of equipment—dyeing skivvies, painting packs and web equipment, and re-covering helmets with burlap and painting these covers to blend with the foliage.

Later news: "We're not going—bad dope." Just another false start. And now training with even greater intensity to catch up on those few last details still unlearned. Then another let-down. . . .

And every day the Colonel climbed those hills and trekked through the jungle to oversee the training. He begged for equipment, ammunition, and replacements, haunted his superiors, won their affection for his men and for the results they were showing. He worked continuously with his staff and talked to his men. They listened and hoped and trusted, and through the sheer force of his character he fostered their faith.

After nine solid months of every conceivable type of training, the Colonel was able to announce to the men that they were going to see a patch of blue sky. That the Third Regiment had been chosen to be one of the regiments in the newly formed Third Marine Division. That they were going to New Zealand to join their parent organization.

"A trained regiment is marked by the way its men conduct themselves. You will be in a civilized country. None of us have seen a white woman in over nine months. Everyone will be watching you. I want you to have fun. I want you to have good chow. You will be taken into homes, you'll have the opportunity of drinking in bars and having dates and going to dances. You will be in a foreign country. The people there will do some things differently from the way we do them in our country. Don't boast. Take pride in your regiment and all the hard work you've been through to make it a great regiment. Don't throw it all overboard. Take pride in your appearance. Practice military courtesy. No matter how you feel, remember you're Americans from good parents; don't let your fathers and mothers down. Remember you're a Third Marine."

For seven weeks the Third Marines "fought the Battle of Queen Street" in New Zealand. The opportunity of training for combat in open country was taken advantage of. And every day we trained. The Colonel kept his promise and insisted that a certain proportion of the regiment be given liberty every day. The men had their first drink of milk in nine months, fresh eggs, steaks. Good people, some of whom had sons still fighting in Africa after three years of war, took the Marines into their homes. The men had dates, drank in pubs, made lifelong friends, captured the hearts of the citizens of a wonderful country, where people discussed the war only in terms of victory—where people said, "That'll be the day," with a proud light in their eyes. Where they sang the praises of their allies and went out of their way to make every convenience and recreational facility available to Marines.

The Third Marines hit New Zealand in the dead of a wet winter, and rain dogged them. But they emerged from their tents in pressed greens and polished Peter Bains, wearing boondockers and carrying their shined shoes in their hands until they reached a sidewalk or the porch of someone's home. They remembered the words of their commanding officer, practiced military courtesy, saluted smartly on the street, walked with pride, and played as hard as they worked. They devoured their seven weeks of civilization!

Nine months of training in the tropics, bad chow, and the absence of white women had left a mark on these men. Good buddies were closer buddies, they had a strong sense of latent power, they were roughed up and ready for combat, they had confidence in their leaders and themselves, and they were well disciplined. But their roughness, their jungle stare, was only on the surface. Beneath it were the same sense of decency, the same tolerance, the same sense of American sportsmanship, and a much greater appreciation of civilization. They were gentlemen of the finer school, loyal to their friends, unselfish, appreciative, rugged in the field, but courteous, kind, and thoughtful in the home. They followed the precepts defined and personally illustrated by the character of their respected regimental commander. And they never let him down. They were Third Marines.

Then the days of moving equipment, loading ships, and embarking came again, and they were on their way for further training as part of the Third Division. Some of the training was the same, some of it new and different and on a larger scale. "Contact Imminent"—the term used for the type of formation involving the movement of a regiment toward an objective when contact with the enemy is imminent—had been adapted to the jungle by the Third Marines. Keeping unit integrity in the jungle, where dispersion is still required, yet sight contact between men is often limited to five feet, is difficult and requires considerable practice. Everyone understood the necessity and importance of these monotonous field problems, but when there's no one shooting at you "a feast is as good as a famine." It was wearisome and dull, and became as unpalatable to the men as the recurrent demand to furnish ship-unloading working parties.

Additional training, working in co-operation with tanks and artillery, supplemented problems in stream crossings, the handling of rubber boats, and other combat exercises. The men were busy but straining at the leash—they wanted the real thing. They felt, as did their superiors, that they were ready for combat. But operations take a great deal of time to plan, the picture in the theater of operations is ever changing, and invasion schedules often have to be modified. More false starts, more let-downs. Good men were lost through medical survey. There were more new replacements. Adversity bound the men in the Regiment more tightly together.

As of old, in times of stress and strain the Colonel would talk directly to the men. Always having his fingers on the pulse of the Regiment, he recognized the highs and sensed the lows. Not merely a good speaker, the Colonel was a fine actor, making transitions from comedy to the serious, never too late or just on time, but always a beat ahead of his audience.

Framing the words they wanted to say, he told them: "Did you ever think you'd see so damn much jungle? If I ever get out of it, I'll never leave the sidewalk." Then the Colonel waited for the laugh and rode into the crest of it with a topper. "Hell—I won't even walk on the grass!" And the Colonel never failed to give the men the truth. No matter how serious, he'd tell them all he was able to tell.

"I know where we're going. You'll know too just as soon as I am able to tell you. But I can say this: our Regiment will be given a tough assignment. I know you never expected or wanted it any other way. You're not trained for an easy one. You're a combat outfit. You'll be given a real combat job. The time is short. This is your last chance to learn everything you can. Don't let down. Don't miss that one detail which may save your life or the lives of your buddies. You won't be here a minute too long!"

More recreation facilities were available here. Major Pappy Whitman burned the midnight oil and toiled through the daylight hours dreaming up and supervising new forms of recreation. Major General Turnage, the Commanding General of the Third Division, insisted that the men be given every available piece of recreational equipment and detailed officers to make this disbursement. Colonel Cauldwell gave Major Whitman the green light: "The lid's off. Whatever the men want, that's what I want them to have. If they don't like one thing, give them something else"—was the Colonel's O.K. to all of Pappy's requests. Baseball, volley ball, basketball, movies, a nightly newscast of world news, shows gotten up by the men themselves, contests with money prizes, beer whenever it was available—these helped us to pass those long waiting hours when the day's duty was completed.

Lieutenant Dave Zeitlin, Captain Fred Finucane, Chaplain Glyn Jones, Chaplain Father Kempker, American Red Cross representative E. O. Godfrey, and Sergeant Freddy Stark, were some of Pappy's most able assistants in the program. Freddy Stark, recalling his promotion days in New York City, planned and executed the most popular diversion of the lot. Given a free hand, he staged a Guadalcanal Golden Gloves Tournament. The regimental champions of each division were given a plaque made by our friends the Seabees out of metal from a Japanese plane shot down near the Third's bivouac area. The Colonel and all officers attended the bouts, which were held in a ring made of coconut logs and scrap lumber. On the final night of the contest, Major General Turnage presented the plaques to the winners. We were proud of our champions: Pfc Alfred L. Lindberg, featherweight; Corporal Howard E. Sozio, lightweight; Pvt. Robert O. Santos, welterweight; Pfc George S. Banks, junior middleweight; Corporal Felice V. Nasti, middleweight; Pfc William and Robert Kervelas, both of whom reached the finals in the light heavyweight division and were awarded the joint championship of that division; Corporal Francis A. Richards, heavyweight.

A few weeks before we sailed for combat Colonel Cauldwell was promoted to Brigadier General. The General was relieved by Colonel George McHenry. The Third now had a new skipper.

"I am proud to be with you," were Big Mac's first words to the Regiment. "The Third Regiment is the best-trained regiment in the Marine Corps. Any regiment trained by General Cauldwell couldn't help but be."

There were few changes, practically none, when Colonel McHenry took over. The Colonel kept the regimental staff intact. He put his stamp of approval on the three battalion commanders and did nothing to disturb the functional smoothness which he seemed to feel was already there when he arrived. The time was growing short. The Colonel wanted to use every moment of that time to continue where the General left off, cleaning up last-minute training details, familiarizing himself with the character and performance of the members of his staff and the officers under his command, and executing the many detailed orders for the impending pre-invasion landing exercises. These were busy days. The tempo of preparation increased. It began to look like the real thing.

Then one day the orders arrived. Two regiments of the Third Division, the Third and the Ninth, reinforced into two combat teams, were to move out, combat loaded, within a designated number of days for a preliminary landing problem off another friendly island in the Pacific. Everyone knew that this was it. Many thought they knew where the strike was to be made. Wild guesses were in the wind. Everyone played the game of strategy.

"What do you think about the big picture?"

"Well, I just got the latest dope from an assistant cook at Division, who got it from a corpsman, who heard a switchboard operator talking to the Captain of the head at Corps, and he said . . ."

Only a higher-ranking few knew the definite picture. One thing was certain, everyone knew it, it was in the air, you felt it all the way through you: the highly trained Third was going to war.

We also knew that General Cauldwell was not to be with us in the initial assault. It was his job to remain behind and insure the movement of the second echelon of the Division. Again the men understood the significance of this very important detail in what must be a difficult general plan; but they were disappointed. Speed had pulled them through all of their adversity. Speed understood every facet of their shining ability. Speed had made them what they were today. They would pay off for Speed. They wished Speed could be there to see them do it. And they knew that Speed also was disappointed.

On the way up from the pre-invasion exercises the convoy stopped one evening for a few hours off the staging base which they had left twenty-one days before. The men saw the boat that carried Speed to the command group transport. They saw Speed board the ship, and they saw him leave. They realized he was there to wish them good luck and let them know he was confident that they were the best shock troops in the world and that they couldn't fail.

When the General's boat pulled away from the transport a smile of confidence curtained his face. But it was a deceptive smile. For the first time Speed felt weary, helpless, lonely. He had given a slice of his life to prepare his boys for the coming bloody plunge. He had taught them everything he knew. Many would be heroes, some would be wounded, and some would be dead before he could get to them again. The time and space between would be an anxious time of hoping, trusting, and praying. The boat churned away from the transport. Speed looked back and waved. He felt a little sad. There was a reason for that sadness. Speed had left a portion of his heart aboard.

The men watched Speed leave and thought of the last time he had talked to them. He had painted with words the picture they so well understood. He had shown them why they had such a strong regimental spirit. He had told the men that it was they that had made the Regiment, that he had never in all his experience seen any organization with such able troop leaders and such truly fine men, men of character, physically tough, men of ideals. He reminded them that they were different. How there had never been a gap between officers and men, never that area so well known in other outfits as "officers' country." That this had been a practical outgrowth of their training background. That they had started out as a combat regiment, had remained the same, and would end their careers as such, when practical necessity dictated that combat training and combat living replace the routine of a barracks regime. They looked different, they thought differently, they felt differently from men in other outfits. And he told them to act differently—better than any who had gone before. No stabbing of their own buddies in foxholes, no unnecessary and useless firing of weapons during an anxious jungle night!

Then they remembered the tears in the General's eyes when he told them that it was they who had made him a General, just as they had demanded to be trained by their own officers for whom through mutual adversity they would carry the shield of pure devotion, true respect, and unimpeachable loyalty. And they heard their skipper, their buddy, their father, say goodbye to them. As the transports pulled away from the island, the last stop before the reckless strike, they gazed back in retrospect and heard again his final words:

"You know I'll never forget each and every one of you. Don't think I've ever left you. No matter where you are—when the going gets the toughest—I'll be right up there with you!"

Early on that morning of the sixth day General Cauldwell left the beach, reported in to the Division C.P., delivered his messages, took off his stars, and sallied forth to the Third Regiment C.P. As he hiked through the knee-deep mud up the newly constructed tractor road, he met an officer from the regimental staff coming the other way. The officer had never been more anxious to salute. But

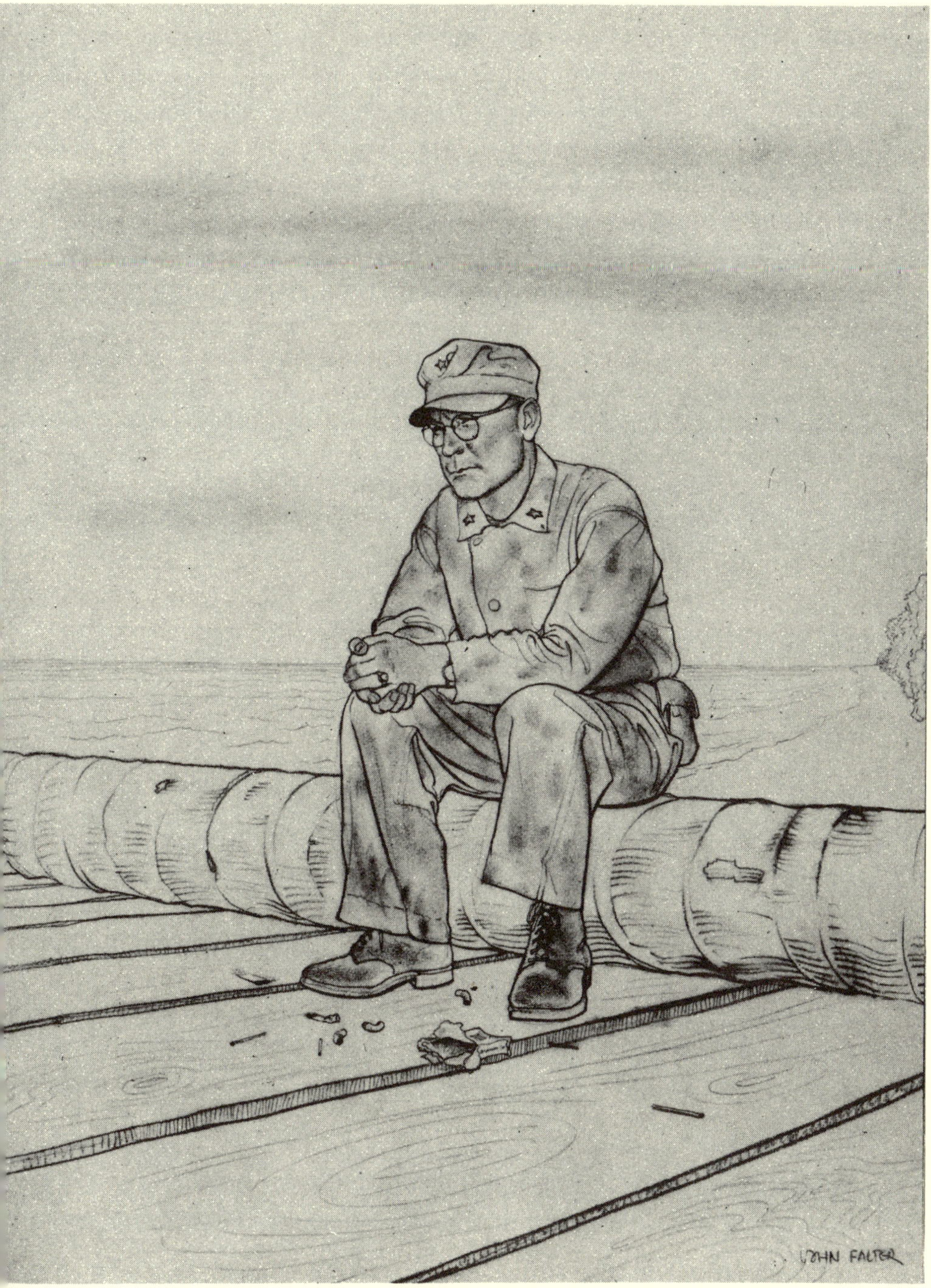
JOHN FALTER

snipers can see and hear, and in the jungle military courtesy is supplanted by the use of first or nicknames only and one doesn't salute. It had to be "Good morning, Speed!" And then—just to see that wonderful smile—the officer added, "What do you think of the boys, Speed?" Perhaps an outsider wouldn't understand, but, to this officer who had seen that look of pride so many times, the General's answer told a beautiful story: "You know what I think."

The officer went on, a wave of well-being passing through him. "Everything's going to be all right," he reflected. "Tojo hasn't got enough men to lick us now. Speed's here. This is a wonderful day for the Third Marines!"

Chapter 9

EARLY ON THE MORNING of the seventh day of the invasion six landing boats, looking almost exactly like our own tank lighters, were discovered sneaking into the beach up beyond the left flank of the beachhead.

All during the day before, landing craft from the boat pool anchored out in the bay since D-day had been streaming back and forth across the bay, out to the newly arrived transports, back in to shore carrying troops and supplies. The men down on the beach had become accustomed to this boat traffic. It seemed as if we had been on Bougainville for months. Things went more smoothly. Supplies hit the beach and were shuttled immediately to the established dumps.

Everyone on the beach saw the six landing boats sneak in. Some of the shore gunners grew suspicious and waited for an order to open fire. But the order didn't come. One shore party officer didn't like the looks of them.

"They could be Jap landing barges," he said to another officer near him.

"In broad daylight?" the other officer returned doubtfully. "There's an outpost up beyond the left flank. They're bringing them supplies."

"What's that screwy-looking boat behind the tank lighter? Have we got any boats that look like that? Gimme those glasses."

"That's a barge, Major—looks like it's being towed."

"You're God-damned right it's a barge," said the officer,. pitching the field glasses back to the owner. "Jap landing barges—" and he dove for the 'phone.

The officer shouted the Division Code name into the 'phone.

But the Division lines were all busy. Very busy. A Japanese landing force had been reported and countermeasures were burning up the wires.

"Bright and early on the morning of November 7th I noticed shell splashes off the point of land to my right, west of the Koromokina River," reports Major Dick Moss, who was in his Regimental Weapons Observation Post on the beach. "Finding out it was friendly artillery, I decided to help, and rolled the two half-tracks out on the beach to engage the target. We put about twenty-five high-explosive shells per gun on the point. It was direct fire at about 1400 yards, and we really bounced them in there."

But by the time the first report of the landing had been checked and fire orders had been given to the artillery and beach defense units, the Jap barges had already hit the beach.

How many barges? Where had they landed? Some had been seen coming in beyond the left flank near and beyond the mouth of the Koromokina River. But how many more had landed west of this area, up near the Laruma, out of sight beyond the point of land west of the left flank of the beachhead? A sixty-man outpost from K Company of the Ninth Marines and a forward observation team from the artillery battalion were down near the mouth of the Laruma River. They had been out of communication all night. What had happened? Had their radio gone dead? What had happened to this outpost? Another platoon from K Company of the Ninth was out on patrol along the Laruma River. Where was this patrol now? What had happened to it? The Third Battalion of the Ninth was holding this left flank of the beachhead. K Company of this battalion anchored the flank to the beach. Their line would be stretched dangerously thin. How large a force had landed? Had some landed during the night? How far inland had the enemy advanced?

These were some of the pertinent questions that must be cleared up immediately. And at the same time countermeasures had to be taken. If that flank was breached and a hard-hitting, fast-moving Jap force poured through the gap, we would be in serious trouble. Action! Immediate action! But where? What was the enemy trying to do? What could we do without weakening any portion of the perimeter? Perhaps this might only be a diversion. The main attack might be made at another section of the perimeter. Messages shot along the jungle lines. Division to the Third Regiment . . . Regiment to the C.P. of the Third Battalion Ninth . . . back to Regiment . . . back to Division . . . then to the First Battalion Third, the battalion in reserve.

The First Battalion had had a bad night. There had been three long bombing raids. The Japs had concentrated on this section of the beachhead. The day before a battery of 90-mm. anti-aircraft guns had moved in right next to their bivouac area. During most of the night the ground shook as the guns blasted the air. Right on schedule the rain had arrived at 3:30 in the afternoon, and it kept up all night. Only a limited supply of rations had been brought up. The company commanders had made their complaints. The men had enough to eat that night, and sufficient rations were on hand for one meal in the morning; but they didn't like it. "Always have an extra two-day supply of rations on hand for an emergency." They were straining to carry out their orders. Company executive officers had tried to get additional rations from the Third Battalion, but the Third didn't have any extras either. The quartermasters were doing the impossible to fill immediate demands. There were just so many amphibian tractors; all were being used. Complaints passed through the chain of command. Regiment bore down on the quartermasters. No excuses. Get those emergency rations up to the lines and the reserve battalion. Supply men worked faster and harder. Tractors bogged down with their heavy, precious loads. Men put cases of rations on their shoulders and plodded through the waist-deep mud. The ugly, gluey, flooded jungle swamp laughed at them.

The men of the First Battalion climbed out of their foxholes that morning, cleaned their rifles, and talked about the night bombing raid. Word had drifted in. One bomb had dropped in the Division Headquarters area. A newspaper correspondent who had been sleeping in a jungle hammock had been killed.

Up to this time a jungle hammock issued to the Army had been a coveted piece of equipment. Some of the men had "borrowed" a few from the Army on Guadalcanal, but all the equipment of the front-line troops (save combat packs) had been left on the beach. A man who had a hammock in his blanket roll down on the beach never expected to see it again. This morning none of the owners cared. Anyone who wanted it could have it for a present. And if any of the men wanted to go over to Division they could get any number of them free. That particular bomb had missed the First Battalion's bivouac area by a few hundred yards. Even with every man below the surface of the ground, they had been lucky.

Before they had finished their breakfast ration the morning's news exploded in amongst them:

"Five hundred Japs have landed on the left flank and have broken through the perimeter."

In a matter of minutes after Major McMath, "The Traveler," had reached Major Chuck Bailey, executive officer of the First Battalion, by 'phone, the First Battalion had gone into action. Chuck Bailey and Major Steve Brody, the Battalion Commander, had issued their orders and were tearing down the tractor road to join The Traveler on the beach. Captain Gordon Warner had assembled his company, had issued his terse orders, and was moving out at the head of B Company. Captain Shorty Vogel and C Company were right on their heels. Here was the emergency. No rations. No extra water. No extra ammunition. Every weapon, all combat packs, and all fighting equipment had been snatched up. No one thought about what wasn't there—men grabbed what there was. Action! Immediate action! Time, man's most precious gift, was running out. The enemy had landed. They had broken through the beachhead perimeter. No one had to define that situation—it was only too clear. This was a time of lightning estimation on the part of the leaders, brief explicit rapid orders, speedy, thorough, immediate execution on the part of the men. Think fast, talk fast and clear, anticipate, act with speed and accuracy. Do something, and do it right now, and do it well—but, by God, *do something!* Two companies of the battle-tested First Battalion smelled urgency. Under perfect control, alert to orders, straining through the mud, determined, keen, vicious, mad, with blood in their eyes, they double-timed toward the beach. The battle of the Koromokina had already begun.

The two company columns halted on the trail running parallel and just off the beach about a thousand yards west of the tractor road. Here, amongst a small clump of coconut trees on the edge of the jungle, the First Battalion had set up its C.P. Here The Traveler was analyzing the situation, with Steve Brody and Chuck Bailey passing on every bit of information that had arrived at regimental headquarters from the Third Battalion, Ninth. K Company of the Ninth had been hit hard by the Japs who, landing over a broad area, had been faced with the choice of taking the time to assemble their forces and organize a full-scale attack, or of attacking immediately hoping to find the line weak enough to effect a break-through and then pour the rest of their forces through the gap as they arrived. They decided on the latter action.

How many of the Japs had already infiltrated through K Company, the remainder of which had advanced and was tied down by Jap fire about two hundred yards in front of its original perimeter line, no one knew. There was no time for preliminary reconnaissance. The plan of action had already been decided on by the time the troops arrived. Steve led the troops into position as Chuck and The Traveler, remaining at the C.P., quickly reviewed the situation and plan to Big Mac, who had just arrived. Captain Tom Jolly, a battery commander who was acting as liaison officer for the supporting artillery battalion, arrived at the same time, together with a forward observation team which was immediately assigned to B Company. But it was a bad situation. An artillery concentration which would harass the Jap forces moving up in support of their troops attacking K Company could not be laid down, for out in front, somewhere between the Laruma River and our front lines, were over a hundred of our own troops: the sixty-man patrol which might have been wiped out or was working its way back toward our lines, and the platoon patrol scouting out the area along the Laruma River. Until reports from these friendly troops could be received, artillery—so precious now—could not be used.

Steve issued his order to his company commanders, Warner and Vogel, and led them into position. Less than fifty yards ahead of the Battalion C.P. a narrow trail led north along the original perimeter line of the Third Battalion Ninth. C and B Companies of the First Battalion, Third Marines, moved up this trail for about 600 yards. They formed quickly into their attack formation. The brief and simple attack order had given the company commanders little to work on. No enemy information. A part of K Company had pushed west, about 200 yards to their front, and was tied down by Jap mortar and machine-gun fire. That was all. The terrain was totally unknown. How much swamp? How much open space? How much thick jungle? All a mystery.

The two companies abreast, covering a front of 600 yards, would attack in a line of skirmishers, each company with two platoons abreast forward and one in reserve. B Company would anchor its left flank platoon to the beach. Both companies would advance immediately on a compass azimuth of 280° until their forward elements struck K Company. They would then halt and await further orders from the battalion C.P.

For two companies attacking, with two platoons abreast, 600 yards means 150 yards of frontage per platoon. In the thickness of the jungle this is a very wide front, and each man in that forward moving line is required to keep contact with the men on his right and left. But 600 yards of front had to be covered. By figuring time and what had already happened, the Japs could be that far inland and ready to attack anywhere along that line.

Warner with the left flank company decided to move forward

with his left platoon. He had a new lieutenant in command, and Warner knew that the Japs could move more rapidly near the beach. He anticipated that this platoon would make the first contact with the enemy. His right flank platoon was under the command of First Sergeant Le Guin. His executive officer, Lieutenant Joe Nolan, would follow with the company command group of about twelve men, directly behind the narrow gap separating the first and the second platoons. His reserve platoon, under Lieutenant Jackson, together with the 60-mm. mortar section from the weapons platoon would follow the command group at an interval of fifty yards. Vogel's company on the right flank was dispersed in much the same way.

Both companies were in position when a lieutenant from K Company came dashing back with the urgent request: "For God's sake, get up there fast. We need help"—punctuated by the sound of firing up ahead. In possession of no information on the whereabouts of the enemy, knowing nothing about the terrain in front of them, Warner and Vogel gave the order to advance. Both companies, moving entirely by compass azimuth, started off through the thick jungle growth.

Joe Nolan and the command group moved cautiously forward in a column of file. Their azimuth led them over dry, dense ground right along the edge of a deep swamp on their right. They had gone about fifty yards through this thick underbrush and were approaching a small clearing when Gunnery Sergeant Duncan, a tall, slow-drawling, seasoned Marine old-timer from Tennessee, signaled to Joe Nolan up ahead. Joe halted the column and everyone took cover. Gunny Duncan pointed out a tall banyan tree overlooking the group about 150 yards to their left front.

"What's the matter, Gunny?" Joe asked him.

Gunny had his head cocked to one side and was squinting toward the top of the tree.

"That's a likely place for a sniper," he drawled. "Yes, I do believe there is one there.'"

Slow and easy, Gunny dropped to a comfortable position on his right knee, never taking his eyes off the target. Then he tucked his carbine into his right shoulder and sighted in. As if he were firing for record on a rifle range and straining for a possible, he lowered his carbine slowly and adjusted his position. That felt better. Once again he raised his carbine to his shoulder and took a bead on the target. Ten seconds built up into half a man's life-span as this slow, methodical, accurate squirrel-hunting expert held that pose and squeezed the trigger a thousandth of an inch at a time. A lone bullet cracked through the air. Still holding his position, Gunny watched the form of a Japanese jungle sniper emerge slowly from the upper foliage of the large tree . . . slowly at first, then—as gravity picked it up from there—plunge through the air and crash into the heavy brush sixty feet below. With the same premeditated slowness, Gunny lowered his carbine and drawled to Joe: "You know . . . I deliberately killed that man."

The sound of the fire fight to their left front grew louder. Joe gave the signal to move forward. The group circled the small open spot, keeping in the shadowed underbrush, and proceeded on their azimuth.

Joe Jackson and Gunner McAlexander with the reserve followed fifty yards behind. Then a new twist occurred. A runner suddenly dashed up to Jackson: "Warner needs your platoon and the 60's over on the left flank. He says, 'Make it fast!' "

"Pass the word up to Joe that Warner has sent for us to reinforce the second platoon," yelled Jackson. Then he pulled out and rushed the urgently needed reserve over to Warner. But the word never got up to Joe Nolan. The group continued to move forward.

As anticipated, the Japs had made their farthest progress toward the perimeter on the left flank nearest the beach. The left flank platoon was hit almost immediately by a Jap force strongly equipped with 50-caliber and rapid-firing Nambu machine-guns. They had immediate fire superiority. Warner had two light machine-guns and a platoon of riflemen. He needed fire power badly, and he needed it in a hurry. Fifty yards to his rear was the regimental and battalion command group sweating over map and field 'phones. A few yards farther back was the field dressing station. Warner knew well what it would mean if the Japs broke through here. He had a fight on his hands.

In the meantime Shorty Vogel's company, presumably moving abreast on the right flank of this new line, advanced ten yards and struck a waist-deep swamp. His orders were to cover 300 yards of front and move on a particular compass direction. He and his men started through the swamp. It was hard, slow going.

The jungle grew thicker. Joe Nolan's command group continued to move forward. The front had been spread much too thin for an advance through thick jungle underbrush. The units on his left were not only tied down by fire but were desperately fighting to prevent a break-through. Vogel's company on the right was bogged down by the swamp. The reserve was no longer following behind them. Nolan with his group of twelve men continued to move forward. He didn't know it, but they were really out on the limb. And they were walking into a situation that would soon separate the men from the boys.

Lieutenant Herron, who had been attached to company headquarters, suddenly appeared from the brush in front of the advancing group and signaled to Nolan. The group halted. Herron rushed over to Joe and whispered, "Japs—up ahead!" He pointed to the front.

Knowing that Herron had started off with Warner, Joe figured that the two forward platoons on his left were keeping up with his rate of advance.

Again they started forward. Three ground snipers opened up. Everyone hit the deck. Three men worked their way off to the left. Selkuski, a B.A.R. man up in front, kept the snipers tied down. Other men moved off to the left. The rest of the group waited patiently under good cover. When the snipers were eliminated, the group again moved forward. The ground started to rise. It was still very thick.

Twenty yards farther, Allicon and O'Keefe, the forward scouts, broke through some heavy underbrush that was screening a recently cleared area on somewhat higher ground. Thirty Japs frantically digging foxholes looked up from their work and into the faces of the two rugged jungle-fighting Marines. The men in the command group would have plenty to tell their grandchildren—they had walked into a Japanese strong point in the process of construction.

Allicon fired. O'Keefe's Tommy-gun jammed and failed to fire. Joe ran forward and shot a Jap in the forwardmost foxhole. The rest of the Japs started yelling, threw down their tools, and sprang for their weapons. Allicon and Selkuski got two of the scramblers before they reached their rifles. O'Keefe threw his Tommy-gun into the bush, screaming, "For Christ's sake, somebody give me a weapon that'll shoot!"

"Six others already in the rear holes opened up," Joe later related. "My first instinct was to charge. But Herron, who had made his way back past them, told me there were more a short distance up ahead. We could hear them cutting trees and jabbering. He knew we had to get possession of these foxholes. Then we could hold them off until Jackson's platoon caught up to us. Thinking Warner was on my left, I knew they couldn't outflank us on that side. I had lost contact with Le Guin's platoon from Shorty's company on my right, but I could protect my own right flank until that platoon came abreast with us. They couldn't be too far behind. I didn't know how wide the swamp was or how far it extended.

"Herron saved our lives. He said if I would hold them down by fire to the front he would outflank them. Herron and four men started off to the left. I tried to roll two hand grenades into the rear holes. But the Japs were on higher ground and had us pinned down. The grenades hit the brush. I couldn't get one in there. We got every weapon on them and covered for each other. Gradually I was able to work the men one at a time into the forward holes. I dashed ahead and reached a hole in the center. Herron had moved off to the left. That was the last time I saw him alive. One of my men yelled that Herron had been hit. I sent another man over to

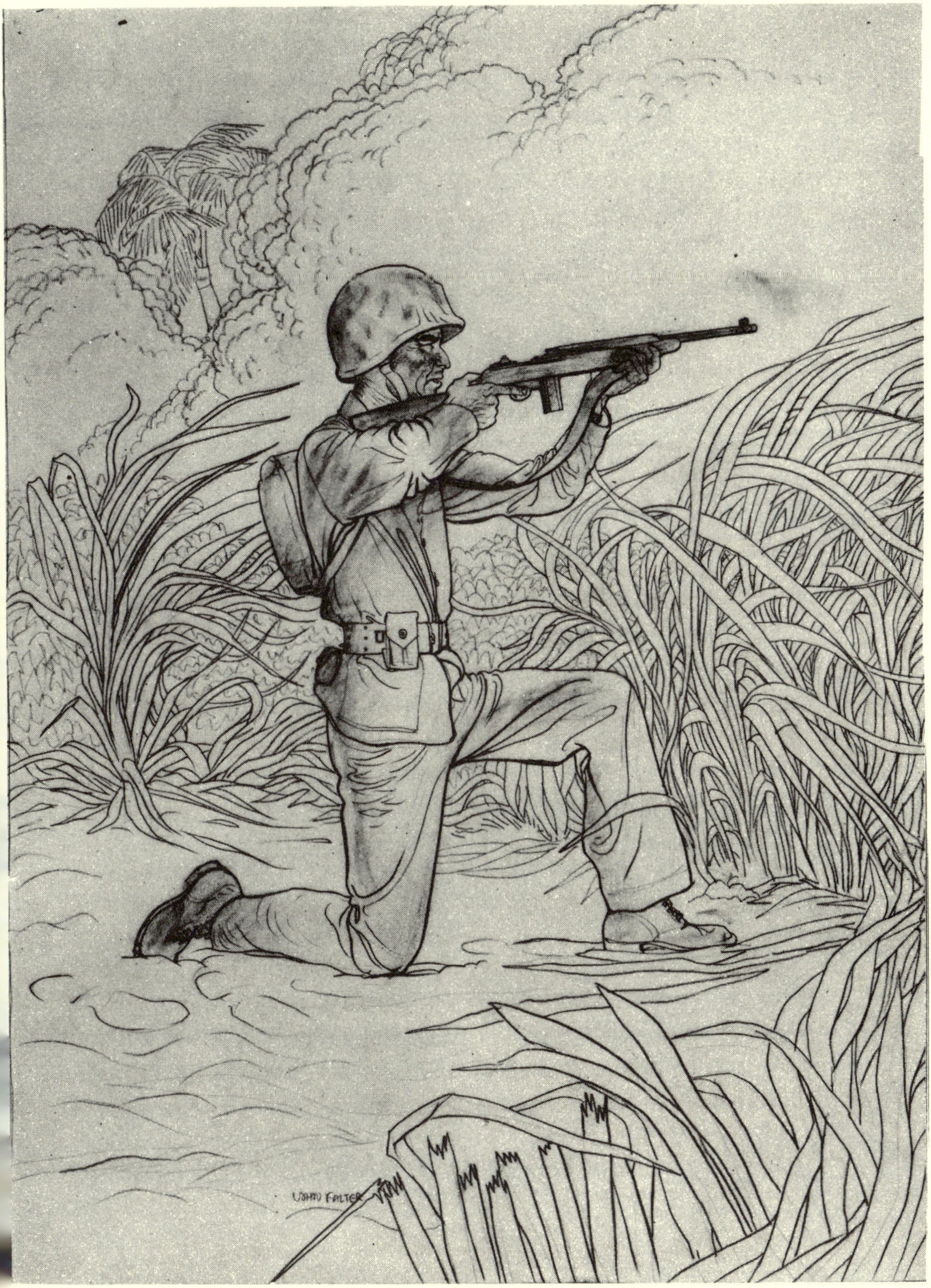
JOHN FALTER

the left to give him a hand. But he couldn't help him. Herron had been shot through the heart.

"Then the Japs charged. I yelled for the men to fire faster. The Japs kept coming with fixed bayonets. I fired as fast as my carbine would work. I don't know how many rounds were left in the clips I kept changing, but I wasn't going to get caught with an empty. One mean-looking bastard charged practically on top of me. I dropped him not more than three feet from the foxhole. A bullet struck the front of Selkuski's foxhole and kicked dirt in his eyes. The bullets tore through the trees as the muzzle of the B.A.R. went skyward. Selkuski slumped in his hole as if he had been hit. I yelled, 'Black John, for God's sake take over that B.A.R.' But Selkuski discovered he wasn't hit and got the B.A.R. back in action. Selkuski told me later that he had thought, as he heard me call to Black John, 'That friggin' Nolan don't care if I was dead or alive as long as the B.A.R. kept firing!' We stopped the charge. Some of the Japs ran to the rear, and some into the swamp to the right.

"Then the Lieutenant from the K Company platoon dashed over. He told me his men were over to our left, badly shot up. He asked me for some help to knock out a machine-gun up ahead of them. I told him that we had just stopped one Jap charge but there were more of them reorganizing behind the cover to our front. I knew they'd be back. I told him to hold tight, that a platoon in his rear was moving up and would soon be there. I asked him to support us with fire while we took the rest of the foxholes. He went back to his platoon, and I signaled to the men to work themselves forward.

"Then I remembered the Japs who had run off into the swamp. I pulled back and worked my way around to the right. I dashed toward Duncan, who was over too far on the right to hear me. As I got off the deck the second time on the way over, I felt as if somebody had hit me in the shoulder with a large hammer. I kept going until I fell on my face alongside of him. 'Watch the right flank, Gunny,' I yelled.

"'All right, Lieutenant, take it easy,' Gunny kept repeating. 'Now take it easy . . . take it easy.'

"The blood started to soak through my dungaree jacket. It didn't hurt, but I kept thinking about going into shock. I wasn't worried about the blood, but I knew I had to get some morphine into my arm. Klinger crawled over to me, opened my first-aid pouch, and tried to get the morphine in my arm. He was fired at. He picked up his rifle and fired back. Then he got the morphine into me and bandaged my arm.

" 'Withdraw! They're going to lay down mortar fire.' The word started from over on the left and passed across the line. 'No one will withdraw!' I screamed back. 'God damn it, *I'm* giving the friggin' orders.' Gunny never moved a muscle. He kept watching a foxhole out ahead. I sent Harberson and O'Keefe back to find Warner and see if any order to withdraw had been given.

"Then the Japs charged again. Gunny changed his position where he could take over. He kept every man firing just as fast as they could. I was still lying on the ground. Gunny and the men stopped the charge.

"I looked down at my arm and tried to move it. It wouldn't work, so I pulled it up and stuck my wrist through the rawhide compass cord I was wearing around my neck.

"We had been fighting for the foxholes about two hours. Things were quiet now for a while. I started to worry about the mortar fire. If that order was correct, we were in a bad spot. Where in the hell was the reserve platoon? I couldn't understand why they hadn't gotten to us.

"I went over to Gunny Duncan and told him to take over. Then I worked my way over to where the platoon from K Company had been catching hell. There was no one there. On my way back I ran into Sergeant Dougherty's squad from C Company. Either they had gotten separated or else Shorty had heard the fire fight and had sent them over to help us out. O'Keefe came running up and told me the order to withdraw was straight dope and that we were about 150 yards ahead of the front line. I sent Dougherty and his squad over to Gunny to help him fight a withdrawing action and pull the rest of the men out. Gunny pulled the men back out of range, made contact with Le Guin's platoon on the right, and set up a hasty defense. Allicon and O'Keefe brought me back. I ran into Lieutenant Crosswell and his platoon. I told him about the foxholes up ahead and the order to withdraw. Later in the afternoon, while I was lying in the field hospital about a thousand yards back of the front line, they brought in Crosswell. He had been blown five feet in the air by the explosion of a Jap 90-mm. mortar shell and was suffering from blast concussion."

Things go wrong in battle. Many Marines believe that more battles are won the wrong way than the right. They learn both ways, and then do their individual jobs so well that a potential defeat is molded into a definite victory. A fighting Irish Marine officer, an old-time cool Gunnery Sergeant, an expert B.A.R. man, and twelve trained men with tons of guts and doing it very well had held off, killed, and dispersed fifty Japs. For three hours they had been separated from the rest of their company. They had saved their hard-pressed company's right flank, and they had stopped the Japs from pouring through a gap in the beachhead perimeter.

Back at the Battalion C.P. Major Chuck Bailey and Major Sid (The Traveler) McMath were planning new moves to meet the developed situation. Watching these two rapid-thinking operation men in action, you knew why it had taken the North four years to win the Civil War. They were the type of officers that Lee must have had. Big Mac would approve or suggest; being the Third's Regimental Commander, it was his responsibility. But Big Mac knew his officers. He had seen them in action on D-day on the Cape; he knew they were good, and he let them call the shots. Major Steve Brody was everywhere, driving units into position, plugging gaps, setting up the various supporting units, sending patrols from the intelligence section to various points along the line for information. It was a good working combination: Steve, the rugged strong-arm man; Chuck, the tactician; and The Traveler, who always had the solution, the supervisor.

Part of the plan was to send a tank lighter to a point between the Koromokina and the mouth of the Laruma River, to dart quickly into the beach at a spot where the Japs hadn't landed, and to locate the outpost and pull them out. The patrol along the Laruma could travel north and work its way east to our front lines.

A short time after the two companies from the First Battalion had begun their advance, General Cauldwell had rushed down from Division Headquarters to personally supervise the eradication of the Jap landing force. Under sniper fire, Speed strode into the forward C.P. no more than fifty yards to the rear of the front lines. The Traveler was straining over a map. Chuck was calling hurried instructions to Warner and Vogel on a conference call over a field 'phone. The air was on fire.

"Well, boys, I see you've got a little fight on your hands," said Speed calmly as he joined the circle.

"Yes, sir."

"Good morning, Speed."

"Good morning, Mac, Chuck, Steve. A little fight on our hands, eh? Well, that's what we came for. Now let's see . . . have you made contact with the enemy? Where the hell are they?" Speed knelt down by the map.

Big Mac and The Traveler hurriedly gave Speed the situation, brought him up to date on the progress so far, and told him their plan. B and C Companies were advancing abreast. When they reached the hard-pressed K Company out in front, they were to halt and reorganize. Jolly was standing by to co-ordinate the artillery. If the outpost could be pulled out, a five-minute mortar and artillery concentration was to be laid down. Then the two companies were to attack through K Company advancing to a designated phase line. A new azimuth would have to be given to each company. Pivoting on B Company on the left and anchored to the beach, the line would turn as it moved forward. C Company would attack toward the beach, driving the Japs out of the area.

"Well, let's drive them right back into the sea," said Speed.

"That's the plan, Speed," said The Traveler.

"Right back into the sea," Speed repeated. "The General wants to have them out of there by nightfall."

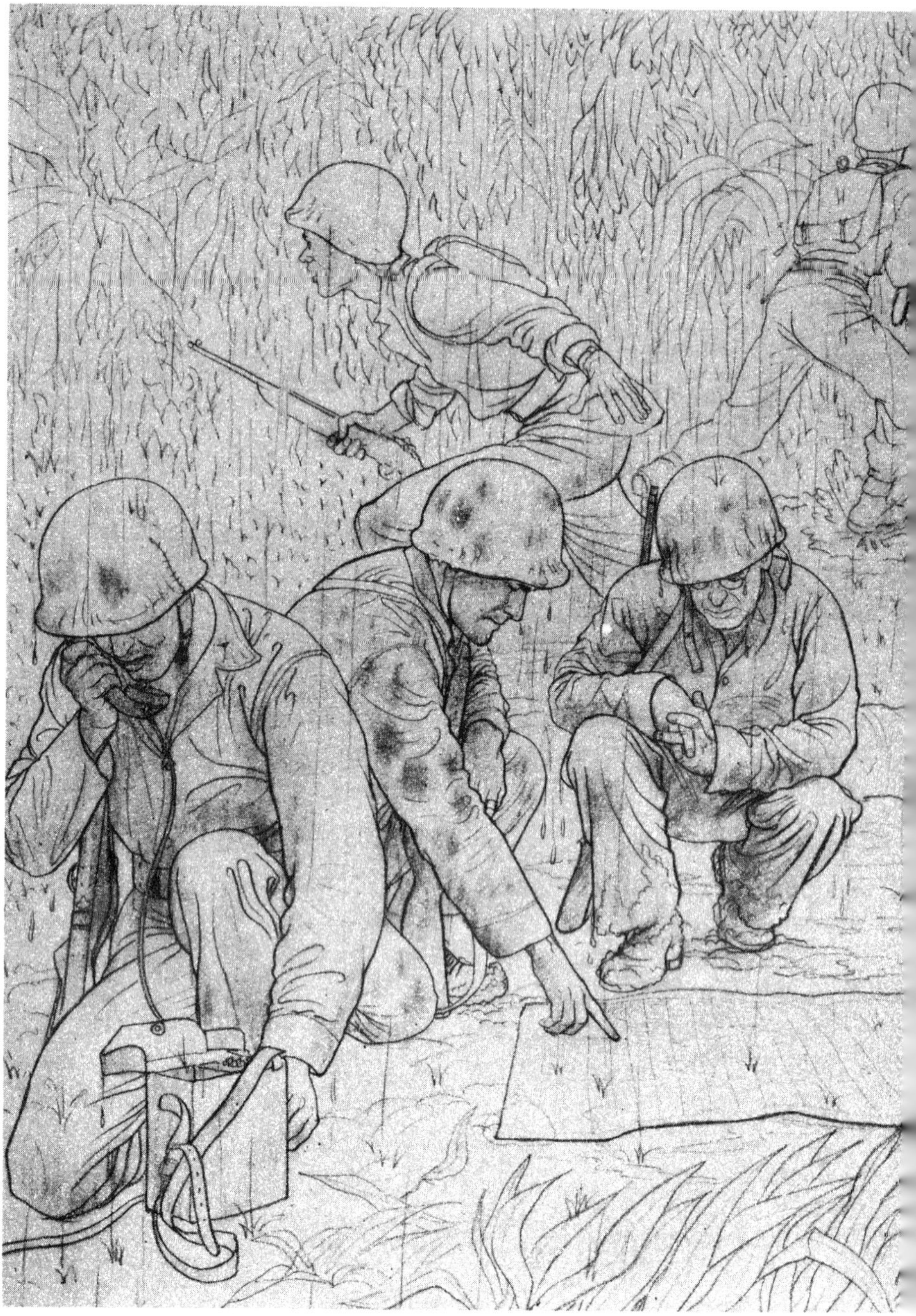

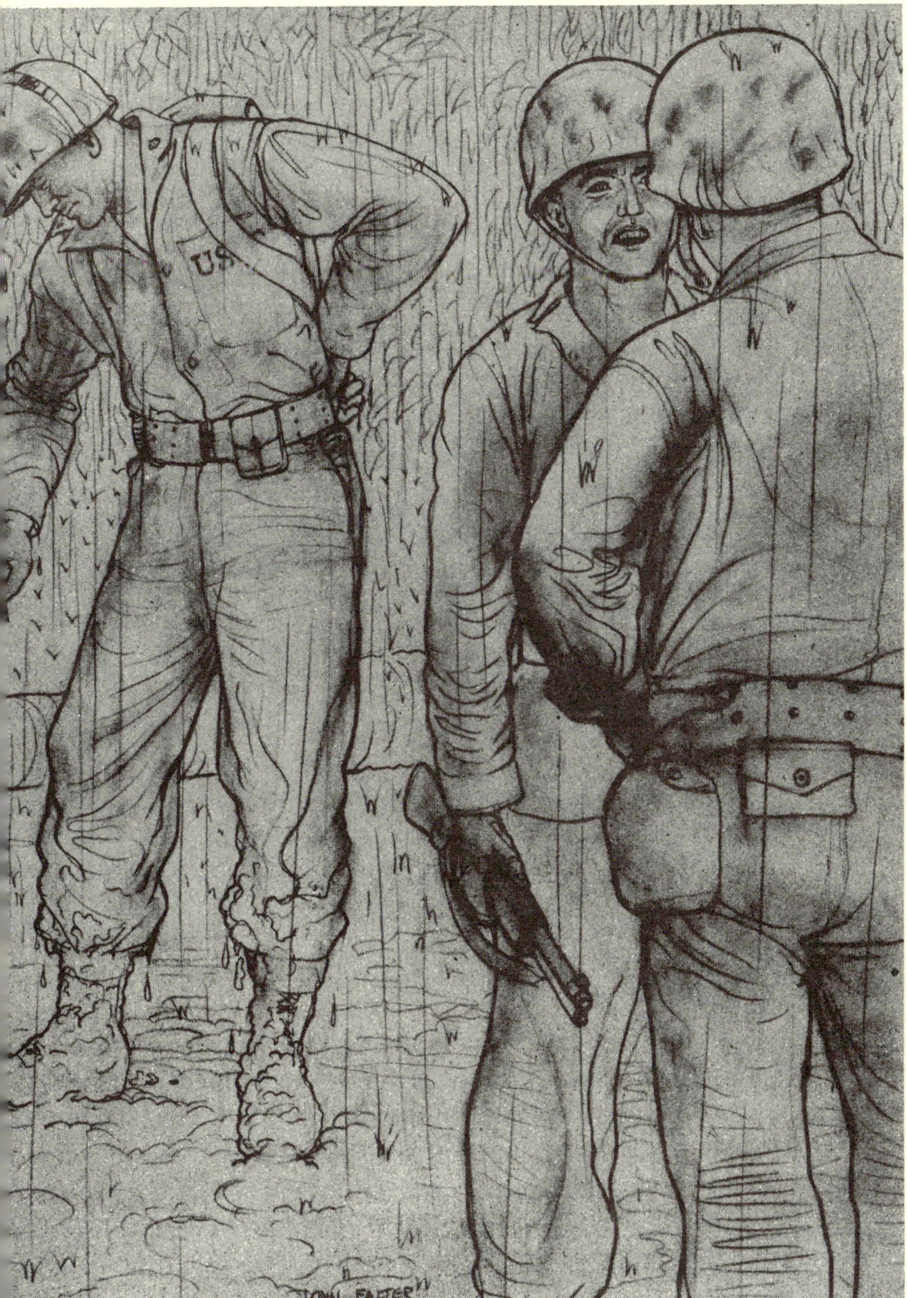
US
VAN FALTER

"Yes, Sir."

"They've got no right on this island," smiled Speed. The officers laughed, then plunged again into their work. Tom Jolly was calling Smitty in the fire control center back at the artillery battalion. Steve was shouting instructions to a Mortar lieutenant. Tom Manion, a clever young battalion staff officer, rushed in with some information for Chuck. The Traveler and Big Mac were working over the map. Doc Willets hurried in to give Steve the location of the battalion aid station. One of the C.P. security men let go a burst with a Tommy-gun at a sniper who had infiltrated to within ten yards of the C.P. Speed calmly sat down on a coconut log near the map and wiped his glasses.

When Warner hit the Japs who had broken through the remnants of K Company and were pouring through on the left flank near the beach, he sent for Jackson's reserves and Gunner McAlexander's 60-mm. mortar platoon. He checked in quickly with Chuck at the C.P. and reported the situation. The area was infested with machine-guns. The left flank was pinned down.

"You've got to hold there, Warner," Chuck yelled over the 'phone. "We'll hold!"

Warner put every man on the line. Everyone fired as fast as he could pull the trigger. Warner ran, crawled, and shouted from one end of the jagged line to the other, pointing out Jap machine-gun strong points, organizing fire teams to outflank a particularly damaging position. The Japs were in the trees, dug in under logs, and one out of every four of them had a Nambu machine-gun. Warner is a Jap-hater of long standing. He had licked them in cabarets in China; he had licked them with swords in Japan; he can even curse their legitimacy—in Japanese. With a helmet full of hand grenades he fought his own personal war. While a B.A.R. man or several riflemen would tie down a machine-gun from the front, he would dash within range of the Nip nest and blow it up with grenades.

This fire fight at a maximum of thirty yards' range went on for hours. Every available machine-gun and rifleman was sent to this flank. Gradually Warner built up a powerful fire line. Then in the midst of the scrap he crawled through to the flank of a Jap fire line and shouted in Japanese for the Nips to fix bayonets and charge. They dutifully obeyed. Thirty-two Japs got about ten feet and fell on their faces riddled with bullets. More Jap reinforcements arrived to supplement this sector. Warner begged Chuck to lay down a mortar concentration in back of the Jap line to prevent their reinforcing. K Company and wounded Marines were still out in front. He was trying to get them out.

Then we got a few breaks. The tank lighter sent to pick up the outpost near the Laruma got in and the men were pulled out of range. Captain Tom Jolly went to work. The boys back at the guns were ready and waiting for the word to throw in the shells. Lieutenant Ben Reed, the forward artillery observer attached to Warner's company, crawled to the left flank of the fire line. The artillery lines were not yet in. Corporal Kowalkowski, acting as scout sergeant, used the infantry 'phone to call in the fire mission to Tom Jolly at the battalion C.P. Jolly relayed the mission in to Captain Smith back at the fire-control center. Ben Reed made all adjustments by sound; it was an amazing piece of jungle artillery firing. Sometimes he would have to crawl farther to the left, out of shouting distance with the man on the 'phone. Then Laliberte, an instrument private, would crawl to a point halfway between Reed and Kowalkowski. Reed would locate where a shell landed by sound, estimate the distance, and shout the adjustment to Laliberte, who in turn would repeat it to Kowalkowski. Kowalkowski would get it to Jolly; then Jolly to Smitty; Smitty to the battery—"on the way." Reed would adjust again by sound alone, through the din of machine-guns, rifle fire, hand grenades and mortar bursts, until he had the concentration placed where he wanted it. But the Japs moved in as fast and close as possible to B Company's front lines. Warner kept calling to Reed to bring the artillery in closer. Reed was afraid of tree bursts. He knew the danger to our own troops, and brought it down a few yards at a time until some of the bursts were no more than fifty yards in front of our own lines. The artillery turned the tide: it stopped the flow of Jap reinforcements.

When the radio with the forward observation team attached to the outpost near the mouth of the Laruma River went out early that morning, the officer in charge of the outpost ordered the forward observation party back to the artillery battalion with the data that would enable the battalion to fire a concentration on the mouth of the Laruma. The Jap landing barges started to stream into the beach. Lieutenant West, O'Connell, Stafford, Hines, Allen, and Wanop were in the party. When the tank lighter picked up the outpost, these men were not among those present; they had started some time before and were working their way back toward their own lines. Little did they know that the Japs had already landed between the Laruma and their own lines and were at this time occupying the area through which they must pass.

As they hurried along the beach they were fired on by a sniper. Thinking it was one of their own men, West held up his hands and shouted that they were Marines. When they were fired at again they did something about it. As they took cover and tried to locate the sniper, they heard friendly artillery firing and saw the shell splashes in the bay. This was Reed starting his adjustment. The shells hit the water about a thousand yards in front of the western section of the perimeter beachhead line. As they moved back toward the beach to investigate, they discovered the Jap barges—looking exactly like one or two of our own broached tank lighters. The artillery in the meantime had moved closer to our own lines. Suddenly it started to work up toward the party. The outpost had been picked up by this time and no friendly troops were believed in this area. Here was one for their war diary—caught in an area marked for an artillery concentration, being fired by their very own battery. Their only hope was to make for the front lines. The only speedy way would be along or near the beach. The Japs moving up in the same direction all morning had had the same idea.

The party split up. West, Allen, Stafford, and Wanop started off first. West walked up to a man he thought was a Marine digging a foxhole, to warn him to get out of the area, and came face to face with a member of the Japanese landing force dressed in the same-colored uniform as a Marine's. Both were surprised—but West had a carbine. Four other Japs ran to the digging Nip's rescue. All five were killed. The four men kept going in a bee line for their own lines and got through in time.

The remaining two men of the original party, O'Connell and Hines, crouched in two freshly dug foxholes. Both were listening, thinking hard, and praying. A shell hit close by. O'Connell was knocked unconscious. Hines rushed over to him, poured water from his canteen over his head, and by slapping him in the face brought him to. Then, through keeping their heads, having a knowledge of artillery, and applying this knowledge to their own serious predicament, the two saved their own lives. Squatting in the Jap holes, they listened carefully to the fire of the distant guns. From the direction of the sound they recognized the battery that was doing the firing. Knowing the pattern this battery would fire, they waited excitedly until the first two shells landed. Then, knowing the next two would land over, they dashed forward toward the first point of impact. On one of these dashes they came across a Jap cleaning his rifle. The two men had been in the mud of the swamp since morning and neither of their carbines would fire. The artillery shells were getting thicker. It was now or never. Both men dashed toward the beach, then up along it toward their front lines. A few minutes later the area where they had been lying in the Jap foxholes was saturated by artillery fire.

In the C.P., Steve and Chuck were working frantically to carry out the Division order: "Take aggressive action against small enemy forces, destroying them or driving them out by nightfall!"

They tried to work two half-tracks from Regimental Weapons up near the platoon on the left, but the terrain was too swampy and they couldn't get through. Every man had been fighting desperately all day. Mortar and artillery fire was now being laid down, but the many close-in Jap machine-guns were still a serious problem. Allicon and O'Keefe, the two men who had brought Joe Nolan back, had later joined Warner's platoon. The two men were buddies. Allicon was trying to eliminate a machine-gun by his rifle fire.

"Crawl back, Allicon—that machine-gun's got you pinned down," yelled O'Keefe.

"The hell with you!" answered Allicon.

So O'Keefe, knowing his buddy couldn't do the job alone and suddenly feeling lonesome, grabbed Allicon by the feet and pulled him out.

Finally two tanks were brought up and dispatched toward Warner. They crashed through to the vicinity of the platoon. They were buttoned up and had brought no hand radios for the infantry officer's use in directing their movements. Warner dashed over to a tank and banged on its side. He managed to point out a machine-gun strong point that had been giving them considerable trouble. The tank wiped it out. Then he dashed over to the other tank. It was in a good position, except for visibility. Warner pounded on the side of the tank. He couldn't get the inside crew's attention. He ran around to the other side, all the time exposed to the Jap fire in front of him. Finally he got their attention. Then a burst of machine-gun fire ripped his knee apart and he went down. The tank located the machine-gun and wiped it out. Two men crawled to Warner and dragged him out. But this brave man's fighting days were over for a long time, for, though they rushed him back to the field hospital, the effort to save his leg was in vain.

E Company of the Third Medical Battalion attached to the Third Division was functioning as the Division Hospital. Division Headquarters was then located in an area behind the left flank of the Third Marine sector and the right flank of the Ninth Marine sector. When measures were being taken to counter the Japanese landing early that morning, Commander Bruce, the commanding officer of the medical battalion, was one of the first to get the call. E Company was the nearest Field Hospital to the harassed left flank. Dr. Bruce knew they were going to have a busy day. While the two companies from the First Battalion were rushing into position, Brucie had gone into action. Doctors Adair, Emert, Peck,

Halley, and Barker, Lieutenant Halatek, a Marine quartermaster, Ensign Mettanet, the Chiefs, and all the corpsmen were hastily rigging new tents, ringing them with sandbagged emplacements, and rushing the necessary preparations for an influx of battle casualties.

Shortly before one o'clock in the afternoon the first casualties from the hard-pressed K Company of the Ninth Marines began pouring in. The field hospital was located about one thousand yards to the rear of the front lines. Japs had already infiltrated through the perimeter, and the dense jungle area between the front lines and the hospital was infested with enemy snipers. The firing on the front was heavy. Bullets and fragments from Japanese mortar shells ripped through the hospital tents. More wounded in rapidly increasing numbers continued to pour in. Chief Lovelace was in the surgery tent busily preparing a critically wounded man for an immediate operation when a Japanese sniper's bullet tore through his shoulder.

Sniper fire became thicker. The doctors were actually operating under fire. Commander Bruce went from one tent to another. He ordered everyone to carry on no matter what happened. He rushed down to the beach and salvaged two machine-guns from a wrecked landing craft. Then he sent for help from the nearest Marine unit, but no one could be spared. Placing the machine-guns in strategic positions on the banks of a small stream less than twenty-five yards from the hospital tents, he manned them with the corpsmen from the medical company; additional corpsmen took a semicircular position between the hospital and the sniper area.

No one in the medical department is spared in the jungle warfare of the Pacific. Brucie knew the history of Guadalcanal too well to have any illusions on that score, but—snipers or no snipers—nothing was going to interfere with the crucial work of the medical company. Wounded men need treatment; and when they are wounded in the jungle, wearing combat clothes soaked with mud and sweat, they need treatment in a hurry. The stretchers were lined up outside the tents. The men suffering on them had been risking their lives all morning to save the left flank of the beachhead. Corpsmen and Marines were risking their lives to get these injured out of the jungle and back to the doctors. These same doctors, defenseless in their scientific labors, faced the same death with the same determination. Dr. Bruce knew what would happen to that Field Hospital if the Japs broke through. He knew what had already happened. He needed every corpsman for medical duty in those tents, but this was one field hospital that was not going to be put out of action—not till the last one of them had been killed. That went for him too. He worked as hard as the lowest-ranking corpsman in the same tents that were being torn by enemy bullets and shell fragments. Then he made another dash to the beach. Snipers saw him go and potted at him from the trees. But he kept right on going and returned with two Marines and seven Seabees. They took over the meager defenses outside the tents and released the corpsmen, who were vitally needed in the operating tent. The Jap infiltrators got dangerously close that day, but not close enough. The two Marines who took over and rooted through the sniper area were found late in the afternoon lying naked and dead in the jungle. They had given their lives for their wounded buddies.

Just before dark Dr. Bruce was able to obtain a platoon of Marines from a battalion moving up in reserve. A defense was thrown around the hospital. The tents were blacked out. Brucie, with his doctors and his corpsmen, operated all through the night, saving the lives of wounded jungle fighters who had rushed toward the attacking enemy, stopped them cold, and saved the left flank of the beachhead.

By the time the two tanks had gone into action with B Company, darkness was beginning to set in. There had been numerous casualties, but the lines were strong. The Japs were still out in front in force, but the artillery and mortar concentrations were harassing the forward movement of their troops and supplies. It was a good time for a counterattack—except for the oncoming darkness. General Cauldwell had been in communication with General Turnage at Division Headquarters all during the day and gave the Commanding General a continuous account of the front-line progress. Steve Brody and Chuck Bailey carried out their orders and attacked. The line hinging on the beach at the left moved forward. More Japs met sudden death for their emperor. A plan previously worked out by Speed, Big Mac, and The Traveler, should darkness prevent the completion of the mission, was approved by the Commanding General and given to Steve and Chuck. The First Battalion of the Twenty-first Marines, which had landed the day before, was assigned to the Third Marines. They moved to an assembly area back of the front lines and dug in for the night. Speed, Big Mac, and The Traveler went back to the Regimental C.P. and worked out the plans for the resumption of the attack. A message arrived from Chuck to Speed: "Operation with tanks successful, but had to stop advance due to darkness."

At dark Shorty Vogel's right flank company was in the swamp. He was tied in with B Company on his left and was in position to prevent any Jap advance from his right flank and immediate front. The enemy that remained was bottled up in an area between these two companies and the lagoon about a thousand yards to the west. They couldn't advance, and harassing fire from the artillery all during the night impeded a withdrawal. There was still a sufficient number of well-equipped Japs left, and during the night they tried to break through the two companies, but they never got through; they were trapped.

Just before darkness enveloped the island, a platoon from Warner's company found themselves in the swamp and cut off from the rest of their company. Their platoon leader had gone to try to make contact with the adjacent unit; his return had been cut off by the Japs. Platoon Sergeant Carter and Sergeant Brackett took over and organized an all-around defensive strong point. They established listening posts out in front toward the Japs and placed the one light machine-gun attached to the platoon in a position to cover an open stretch in the swamp.

It had been raining since early afternoon but, as the night settled in, the rain let up and the swamp grew lighter. Brackett was crouching near a log keeping an all-night vigil on the open stretch. The Japs might try a surprise break-through during the night. Strange things happen. What happened to Brackett was quite unorthodox. A man walked up to Brackett and in perfect English asked him what gun position that was. It was light enough for Brackett to see that the man was a Jap. He fired two quick shots with his rifle, dove for the deck, and rolled out of the line of machine-gun fire. Still, the machine-gun squad leader had seen the action, heard the Jap, and held his fire. Then he opened up. Brackett jumped up, dashed past the dead Jap and over to the machine-gun position. He was a trained man with sufficient presence of mind to utilize the lessons he had learned. He ordered the machine-gun moved immediately, where it could still cover the open space but in an entirely different position. No sooner had the order been carried out than the Japs charged. The platoon had established a good strong point. The machine-gun, B.A.R.s, and rifles swept back and forth through the open stretch of swamp. The Japs kept coming. They were greeted by a shower of hand grenades. The men fired faster. Five minutes after the machine-gun had been moved, two Jap grenades landed in the midst of the old gun position. Had it not been moved the gun would have been destroyed and every man in the squad wiped out. The Japs kept coming until there weren't any more to come. The next morning the platoon of Marines was intact. No one had been even wounded. Twenty-seven dead Japs were starting to rot in the swamp.

As soon as Shorty Vogel had his company in position the first day of the Koromokina battle, he had ordered one of his officers to take his platoon, to move out on a particular compass azimuth, and locate the flank of the friendly forces of the Ninth Marines, who were somewhere out in front of him. Lieutenant Bob Harvey started off. They struck the swamp immediately. It was tough and slow, but they stuck to their azimuth and kept right on going. Somewhere along the line they passed the flank, or else a part of the friendly unit was no longer where it should have been, for

Harvey never made contact. After he had gone some distance, he sent out small patrols to his own right and left. The platoon had started off from a point considerably to the right of the Jap line of attack. Moving west and parallel to the coast line they continued to the right of it.

The patrols returned. They had not made contact. Harvey decided that the unit for which he was searching must have moved forward in an attack. His mission was to find them. He continued through the swamp. Later in the afternoon, when mortar and artillery shells began dropping in close, he had to make one of two choices: To abandon his mission and pull his men off through the swamp to the right, or to remain on his original azimuth and keep going. He took a deep breath and decided on the latter. Darkness caught the platoon patrol over a thousand yards ahead of the present front lines and on the banks of a river. He knew he had missed his objective. Judging the impact area from the sound of the exploding shells, he knew he would have to spend the night in back of the Japanese lines worrying how he was going to get his men out of a bad spot early the next morning.

At daybreak he had an immediate problem. The men had nothing with them but their arms and ammunition. They had been plodding through a deep swamp the day before, they had crossed areas up to their armpits in mud, and not a weapon in the entire platoon would fire. Following the river, Harvey led his platoon to a point near the beach, on which there was an abandoned Jap landing boat. Two volunteers crept out to the boat and drained a helmet full of gasoline from its tank. They got back still unseen, and the men in the platoon hurriedly cleaned their weapons. Harvey had no communication. He tried to visualize what had happened to the two companies which had started a counterattack against the Jap landing force the day before, and wondered what the plan of action would be today. Then he anticipated the continuance of the attack and realized with frightful potency that it would be prefaced by an artillery preparation. He and his forty men were right in the area of concentration. It was getting lighter.

The sands of time were running low. Anyone in that area would be blown to bits. There was only one fast escape route: by sea.

Harvey noticed that one of the daytime fighter coverage planes was flying rather low. Word of their predicament might have been sent to the fighter command through Division, but the plane would never spot them through the thick jungle growth. John Perella, one of the men in his platoon, wanted to take a chance. He crept to the beach and dove into the bay. Then he cut through the open water. The Japs had a lot on their minds that morning and weren't down for their morning dip. The planes dipped low over the water. Perella stripped off his skivvy shirt, trod far out of water, and waved the white cloth desperately. The plane dipped its wings and flew toward the boat pool anchored in the bay 1500 yards to the east. Perella waited anxiously. A tank lighter sped parallel to the shore and headed for the point of land on the west side of the bay; then it suddenly turned toward the shore and raced in. Perella shouted the direction as the boat shot past him. When the lighter touched the sand Harvey had his men at the edge of the jungle. The ramp slammed down and the men tore across the beach and into the boat. As they picked up Perella the shells started to fall, one striking the abandoned Japanese landing boat. Then the area they had just left was saturated. The lives of forty trained Marines had been saved.

At H-minus-five-minutes that morning the artillery unleashed its blasting fury and plowed up the enemy-infested area of the jungle swamp ahead of the two front-line B and C Companies. Five batteries of artillery, two of which were 105-mm. caliber, saturated a rectangular area 500 yards deep by 300 yards wide. Heavy and light mortars from the First Battalion plowed up the close-in area. The artillery threw in 180 shells. The mortars were fed as fast as one could throw shells in the tube—and that's *fast*.

The situation was slightly different this second morning. The day before had been one of partially planned but immediate action to counter fast-moving shock-troop enemy action already rolling toward its objective. The Japs had not met a defensive force taken by surprise, but had been hit by attacking Marines who write several chapters in the shock-troop textbooks themselves every time they go into action. The Japs had been stopped, counterattacked, and herded into a confining area. Hundred-pound packs loaded with rice and ammunition, stacks of 90-mm. mortar shells, mortars, tools, and medical supplies made one suspect that they had counted on a longer stay—or at least a longer run for their money. It was dog-eat-dog the first day, but the Jap hadn't snarled loud enough. The second day's medicine was a more potent mixture, for the number of enemy troops and their location were known and time had permitted concentration of a more deadly opposition.

At H-minus-one-minute, every original machine-gun and a great many more that had been brought up to the two companies from the First Battalion opened up on the line. They ripped through the jungle and raked the upper foliage in the trees. Not a sniper lived to tell about it. At H-minus-ten-seconds, while the machine-guns were still firing, every man on the line threw a hand grenade. Then—on schedule and according to plan—the entire First Battalion of the Twenty-first Marines, moving up during the five-minute artillery preparation, struck the lines held by the two companies of the First Battalion, Third. At H-hour, shortly after daylight, this fresh battalion, held in reserve, passed through the lines of the First Battalion, Third and moved through to the lagoon 1500 yards west of the Koromokina River. The movement was opposed only by four or five screaming, crying, cringing, shell-shocked Nipponese maniacs. The artillery concentration had churned the jungle swamp into a thunderous inferno. One Japanese assembly area of about seventy men had suffered two direct hits from 105-mm. shells. Nothing remained but bloody bits of arms, legs, trunks, and heads clinging to the larger trees splintered into jagged ugliness.

The two companies that had fought so hard the day before and had held the Japs bottled up during the night followed in reserve. But the fighting was over. Upon reaching the objective, combat patrols were sent north through the swamp and as far west as the Laruma River. No Japs could be found.

The two companies from the First Battalion, Third Marines, moved back to a reserve position behind the Second and Third Battalions. They had done another great job, their second triumph in eight days. They had lost more of their officers and men; they were still in the swamp; they were tired; many were sick; they still had many rugged days ahead of them—but they were still dangerous. These were very tough gentlemen. They had already proved it.

For some days, Japanese combat patrols had been feeling out the lines in the northeast section of the semicircle, but their way had been blocked by the Raiders. The beachhead was still intact. Work on the airfield went feverishly onward. With the terrific, devastatingly accurate support of the artillery, the gallant men of the First Battalion with two-thirds of their strength had again, if only temporarily, "secured the butts."

Chapter 10

WHEN THE FIRST BATTALION returned to the regimental fold there was a reward waiting—the best reward that can be given to a fighting man while he is away. Back in their bivouac area, back in the swamp, the First Battalion found mail. Manna from heaven! During the morning of the day before, the men of the other two battalions up on the line had heard that glorious shout from the First Sergeants' foxholes: "Mail call!" Happy days were here again. Letters from home. Letters from the best girl. Letters from buddies. There were even a few home-town newspapers.

Harberson sat on a log and read the *Philadelphia Inquirer*. He had been Lieutenant Joe Nolan's runner. They'd been together a long time. The Lieutenant thought a great deal of his runner. "All during training I used to explain everything I did to Harberson. 'Harberson,' I said, 'you've got to know everything I know. Some day I might get hit and you might be the only one who would know what to do. You could carry on. You've got to know the reason why it's being done. Ask questions. That's the way I learned. I'll always tell you everything you want to know.'" And it had paid off. Harberson could find his way through the jungle as if he had been born there. He always found what he was looking for. When he got there he was able to give an intelligent picture of the situation. He had been the man who had helped pull the B Company command group out of a tight spot, the man who had gone back, found Warner, checked the withdrawing order, and returned in time to get the men out of the mortar impact area.

Now Nolan, his boss and buddy, had been severely wounded

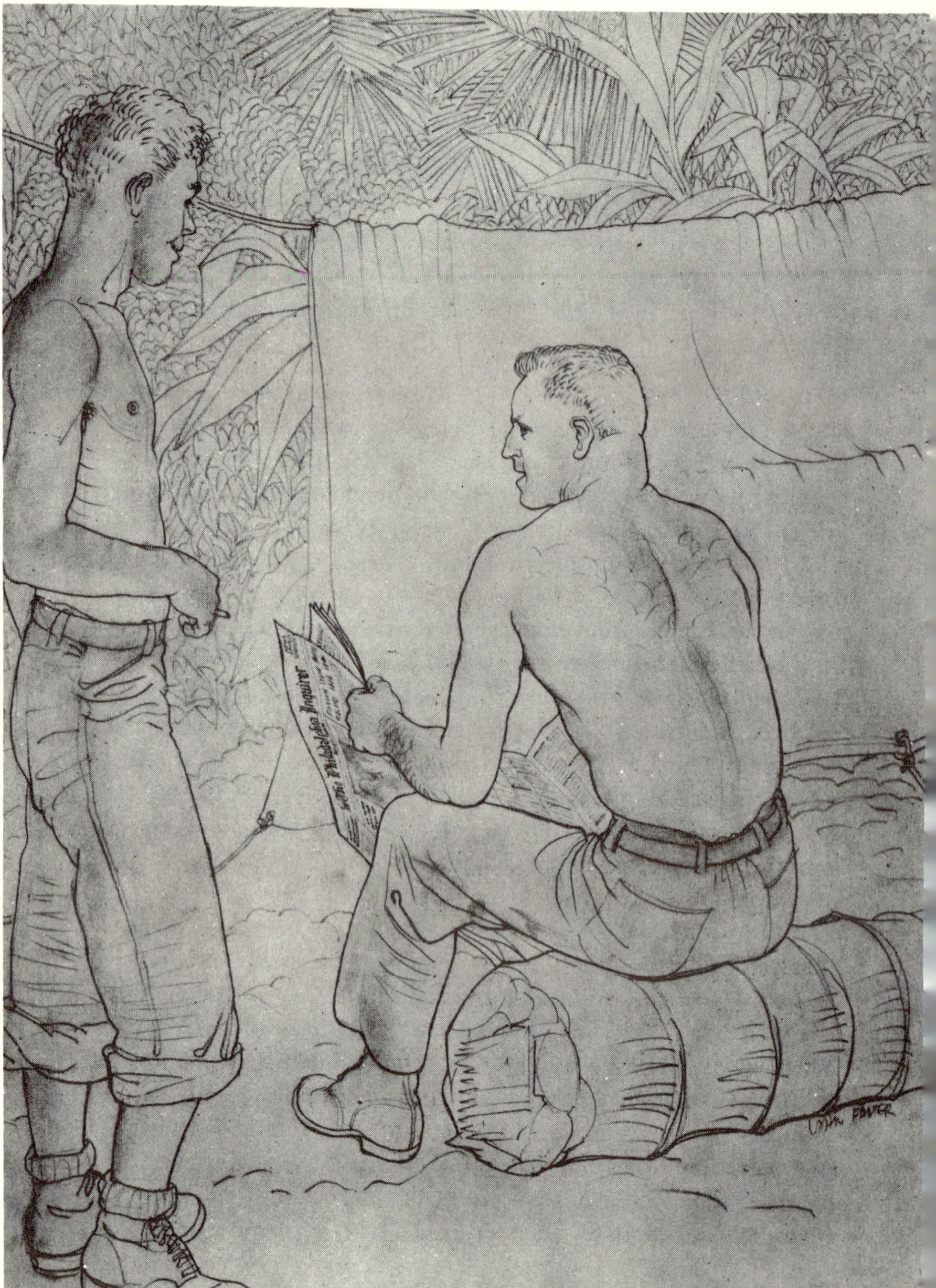
Philadelphia Inquirer

and was lying in the field hospital. In a day or two Nolan would be evacuated. Harberson might never see him again, and he missed him.

A buddy came up to Harberson and glanced over his shoulder. "What in hell are you reading, Harberson?"

"A newspaper. What in hell does it *look* like?"

"But that's the want ads. Lookin' for a job?"

"Yeah."

"How many years you done on your cruise?"

"Two."

"You got two more years to go. You wouldn't be able to take a job for two years even if you could get one," said his buddy.

Harberson looked up slowly, deflated. "Well, I can dream, can't I?"

Back in the communication repair section at the Regimental C.P., Red Neidermier was in trouble.

"How do you like that?" He threw the letter he was reading on the deck.

"What's the matter, Red?"

"How do you like that? She's found a guy she thinks is 'more congenial.' How do you like that? 'More congenial.' For four years I've been goin' with that dame. Wait till she gets my letter. Lend me some stationery."

"Burn her up, Red."

"Wait till she gets this letter!"

All afternoon Red worked over the letter to his girl. She was the finest, most wonderful girl he had ever known—but they were through. (The wonderful plans they used to make. . . .) Here he was stuck on a stinking island in the Pacific, risking his life for her, for their future, and she couldn't wait. He'd have her in tears. That was all right with him. Dames were a dime a dozen. Wait till he got back—he'd find ten that would be "more congenial." More beautiful, too. *Women!*

A week later another letter from his girl arrived, having crossed his on the way. She told him how sorry she was, that she never should have written the other letter; she didn't really feel that way at all. There would never be another guy like Red. She loved him. She'd wait forever.

"What's the matter, Red?"

"How do you like that? Why did I go and write that letter? War is sure complicated."

Up in the lines a sergeant put his letter down and called to a buddy nearby, "Things are sure screwed up back in the States."

"They ain't no bargain here," answered his buddy.

"Listen to this," said the Sergeant, looking at his letter. "My wife's going to get a job, but she can't make up her mind which one to take. She can be a driver on a Greyhound bus, *or* she can drive a tractor in an Army camp. Hell—when I get home, she'll throw me out of the house!"

By November 9, B Line of the beachhead perimeter 1900 yards in depth was reached. The Regiment had been almost constantly on the move. Time had been taken out for the two companies of the First Battalion to fight the battle of the Koromokina. Actually no time was taken out, since the Second and Third Battalions were manning the line and had kept on the move. On the day the battle ended, the First caught up with them and went into reserve for reorganization. Meantime the Third Battalion was preparing defensive positions all along its sector of the line. On November 9 these positions were turned over to the 148th Infantry Regiment of the 37th Division of the U. S. Army who relieved them. The picture now changed a bit.

The beachhead was growing deeper and the semicircular line was getting longer. The perimeter was theoretically split in halves, with the Army taking over the Marine sector on the left half and the Marines manning the continued semicircular line extending to the right.

Lieutenant Joe Gehring and his company of Seabees attached to

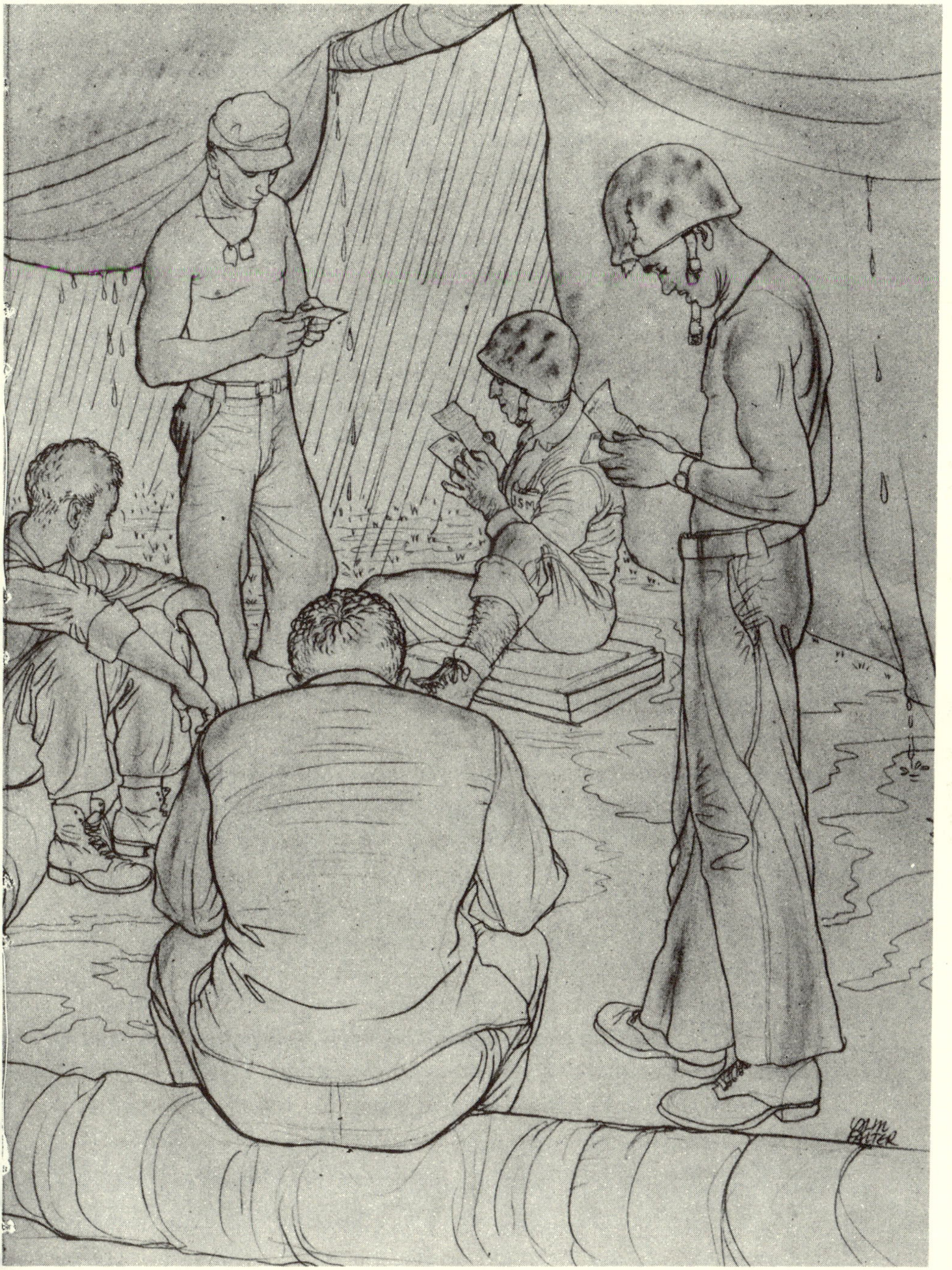

the Third Battalion had pushed a road through to the Third. This was joined by an amphibian tractor trail which they were pushing across the front of both the Third and Second Battalions. The shift toward the northeast "Coffin Corner" began in earnest. While the Seabees, screened by a combat infantry patrol, were pushing this lateral trail across the front, the Second Battalion moved forward another thousand yards. The Third Battalion began their shift to the right, moving to the right of and tying in with the right flank of the Second Battalion.

There was a small pot of gold waiting at the end of this last forward move by the Second Battalion—or a few nuggets, anyway. The ground was much better here. The men let out their first sigh of relief since D-day, and squared away with the joyful anticipation of being able to dig positions and foxholes more than six inches below the surface before striking water. A good-sized stream in this new area augmented their joy. The men had their first baths since hitting the beach. Clothes were washed for the first time. Razors were brought out after only slight pressure from Regiment, which voiced its preference (though not a formal order) for clean-shaven faces. But many of the men of the Third were youngsters who had only recently graduated beyond the fuzz stage, and every man harbors a secret desire to see just what his beard will do if given a proper chance. They were growing beards, so they explained, for facial camouflage and protection from mosquitoes. Actually a beard isn't worth the trouble. It has to be a full job to have any real value, and a man is able to keep cleaner and feels better when he's clean-shaven. A short time after the men had a chance to see what the collection of goatees, mustaches, and scrub growth looked like, practically every face was surveyed back to normal duty; but the more successful crops were long remembered with satisfaction and a feeling of confidence. It was one more diversion.

There had been few diversions. Men had been pulled out of the swamp with pneumonia, jungle ulcers, and fresh attacks of malaria and filariasis. The swamp was beginning to take its toll. It rained on seventeen of the first eighteen days. Many of the men had not had a hot meal since the morning they had left the transports; and only one battalion in the Regiment, outside of some night Jap patrol actions, had tasted combat. The battle of the swamp had been a tough battle, both as a living problem and as a problem of logistics. The men had maintained active patrols beyond their lines. They were searching for friend and foe. The foe was the Jap, the left-over Jap, the hungry Jap, the curious Jap. The friend was higher, better ground. This would at least be something to look forward to, and tired men need to look forward to blue sky ahead. Returning patrols in the evening could promise nothing. The swamp seemed to always extend beyond their limit of reconnaissance; the hills were much farther away than they looked from the first glimpse from the transports. Captain John Scott, the Battalion operation officer for the Third Battalion, describes their feelings:

"Occupy line Baker. Occupy line Charlie. The first eighteen days were depressing. We patrolled for Japs, grabbed at the least sign of the enemy. The First Battalion was engaged first on our right—the battle for Cape Torokina; then on our left—the battle of the Koromokina. But *we* found no enemy. All our foxholes were little lakes. Nobody was happy. There were Japs at Buin and Kieta, at Kahili and Jaba, on the Laruma River and the Numa Numa trail; but *we* hadn't even seen a dead one. The only things we had to fight were jungle, swamp, and rain—and we'd had all that in Samoa and Guadalcanal. What the Third Battalion needed was a Jap. We didn't even have a good rumor."

But the Third Battalion would have to wait a while—not long, just a little while longer. There must be Japs out there, even a few sick ones. The trick was to find them.

Lieutenant Billy Langdale was a great patroller. He begged for the chance to get out in the boondocks. There were always more men wanting to go with him than he would take. But you had to be rugged. Billy had been an outdoor man all of his life. He hails from a large plantation in Georgia and has hiked, hunted, fished, and ridden over practically every inch of the State. When he talked

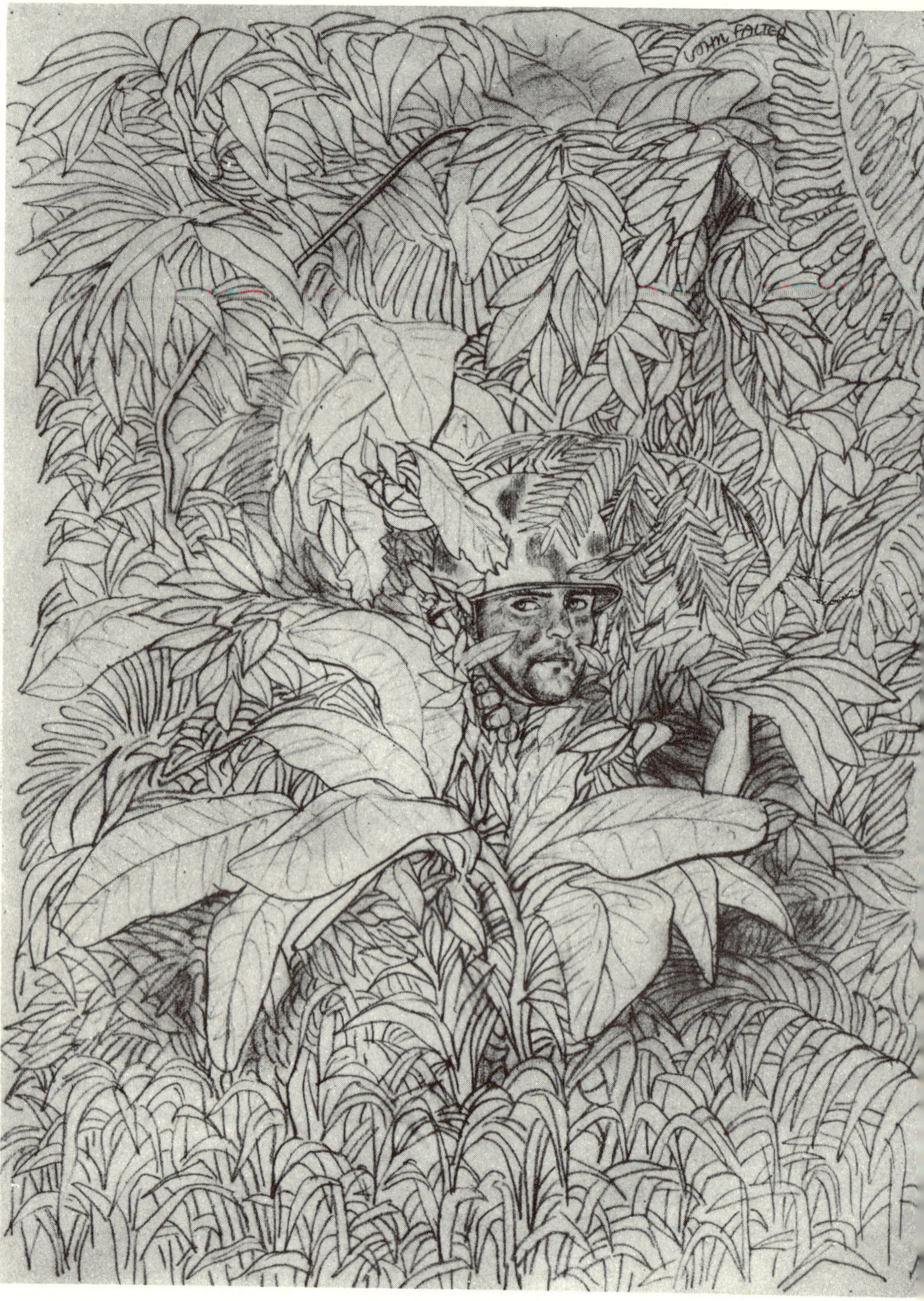

JOHN FALTER

about the bird dog he had left back home it was a sonnet. Everyone gets flashes of the reason why he is in the war, of what he's fighting for. Often the reason isn't very satisfying. But Bill's reason was cut and dried, simple and worth while: he was fighting the war for his dog, a beautiful Irish setter who was waiting at home—patiently, loyally waiting for Billy to return. Then they could go back to work and know the joy that only the two of them could really understand.

Billy Langdale is a man who has to know; he can't stand not knowing. But the industrial revolution had never caught up with him. He had always been at home in the woods, and now the jungle was his element. When Billy returned with a negative report you knew it was negative, for what he couldn't see or hear he could smell.

The Langdale patrol had reached their day's limit and were starting back by a different route. Day after day they had gone out in front of the jungle front line, each time by a different route, patient hunters looking for game. And this was an open season. They moved quietly through the maze of heavy underbrush and jungle vines. Suddenly Billy had that feeling. There was human life up ahead . . . Japs . . . that smell. The patrol halted. Billy whispered some orders. Two unarmed Nips were lying under the shelter of a large bush. They were completely hidden—so they thought, until one of them heard a sound. It spelled immediate danger. The two frightened Sons of Heaven looked up into the cold, dead-pan faces of five very tough Marines.

"Don't move! We'll blow your God-damn heads off!"

The words weren't necessary. The cruel look of five unshaven jungle fighters speaks the same language all over the world. Two of the Marines moved in slowly and searched the trapped Japs. One was a mess of blood and pus and stank terribly. The unwounded one spoke some English; he told Langdale that he had attended the Imperial University in Tokyo. He was an officer cadet in charge of about forty men and would be made a commissioned officer when he had more overseas time behind him. He begged

Langdale not to shoot them. They had no arms; they had been hiding in the jungle for a week without anything to eat. The sole survivors of the landing force that had landed over a week ago, they had survived the artillery barrage during the first day of the battle of a week ago and were now trying to escape through the pass in the ridge to the north coast garrison at Numa Numa. His buddy was dying. He couldn't leave him. He had tried, but they were good friends.

It was growing late. The rest of Langdale's patrol returned from searching the area. They had a long, hot hike back to the front lines, and they must be starting. Langdale asked the cadet if the wounded man could walk.

"He is in great pain—very sick," replied the student officer.

"Well, he will have to walk," Langdale said.

The Jap relayed the message to his buddy. A Marine helped the wounded man to his feet. Langdale shot an azimuth with his compass; then he beckoned to the cadet. "Let's go," he ordered.

The patrol started off. The wounded man groaned and fell on his face. There was a large hole in his back. Langdale looked down at him. Then he spoke kindly to the young officer. "Your friend is dying," he said soberly.

The cadet looked down at his buddy—just stood there, dry-eyed, expressionless. Then he spoke to him in Japanese. The wounded man tried to rise, but fell back groaning with pain.

Langdale looked at his watch. "Let's go," he said.

The patrol started off. The cadet turned quickly away and followed silently. A Marine again helped the wounded man to his feet. He screamed with pain, sat down slowly on a log, and began to cry. Langdale went back to him.

The two Japs talked together in Japanese. Then the cadet said to Langdale in English: "My friend is very sick. He says that he cannot go any farther."

"Tell him that if he will walk I will send him to the hospital."

The cadet again spoke to his wounded buddy. But the buddy just sat there and cried. The cadet shrugged his shoulders. Langdale whipped out his raider knife. He walked over the wounded Jap and held it out before him. Then he reached back, grabbed the cadet, and pulled him up closer to the wounded man.

"Ask him if he wants to commit hara-kiri," said Langdale.

"I do not understand."

"Ask him if he wants to commit hara-kiri," repeated Langdale, with gestures.

Then the two frightened Japs talked simultaneously in Japanese.

"We do not understand," said the cadet to Langdale.

Langdale put his knife back in his sheath and started off. The unwounded Jap stood watching his buddy cry with pain. He said nothing. A Marine gave the young cadet a starting shove. He never looked back, but followed after Langdale like an obedient puppy dog.

Hours later the tired patrol walked into the Company C.P.

"We got a prisoner," shouted Langdale to Lieutenant Stets Holmes, pointing to the 110-pound Jap who was hanging close to the patrol leader like a frightened child. "Where's Bert?"

The prisoner noticed from Stets Holmes's manner that he was an officer. He came smartly to attention and held a salute.

"Don't salute me, you no-good slit-eyed son-of-a-bitch!" flashed the angry Holmes. Then to Langdale: "Bert's at the Battalion C.P."

The men crowded around. Billy sat down, the prisoner following him. When Billy stood up, the prisoner stood up.

"College man," said Billy. "*My* platoon only takes high-class prisoners."

"Strike yourself a medal," suggested Stets.

"Give him something to eat and then I'll take him over to the C.P.," said Billy

One of the men threw the prisoner a can of C ration. The Jap wolfed it; for a starving man he was good casting. A Marine offered him a cigarette, but the Jap was too scared—there were too many Marines. Instead, he looked at Langdale, who took the cigarette and handed it to him. The men tried to ask the Jap questions. But he kept looking at Langdale as his only benefactor and protector.

Finally Langdale got up, the prisoner following eagerly, and the two of them walked silently to the Battalion C.P. There he turned the Jap over to Fox, a battalion staff officer. After a while, he was taken to the Regimental C.P., standing silently in the middle of the amphibian tractor as it plowed its way through the jungle, and opening his mouth in wonder when it swam through an open space of water. Gradually he grew depressed, apparently doubtful now of Japanese victory. How could any nation fight against equipment like this? He looked completely disillusioned. He loved his country, but he no longer believed in his leaders—they had lied. He was glad the young Marine lieutenant had spared his life. But his gratitude was mingled with hatred. The lieutenant was an American—and a Marine. He hated Americans—especially Marines.

A few days later Langdale received a letter of commendation from Colonel McHenry. The cadet officer was not only the sole captured survivor from the Second Battalion of the 54th Japanese Infantry, which had been rushed down from the north and had fought the First Battalion of our regiment on November 7 and 8; he was also the first prisoner taken by the Third Marines.

Of course Langdale had to repeat the story of the capture many times. Billy is a straight-line, honest thinker. He tells a good story, but doesn't waste his great store of energy on emotional gingerbread.

"Why did you ask the Jap if he wanted to commit hara-kiri?" asked a fellow officer.

"I wanted to see what it looked like."

Chapter 11

WHEN THE ARMY first moved in to take over some of the Marine positions on the left flank, the first thing that greeted them was the sight of Marines working all along the beach unloading freshly arrived supplies, vehicles, and equipment. Some were taking a bath in the bay, and there was considerable beach activity, though not of a combat variety.

The Third Marines had always had good luck with the Army. They had done a little borrowing from them in the past, but usually it wasn't necessary. Army units with which we had come in contact up to this time had been most liberal, and when we weren't able to obtain certain items from our own quartermaster the Army had been generous. The old rivalry between the two branches of the Service still existed and now was carried into Bougainville, the same ribbing—jokes such as "Did you bring the U.S.O. with you?" from the Marines; and the same answers, such as, "You Marines are good fighters, but—like our other allies, the Chinese—you don't have much equipment." But the rivalry was friendly. It's one thing when men of two different branches of the Service run up against each other in a liberty port barroom, and quite another when they're together in close proximity to a dangerous enemy. The latter situation is more conducive to friendship; even if you didn't volunteer, a Jap bombardier or machine-gunner doesn't ask. When the shooting dies down the rivalry springs up again. Each man is proud of his own unit, each is willing to help the other, and at the same time each is trying to "do" the other if he can get away with it. Sometimes the have-nots in dealing with the haves use the brazen "borrowing" approach.

One day a couple of Third Marines were walking along the beach, and it happened that their unhurried mission took them past a large ration dump recently set up and guarded by an Army sentry. One Marine turned to the other and remarked:

"I'm thirsty. I think we ought to have a can of pineapple juice."

"You're so right," agreed the other.

The first Marine walked quickly up to the sentry, the earnest look on his face implying that he had been sent on an errand for the commander-in-chief of all the armed forces in the world.

"Say, Bud, what's this?" he demanded authoritatively, pointing to a case plainly marked PINEAPPLE JUICE.

"Pineapple juice," replied the sentry.

"That's it!" snapped the Marine, taking the case and walking off with it on his shoulder. (He wanted to halt and snap back, "Carry on!"—but that would have been overdoing it.) The two Marines walked smartly away, and the sentry resumed his guarding.

Later in the campaign a Marine liaison officer working with the Army was accompanying a Colonel from the Army Division's intelligence section. The Colonel was in the forward jeep, and the Marine officer was following close behind in another. Both jeeps stalled in the mud near a supply tent of a Marine artillery unit. The Colonel, suddenly recalling the various borrowing tactics, turned around and called back good-naturedly to the liaison officer: "I'll say one thing for the Marines."

"What's that, Colonel?" asked the Marine officer.

"They *never* steal a stove while it's still hot."

At which the voice of an unseen Marine called out from the tent: "Put some handles on it, Mac, and we'll get that too!"

The Colonel laughed. They were on the same team.

Ed Godfrey, a Red Cross field man attached to the Third Marines, had been saving his cases of ditty bags—those very handy little cloth bags containing toilet articles, a pack of cards, a paperbound novel, and other small items—for distribution to the men in the Regiment after they had been in combat. It was his experience as a combat man in the last war that had led to this decision. He had carefully guarded the cases for months and took special care to see that they got safely on the beach. But since getting them there he was having a difficult time. Ed is a soft-spoken man and very liberal and popular, but not even this did any good. Marines of other units didn't know him, and all Marines have the same borrowing propensities. But he knew his boys were going to need those things, and he was going to hang onto them until the right time. He decided to change his tactics and fight fire with fire. Borrowing some dungarees and a raider cap, he took his post near the equipment. "Get the hell away from that gear before I knock your friggin' head off!" he barked at the next man who tried to borrow—and the gear was saved.

After the Third had lost everything they owned in their last battle later in the campaign—soap, toothbrushes, and razors being practically nonexistent—Ed's Red Cross ditty bags came in handy. And somehow or other Ed always had letter-writing material for his boys when none could be found anywhere else. Ed had been with the Third since New Zealand, and he had spent every waking minute working for the little man. The Third Marines think of Ed Godfrey as a good Marine. What better compliment could we pay him?

Our second experience with the Army on Bougainville occurred on the evening of November 16 when the Second Battalion of the Third was attached temporarily to the 129th Army Infantry Regiment. This Regiment had recently arrived and gone into position in the Army sector to the right of the 148th. That evening the Second Battalion had gone into a bivouac area behind the newly arrived 129th. Just before dark it was discovered that their right flank was open and dangling dangerously near the Numa Numa trail. "Call out the Marines!"

The men in the Second Battalion had just finished digging their foxholes and were in the midst of heating some canned C Ration in their steel helmets. Just before dark, F Company of the Second got the call to pull out and high-tail it for a thousand yards through the jungle to the exposed flank. There was plenty of gum-beating that night. Rifle in one hand, and helmet half-full of hot stew in the other, the Marines paraded up to and along the Army's front lines. They were a tired, ugly-looking crew as they marched away from the Battalion bivouac area. Private Red Viggers of Headquarters Company serenaded them off:

"*Good-by, dear. I'll be back in a year,
'Cause I'm in the Army now!*"

Construction on the fighter strip down at the Cape went rapidly forward. The Seabees were out to beat all existing records. But an additional project had been planned by the higher command. Patrols had located a large section of dry and comparatively flat ground extending from a coconut grove northwest of the present northeast sector of the present perimeter—through the jungle for a considerable distance to the west. And an even greater undertaking was being conceived, though the ground was better and could be worked more easily. A full-sized bomber strip with an adjacent fighter strip was being planned for this area. Another Seabee battalion was on its way to Bougainville. The proposed site was still a considerable distance beyond the beachhead front lines; the ground was not yet in our possession. But new beachhead lines were already drawn on the situation maps of the higher echelon. D Line, to be occupied on November 15, called for a depth of 5500 yards. E Line, a depth of 6500 yards, was to be occupied on November 21.

Since D-day the Japs had been hitting the northeast sector of the perimeter. First combat patrols of small strength, then increasingly larger forces, hit the sector as the semicircle moved forward. The junction of two trails was located in this northeast sector. The Numa Numa trail mentioned previously—leading through this sector, then winding off to the northwest through the gap in the ridge to Numa Numa and Kieta on the north coast—joined another trail from the east appropriately named the East-West trail. One action instigated by a Jap force of unknown strength (later believed to be a strong combat patrol which had jumped the gun and opened up on a battalion of the Twenty-first Marines) had already caused a tussle, and the Japs had retired—but not very far. Information obtained by reconnaissance had aroused a dark suspicion that the Japs were moving up forces from the east, assembling in the hill mass to the north and east of this trail junction, being joined by forces from the Numa Numa area, and generally cooking up a situation that would have to be met by strong counteraction if the beachhead area was to be extended to the proposed new lines. And the beachhead lines were going to be extended, and on time. In other words, two parties had conflicting ideas. One party was the Japs, perhaps assembling a large force bent on piercing the beachhead at this northeast sector and driving through to the fighter strip in process of construction on the Cape; the other party was the Marines, definitely intending not only to hold what they already had but to extend the area for additional construction of vital military installations—the new bomber and fighter strips. When two parties have such conflicting ideas there is bound to be an argument.

The Third Marines were making rapid progress toward the area of dispute.

On November 15 the First Battalion of the Third Marines, having completed their shift to the right through the jungle, went into position south of the Second Battalion of the Twenty-first Marines, which had now passed to the temporary control of the Third Marines. The Second Battalion of the Twenty-first held the line to the left of the First Battalion, Third; their lines extended north, then bent toward the west. On November 16 the Third Battalion completed its long, hard shift to the right, broke out of the jungle, and connected its lateral road from the west to amphibian tractor trails leading up from the beach from the south. This meeting occurred near the junction of the Numa Numa trail and the East-West trail. The Third Battalion set up a defensive position and tied in with the Second Battalion, Twenty-first Marines, on their right. As the semicircular line bent and extended to the west, the front of the Third Battalion, Third, faced north. They tied into the Second Battalion, Third, attached to the Army sector on their left.

The Third Regiment C.P. moved into a position behind the trail junction, in approximately the center of the Third Marine northeast sector of the beachhead. General Speed Cauldwell moved into the Third Regiment C.P.

"It's sure good to see you, Speed."

"Getting tired of visiting you folks," grinned Speed. "Every time I come you get into a fight."

"When the going gets toughest I'll be right there with you!"

Everyone remembered.

The Third Regiment had already fought two battles on Bougainville. They had been constantly on the move for seventeen days. All that time they had been battling the swamp and the rain, cold chow and cumulative fatigue. They had lost a sizable proportion of their officers and men through battle casualties and tropical illness. They had over a year's severe training in the tropics, they were tired, they were sick; but what the Third Regiment had already gone through was a prep-school outing compared with what was on the immediate docket. The "valley of the shadow" was coming up. The Battle of the Piva Forks was about to begin.

When does a battle start? Is it the time you decide what the intention of the enemy is and make up your mind to do something about it? When you start to co-ordinate the many units to be involved in the action, begin arrangements for the thousands of details, prepare plans of attack, arrange for the evacuation of wounded, and so forth? Or is it after these details have been completed and your attacking force first makes contact with the enemy? Who knows? And what does it matter? The fundamental rules remain the same. You plan to destroy the enemy, drive through a certain land distance, and consolidate your gains. But first you must find the enemy; and, in terrain as formidable and as unsuited for fighting as the thick, walled-in jungle swamps of Bougainville, this is quite a stunt. Then, after you find him, you must determine his strength; for not until then will you know the size of the force you must pitch against him. Only then are you able to go ahead with the actual detailed plans of attack, which must be simply devised so that they may be carried through to a successful finale. Where is he? How much has he got? How has he dispersed it? What will you do? How will you do it? *Do it*—just like that.

Here's how the Third Marines did it on Bougainville in the Battle of the Piva Forks. Here are some of the incidents that occurred; some of the things that went wrong; some of the things that broke in our favor, through blind unadulterated luck; some of the things done skillfully under the most severe conditions. Not that any battles any place are easy—they're only "tough" or "tougher." But this is not only the story of the able planning of leaders, though this is an important part of it. It is also the story of the little man with the rifle, machine-gun, mortar, hand grenade, B.A.R., Tommy-gun, carbine, flame-thrower, knife, foot, fist. It is the story of the noncom. It is the story of the junior officer who fought and died with his men. It is a tale of men who had been trained to fight—but not to die. For every one of these men wanted desperately to live, yet knew certainly that some of them would have to die. Each hoped that he would not be among these. All of them knew fear. All of them controlled it. They faced a ruthless opponent . . . thinking: "It's you or me—and I'm the better man. A fight will decide. Let's go!"

Battle of the Piva Forks

1 ⊠ 3 = 1st Batt. 3rd Mar. Reg. L ⊠ 3rd RDR = L Company 3rd Raid.
2 ⊠ 3 = 2nd Batt. 3rd Mar. Reg. 2 ⊠ = 2nd Raider Batt.
3 ⊠ 3 = 3rd Batt. 3rd Mar. Reg. 23(JAP) = 23rd Jap. Reg.

Chapter 12

THE PREPARATION for the Battle of Piva Forks had begun as far back as November 11, when the Third Marines had received definite orders from the next higher echelon, the Third Division, to maintain aggressive patrols 1000 yards to the front of their forward positions and to establish ambushes after dark on any and all trails where they had encountered enemy movement. This had been done.

On the 17th, when the Third Battalion had taken their position on D Line, reconnaissance patrols verified the fact that the Numa Numa trail (leading to the large Japanese garrison on the north coast) lay directly in front of the Battalion's defensive sector. Lieutenant John O'Neil was ordered to establish and maintain a combat outpost 600 yards forward of their lines astride the Numa Numa trail. O'Neil laid wire behind him and set up a platoon ambush. The outpost spent the rest of that day and the night patiently waiting. Nothing happened. About noon of the next day, a force led by a young Japanese officer wearing white gloves and a Samurai sword came down the trail. One of the men drew a bead on the officer and squeezed one off.

Captain John Kovacs, O'Neil's company commander, heard a fire fight up ahead and got O'Neil on the 'phone.

"What's going on up there, John?" asked Kovacs.

"Got a little fight on our hands."

"Everything all right?"

"Yeah—we've got a good position," replied O'Neil. "Got our first Jap, an officer."

"Great! Who got him?" Kovacs asked him.

"Curry, my runner—right between the God-damn eyes."

"Is he dead?"

"I don't think he'll take any long walks any more."

The sound of the fire fight going on during the conversatio could be heard plainly over the 'phone.

"Do you need anything, John?" asked his company commander.

"We could use some ammunition."

"All right I'll get it right up to you. Anything else?"

"Water would come in handy."

The platoon had had no water since the day before, and one canteen per man in the heat of the jungle doesn't last very long.

"Right. You've got it. That all?" said Kovacs.

"That's all we need now."

"Take it easy. See you later."

"Yeah. See you later for a drink at Paddy Clark's." Paddy Clark's was John O'Neil's favorite barroom in New York, O'Neil's home town.

The sound of the fire fight up ahead of the Battalion's position grew more intense. O'Neil got on the 'phone whenever possible and gave a running account of what was going on. During one of these conversations he requested mortars. They were promptly dispatched under Lieutenant Railsback. O'Neil and Railsback and the men with them held the position against strong Japanese resistance all that day. The Japs tried to outflank them; they were slaughtered. Some got in and around back of them, but O'Neil had prepared a watertight ambush and more Japs were slaughtered. Over seventy-five Japs died trying to force O'Neil's road block. By nightfall all was quiet. The few that were left had withdrawn. O'Neil had lost one man.

A map taken off the body of the Jap officer was promptly dispatched to Regiment. It showed a full plan of attack involving a Japanese regiment. It was impossible to orient the map, but the terrain—draws, ridges, streams, and swamp—looked suspiciously like the terrain centered around the forks of the east and west branches of the Piva River, east of the Third Regiment's position. The map was of great value—it could be used as another clue. Maybe that's where the enemy was, and maybe an attack was his intention. We would have to find out. The map was promptly sent to Division Headquarters, and later proved to show the true plan of attack. At the moment there was enough evidence to inspire a decision by the Commanding General to beat them to it.

An order arrived from Division Headquarters for the Third Marines to move against the enemy, discover his strength, disposition, and intentions, and prepare to attack and destroy him on order.

The next day our old friends the Third Raiders moved in and took over the lines of the Third Battalion. The Third Battalion moved forward in attack formation astride the Numa Numa trail. Two tanks sent in support of the Third moved out with them. The Battalion moved forward unopposed, picked up O'Neil and Railsback, moved forward 300 yards farther, but encountered no opposition. The only Japs seen were dead ones, in and around O'Neil's position. The Battalion went into an all-around defense with the tanks covering the trail, and spent the night unmolested.

Meantime, patrols had been ordered by Regiment to reconnoiter in front of the line along the west branch of the Piva River. They encountered resistance in front of the outposts of the battalion of the Twenty-first Marines. The patrols returned with additional information regarding the disposition of the enemy's forces.

On the morning of the 20th, Colonel King, commanding the Third Battalion, sent out two platoons with Major Ed Hamilton, the quiet-spoken, clever, popular executive officer of the Third Battalion, to locate the limits of the new E Line to be occupied on the 21st and to arrange for a route of supply to this new position. One platoon under Lieutenant Morris was to locate and garrison the right flank of the new line. The other platoon under Lieutenant Hendershaw was to screen a bulldozer cutting a road to the new position. Both of these platoons moved back down the Numa Numa trail, then proceeded off to the east. A patrol under Lieutenant Taylor was ordered to establish the Division left flank, which was also the Third Battalion left flank at a certain stream junction east of the Third Battalion's present location. Another platoon patrol under Lieutenant Messer was ordered to investigate a trail which led from the rear of the Third Battalion's present location off to the east, apparently crossing the Piva River and leading to the new position of the Battalion on E Line. Both these patrols started off.

Lieutenant Messer's patrol had advanced about 125 yards when they were hit by a platoon of Japs who had worked around the rear of the Third Battalion during the night. He called for 60-mm. mortars. Lieutenant Railsback and the two tanks moved back into the fight. The scrap lasted six hours. All the Japs in that area were either killed or routed; eighty dead ones were counted. Lieutenant Messer lost all of his squad leaders in the action. The results of O'Neil's and Railsback's efforts on the 18th and those of Messer and Railsback on the 20th were now apparent. The Jap defensive position or road block (estimated strength, about a company) which had formerly held this sector had been knocked out. This important Numa Numa trail area included part of the site for the new bomber strip, and it now belonged to the Marines.

All morning the bulldozer manned by a brave Seabee and screened by Lieutenant Hendershaw's platoon plowed through the jungle a few yards at a time, pushing through the supply road which would soon play so important a part in the coming operations. Major Hamilton was back and forth picking the only negotiable course toward the new line and supervising the work's progress.

At about 12:30 that afternoon Sergeant Nasti, our hard-boiled regimental middleweight champion, was out in front of the bulldozer shooting a compass azimuth and guiding the cat toward the line when he suddenly heard firing off to the left front. "That's either artillery or mortars—and it's in the wrong direction to be friendly," thought Nasti. The heavy, air-splitting explosion of a Japanese mortar shell about 400 yards to their right confirmed his deduction. "That's Jap!" A few seconds later another shell exploded 100 yards to their left. Major Hamilton ordered the cat to cease operations—the Japs up in the hills to the left front must have them spotted. The men were ordered to spread out and take cover. Then another shell landed, and a hole four feet in diameter a few yards from the bulldozer marked its point of impact. Nasti yelled nervously to the Major, "Big hole!"

"Sure is," answered Major Hamilton.

No one remembers how many more shells came in on them. But they came thick and fast. The ground shook; the air was churning so fast they could hardly breathe; thunderous explosions burned their ears. Nasti felt a shell fragment strike the back of his helmet. He dove alongside Major Hamilton.

"I've been hit," yelled Nasti. Big, yellowish orange balls the size of Christmas-tree ornaments kept popping out of the air in front of his eyes. "Like seeing stars after you run into a right hook—only *big* stars," Nasti related. "My ears were ringing. The noise of the explosions was so loud you could hardly stand it. I saw Major Hamilton get up. He was holding his back, and blood was dripping off his hand. The Major started limping off to get help. Then I saw some men crawling through the bush. I thought it was the Japs."

"Here they come!"

Then Nasti recognized Berry, the corpsman. Some Raiders rushed down to give them help. Major Hamilton was lying on the ground holding his back; a large shell fragment had torn through his hip. Berry rushed up to give him aid. He was bleeding badly. Major Hamilton (being Major Hamilton) asked Berry to take care of the others; he could hear them groaning, and knew there must be many wounded.

More shells exploded in a thunderous roar near by. The Japs had the area well marked and were pouring it on. Berry refused to leave. The Raiders and the rest of the platoon who were uninjured carried the men out. Major Hamilton, with his hip ball-and-socket joint sheared away, walked to the aid station. Nasti walked around in a fog. His head felt as if it would burst wide open. "I'll help you . . . I'll help you," he kept saying to Berry.

Berry went right on bandaging the men and giving them morphine. A Raider helped Nasti walk back to the aid station. Lieutenant Hendershaw was lying on the table; there were large open wounds in both of his legs. A doctor was having trouble deciphering the number on the rusty dog-tag of an unconscious man.

"I can help you," said Nasti.

"What can *you* do?" put in Hendershaw from the table.

"He was always riding me," said Nasti later in the hospital. "What a guy . . . even hurt so bad! There'll never be another platoon leader like Red Hendershaw."

A doctor came over to Nasti. His ears were still ringing. The doctor recognized the middleweight champion.

"How do you feel, Nasti?" he asked.

"I've got an awful headache."

The doctor took a look at Nasti's head. There was an open, elongated wound the size of a cigarette across the back of it. The doctor smiled. "Yes, Nasti, I guess you have!"

One battalion executive officer, one platoon leader, and eighteen men and noncoms out of one platoon of L Company made the road to the Third Battalion's new position an expensive highway.

The Second Battalion was detached from the 37th Infantry Division of the Army on November 19 and ordered to rejoin the Third Regiment the next morning. They were to proceed east to an assembly area in the rear of the line held by the battalion of the Twenty-first Marines. Early in the morning, as the Second Battalion prepared to move out, down came the rain. Whenever the Third Marines were going to move on, for some reason or other it had to rain.

E Company at the head of the Second Battalion column moved into the assembly area near the west branch of the Piva River about noon. G Company, following, was filing into position when Jap mortar fire began to register on the route of approach. Two shells landed in the F Company column. Two men were instantly killed, and six severely wounded. The men in the company moved on. The Jap observer followed that marching column into the assembly area and poured it on again. F Company again took the rap, and eight more men were severely wounded. Staying there and taking it when the enemy has you bracketed is bitter medicine. The men started to dig in and broke all existing records.

They had barely finished when orders arrived for the Battalion to move through the lines of the Twenty-first Marines, to attack across the east branch of the Piva River guiding on the East-West trail and knock out a Japanese strong point located in a small village—some five native huts—with the fancy name of Kugubikopoi. The village was located in a triangle formed by two streams. According to the map a tributary from the north joined the east branch of the Piva River at a junction about 200 yards southwest of this village, this junction being called the Piva Forks. The battalion was to attack across the river and secure the village by dark. H-hour was at 3:30 that afternoon.

As the Second Battalion moved out an order passed down the lines: "Load and lock!"

Not a sound of execution could be heard. Those rifles had been loaded and locked for days. Grim, determined faces revealed the thoughts of the men in the Second Battalion moving forward in their first attack. Only a few hours before, they had seen the poignant pain registered on the faces of their wounded buddies, had heard their agonized groans through the din of Jap mortar-shell explosions; and there was nothing any of them could do about it. Not then. But now, as they moved forward, these men had blood in their eyes and revenge in their souls.

The plan called for G Company to move along the East-West trail until they hit the river. They would establish their left flank at this point and extend down the stream for 200 yards. E Company would remain in a column of platoons preparatory to crossing the river. Downstream from E Company a platoon from the Twenty-first Marines would set up on the river bank, and to their right the line would be extended farther downstream by a platoon from A

Company of the First Battalion, Third Marines. After a short artillery preparation, G Company and the two platoons to the right of E Company were to cover the opposite bank of the stream with machine-gun and rifle fire for two minutes. E Company would then cross the river, move into the bush for about a hundred yards, turn left on an azimuth of 15° and proceed obliquely across the front of G Company. They were to take possession of the village and set up security for the night. G Company would then cross the river, followed by F Company, and establish contact on E Company's left.

By the time all the platoons on the right had moved into position on the river bank it was five o'clock in the afternoon; less than two hours of daylight remained. Suddenly word arrived that the attack had been called off until the following morning. Runners dashed out to the front-line platoons to tell them to hold their fire; but, before all of them could be reached, the platoon on the extreme right opened up with everything it had. Immediately the firing spread all along the line. Then the Japs opened up with machine-guns and rifles, and a fire fight was on. Though of short duration it was long enough to add to our growing list of casualties. Two men were killed and seven wounded. Darkness was settling in. Getting the casualties out before it became pitch-black was the immediate difficult problem. One man had a badly shattered left arm, and darkness had come before he was found. He needed immediate surgical treatment. A corpsman named Smith crawled out to the wounded man, administered morphine, and released the tourniquet on his arm at regular intervals all during the night. The man would have been dead by morning. Smith saved his life.

Back in Samoa, Lieutenant Kay of the Second Battalion had led his battalion commander on a merry chase during a problem, and from that time on he had been called "The Swamp Fox"—first in friendly sarcasm, and now always as a term of praise. Neither the jungle nor the Jap was any mystery to The Fox and the boys of his section. They knew what to look for, and they always found it.

Their keen efficiency paid off for their battalion and their regiment. On November 20 The Fox and some of his scouts were making an important reconnaissance of the area to be occupied in the near future by the Second Battalion. Off to the left of the East-West trail and forward of the Battalion's position they spotted a ridge rising sharply to a height of 400 feet out of the thick jungle. A happy shiver ran up and down The Fox's spine. In the jungle the faculty of observation is a valuable gift. What a prize this ridge would be for the Regiment! The Fox rushed back to the Battalion C.P. with his discovery. And this *was* a discovery: the first piece of high ground that had appeared near the front lines of the beachhead.

Lieutenant Colonel Hector "Joe" de Zayas, Commanding Officer of the Second Battalion, ordered Major Buck Schmuck, F Company commander, to occupy it. Lieutenant Steve Cibik of the first platoon got the call. Shortly after Steve received orders to take his platoon together with a section of machine-guns on this mission, F Company was hit by the Japanese mortar fire. A long hike from the Army sector through the muddy swamp . . . shelled on the way . . . shelled again in the midst of the preparation for an important mission—such were the events that prefaced the departure of this rugged band of jungle warriors who started out late in the afternoon to climb into the unknown.

The Fox guided the platoon to a spot in the jungle where he could point the hill out to Steve. Steve shot an azimuth; then ordered his scouts to move out. His runners continued laying a combat wire from the rear of the column. Steve was moving just behind the forward scouts when they hit the base of a sheer, almost vertical rock cliff. Steve ordered the scouts to work off to the right. Finally they located a spot that looked negotiable. Darkness was rapidly closing in. They were in enemy territory. They had been on the move all day. They were tired. They all knew the situation. They knew what to expect. And every one of these trained men realized the importance of the mission ahead of them.

The men up at the head of the column looked at their platoon leader. They had been together for months, and they knew him well. They liked his toughness, knew he could do anything any man in the company could do, and do it better. They liked the way he looked after them when they needed a friend at court; his restless, searching energy, his gift of rapid analysis, his dogged drive. They liked his sense of humor and fairness, and his loyalty to his superiors and to the Corps. They liked his ambition. They knew he had risen from the ranks: private, corporal, sergeant, first sergeant, sergeant major, second lieutenant, and first lieutenant; that he had been in a guard company, sea-going, a Captain's orderly aboard ship, an anti-aircraft gunner aboard an aircraft carrier, a weapons expert, a crack jungle-fighting instructor, the top-ranking platoon leader of their company. They liked the way he beat his gums. They admired his guts. The men of the first platoon of F Company *liked* their leader.

"Let's go!" said Steve Cibik.

The men followed the scouts and Steve up the hill. Most of the men were carrying nothing but their rifles, B.A.R.s, and carbines. All packs had been left back at the battalion bivouac area. The hill was steep and slippery. But Steve knew that if he was tired the men carrying the machine-guns, tripods, and ammunition—the same men who had been carrying them all day—would be bushed. He had to get there before dark. He knew nothing of the terrain or what was up there. He had to get there "fust with the most," but he knew what it was like to carry a machine-gun—he had carried one. Steve ordered several halts.

They started off again. The hill kept going up—it seemed the highest hill in the world. They slipped and fell, cursed under their breath, grabbed vines and bushes, and pulled themselves forward. It was a contest of men against darkness. Darkness was a champion, but these men were out for the title. As the last light of that rugged day melted into the blackness of the jungle they reached a place where the ridge leveled off into a narrow crest. The scouts crept cautiously forward. Not a sign of a Jap. Steve made a rapid reconnaissance. Then he looked up at the darkening sky.

"Now what?" asked Platoon Sergeant Kennedy.

"We're going into a perimeter defense," said Steve. "Dig in!"

The men remembered the dozen or so craters made by our own artillery; they had passed them on the way up the hill. They yanked the liners out of their helmets and pulled out their bayonets. At the moment they were vulnerable trespassers. Four hours later, in a circle of shallow foxholes, they were the undisputed owners of Cibik's Ridge.

Chapter 13

LIEUTENANT TAYLOR of the Third Battalion, who had taken a patrol to locate the left flank of the Battalion's future position, had experienced considerable difficulty finding the correct stream junction. The only available maps of islands in the Pacific are inaccurate, to begin with, and in the jungle a stream is likely to change its course every time it rains. Taylor finally found what he believed to be the right stream junction among many. A section of machine-guns were dispatched to him and he was ordered to garrison this left-flank position. Lieutenant Morris's patrol had successfully located the right flank and was garrisoning that position. The stage was now set for the Third Battalion's advance the following day and its occupation of E Line. Captain Frost was to take the rest of I Company, join Lieutenant Taylor on the left, and extend his defenses to the right. Morris on the right flank was to extend to the left. The rest of the Third Battalion would move northeast, cross the west branch of the Piva River, move up to the center of the line, and extend right and left until they tied in with Morris and Frost on the right and left. Distances and directions had been carefully worked out.

All during the day the Japs had been throwing 90-mm. mortar shells into the Third Marine positions, and they kept it up all during the night. Back at the Regimental C.P., Speed, Big Mac, The Traveler, Major Bob Armstrong (the artillery liaison officer), Bob Walker (communications officer), Pappy Whitman—all members of the Regimental Staff; all the communicators with their heavy drums of wire; all the headquarters men—all were straining over the thousand details of the planning of succeeding moves, co-ordinating all the attached units . . . supply, communication, digging in a C.P., and so on. No one was idle. Lieutenant Jack Foley, his assistant, Lieutenant Neugent, and the entire map section were working from dawn into the hours of darkness, bringing up to date the rapidly changing terrain and situation maps as the three front-line battalions moved into unknown territory. From excellent terrain sketches carefully drawn by the battalion map sections and dispatched quickly by Lieutenant Stevens, an officer of Third Battalion Headquarters; from Lieutenant Kay, The Fox, of the Second; and from smiling Lieutenant Tom Manion of the First, Jack Foley had corrected the available maps. He stuck to his guns when questioned about the location of a certain potential enemy strong point, a native village, a disputed boundary between units, a stream junction, the direction of a trail, an enemy supply route. The reconnaissance men from the three battalions scouted out, drew sketches, and brought back information; and day after day Jack sifted, analyzed, and plotted all of this information. When the tools for planning were needed by Speed, Big Mac, and The Traveler, Jack had them there. The kit was complete, up to date, and quickly accessible; and it was Jack Foley and his boys who made that possible.

Communicators with their coils of wire, compasses, field 'phones, and climbers—plus their packs and arms—constitute a group of men who take some beating. For some reason the jungle stifles radio communication. This weakness, though widely discussed, has not yet been overcome. If good communication between units isn't number one on the list of important requisites in a jungle combat operation, it is crowding the top-flight priorities very close. Miles of wire have to be laid and maintained. The communicators are the rugged band of technicians who go out all during the day and night performing this important drudgery: carrying the wire, providing their own security against the enemy, running the omnipresent risk of being mistaken for the enemy and being shot by their own men (they sometimes are), climbing and tying wire in trees, tying-in the various units, following a wire down to a break and effecting the repairs after the wire has been torn down by an amphibian tractor or one of the other vehicles battling through a muddy jungle trail bringing up the badly needed supplies of chow and ammunition.

Bahe, one of the great lightweight boxers in the Regiment and a regimental communicator, had been out all day laying wire. Being an Indian he is a natural in the boondocks. A perfect little athlete, he is rugged and can keep pushing forward when the average man is bushed and has to stop for a blow. Like most Indians he is sparing of speech, and when he does speak it is usually an understatement. Bahe was beating his way through the jungle on a wire-laying mission. A Japanese mortar shell exploded near by. He was lifted off the deck and thrown bodily against a large banyan tree. His helmet went in one direction, his rifle in another, the coil of wire in another. "Uggg! . . . too . . . close!" said Bahe, and gathered up his gear and continued on his mission.

Darkness had enveloped the entire sector. An officer had arrived at the busy Regimental C.P. Jap 90-mm. mortar shells were dropping dangerously close. Lieutenant Brannon, the regimental adjutant, had a large hole dug into the side of a bank. He offered refuge to the newly arrived officer messenger, and the two of them curled into their ponchos and lay on the deck in the hole. It had been raining for some time and water started to drip down through the palm-leafed shelter, splashing down in the officer's face and, seeping in through the edge of the poncho, making the visitor generally miserable. The foxhole he had left down nearer the quieter beach section had been reasonably comfortable.

"Hell, Brannon—you've sure got a wet foxhole," said the officer.
Another mortar shell exploded very close. The ground shook.
"Yeah . . . but it's deep," said Brannon.
There were no more complaints.
Friendly artillery rushed through the air overhead and exploded out into the unknown in front of our lines. The men of the First Battalion, scheduled to move up to their new line the next day,

watched and waited out the rainy night. The men of the Second Battalion listened to the sound of the Jap mortars mingled with the sound of our own artillery passing overhead and tried to catch a few moments of precious rest before their attack the next morning. The men with Steve Cibik on the ridge wondered why they had found it deserted and prepared for a scrap in the morning. The men in the Third Battalion, having destroyed the Japs who had tried to envelop the rear of their present position, listened to the lullaby of the shells and thought about their buddies out on the left and right flank of an imaginary line in the jungle to which they must fight their way in the morning. They listened to the mortar shells explode near by as the Japs returned the harassing fire. Everyone tried to snatch a few moments of sleep—that precious, rare, expensive jewel in combat—but few slept. The night was long and wet and menacingly noisy. There was a tough day ahead. The weary men of the Third Marines waited out the night.

On the morning of the 21st the artillery laid down a five-minute artillery preparation before the Second Battalion jumped off on its reconnaissance by force across the Piva River. A Company of the First Battalion was to move up behind E Company of the Second as the latter moved forward and establish a defensive line along the river. When G Company moved forward, B Company, now tied into the left flank of G Company of the Second Battalion, would tie in with A Company on their right and extend their defensive farther to the left.

After the artillery fire had lifted, supporting mortar and machine-gun fire opened up. Then E Company started across the river. As the rear platoon passed 50 yards beyond the opposite bank it struck another large stream flowing into the east branch of the Piva. Captain Coupe, thinking this must be the tributary marked on the map, issued orders for the two leading platoons to execute their turn immediately and attack on an azimuth of 15°. To go too far beyond this stream junction would put the leading platoons too far to the right of the strong point in the native village which was their first objective. The rear platoon also executed a turn toward the north, and the three platoons started off abreast toward the village.

For the first 200 yards nothing of moment occurred. Then word came back along the line that Nip bunkers had been sighted by the first platoon. A Jap was spotted squatting down in the bush across a small stream. The noise of talking and the rattling of mess gear came from the direct front. The platoon moved up cautiously and spotted two bunkers and a chow line just across a stream. There were fifteen Japs standing in line for chow no more than thirty yards away. Hendricks, a Pfc who had made the discovery, reported it to Sergeant Renthal. The men waited until all of their B.A.R.s and machine-guns were in position. Renthal gave the signal and the skirmish line opened up. What was left of the chow line disappeared in the smoke and confusion of the fire. More jabbering, and then fire was returned from across the stream. One of the bunkers was silenced but the other kept firing at regular intervals. It was impossible to make a stream crossing until that bunker was knocked out.

In the meantime the second and third platoons of E Company, farther to the right, had crossed the stream and discovered several deserted bunkers. As they moved on they received fire from another bunker and, on attempting to outflank it, received fire from the previous bunkers which had been reoccupied. In moving forward the third platoon came to a small rise in the ground. The two scouts, Walter Walker and Charles O. Bullis, crossed over the rise, and Sergeant Yuhasz followed at the head of the platoon. There was a sudden burst of machine-gun fire close at hand, and Yuhasz fell badly wounded right in the fire lane of one of the active bunkers. It was risky business to give him help at this time, but he needed help badly. Lee, a plucky corpsman, never hesitated.

"Here I go," said Lee and moved out into the fire lane. He lay down beside the injured Yuhasz and coolly bound up his wounds. The Jap machine-gunner watched him work. As he tried to drag Yuhasz back toward some cover the machine-gun cut the two men down. Lee had known what he was walking into. Here was another heroic incident where a Navy corpsman attached to the Marines, a boy of great courage and devotion to duty, heard the moan of a wounded man, defied all risks of personal safety, and moved out into sudden death to bring relief to the suffering. Corpsman Lee gave his life to help a wounded comrade. Yes—but these are cold, stark words to describe heroism, to use in telling the tale of an unselfish answer to the call of duty and humanity.

G Company, as planned, had moved across the river and had advanced to contact the left flank of E Company. They found that E Company was held up by the dense fire from the bunkers. Both company commanders agreed that the bunkers would have to be outflanked if further forward progress was to be made. Corporal Haranka was sent out with a small patrol from G Company to try to discover the enemy's right flank. He ran into some more bunkers. Then Lieutenant Billy Langdale was ordered to take his platoon and develop the situation and find out just how much strength blocked the way. Billy took his platoon and moved off still farther to the left. He deployed his platoon for an attack. As they moved forward, several men including Platoon Sergeant Brazleton were hit by sniper and machine-gun fire. Brazleton lay just alongside of one machine-gun fire lane. He had a bullet in each leg and one in his right arm. Two men started out after him. Brazleton saw them coming. Cursing in true Texan fashion, he pointed out the fire lane and told the men to stay where they were and leave him alone. The men knew if they didn't soon get him out he would bleed to death. And Brazleton knew that if his rescuers moved toward him they would be mowed down. He knew the Jap mind and every one of his tricks. He knew the machine-gunner who had got him was covering his wounded body; the second a man stepped across that fire lane, the gunner would open up.

Brazleton lay there bleeding rapidly, holding a .45 pistol in his left hand . . . waiting . . . hating just as intensely as that slant-eyed Nip behind the Nambu machine-gun. He knew he was in bad shape, and while that Jap machine-gunner still lived he didn't have a prayer of getting out of there. O.K.—he might bleed to death, but here was one Nip that was going with him! Brazleton shook a bush on the edge of the fire lane. The Jap lost his nerve and opened up. The rugged Texan put a bullet through the Jap's head. Two men dashed forward and dragged Brazleton to cover. A corpsman went into action with tourniquets and blood plasma. Back at the battalion aid station, Dr. Dingman and Dr. Etheridge, the two battalion surgeons who were always up close to the front line, added their skill to save the platoon sergeant's life and shuttled him back toward the next dressing station. More blood plasma. . . .

Some days later, Brazleton was evacuated to a hospital on an island farther back. By the time he had reached the rearmost mobile hospital before evacuation to the States, he had been given twenty-six blood transfusions. He had gone from 190 down to a mere 90 pounds. He cursed everyone who came near him. When the doctors thought he was strong enough, a Naval officer paid him a visit to present him with a Silver Star. He cursed so loud that the officer had to leave. Doctors all along the line wondered how he could stay alive. But he was too mad to die. Mad at getting hit, mad because he couldn't kill more of the Japs who cover the wounded and murder defenseless corpsmen as they perform their lifesaving deeds of mercy. He's still mad—and he's still alive. And when he gets better he'll be back in there fighting for the Marine Corps and the State of Texas . . . and God help the Japs!

Langdale moved his platoon skillfully through the swamp and surrounded a series of bunkers. The Japs, waiting behind their guns and covering their carefully cut fire lanes, could hear Langdale's men as they closed in and around them. They waited silently for a target to cross one of the deadly lanes. Little did they know that they were being surrounded by a platoon of jungle-wise men who had been patrolling together for days. This same platoon had already surprised and killed a dozen or so Japs in a patrol action on the 18th, fighting an able withdrawing action and disappearing into the jungle without losing a man. Finally the Japs' patience was exhausted. They could hear the Marines, but they couldn't see them.

"Come on out, you American sonsabitches, and fight," squeaked the Japs.

"You're the ones that're pinned down, you bastards! *You* come out and fight," drawled Langdale.

B Company, holding the sector left of G Company's take-off position on the bank of the river, extended right and left and began to consolidate their defensive line. By this time all the companies in the First Battalion were considerably under strength and growing slimmer daily. Their lines were spread very thin.

Some time after G Company of the Second Battalion had shoved off across the river, Le Guin's platoon of B Company, holding a sector along the river and near the East-West trail, began receiving heavy machine-gun fire from a Japanese position to their immediate front. The fire got heavier, and Le Guin requested support. Two platoons of F Company of the Second Battalion were not yet committed. Captain Don Baker, the executive officer of F Company, was ordered to take Lieutenant DeLamar's platoon and a machine-gun squad and destroy the Jap positions. Baker and DeLamar moved quickly to the B Company position and sized up the situation.

Baker decided to outflank the Jap machine-guns. They moved off to the left of the East-West trail, crossed the river, and started east. The Japs anticipated the move and withdrew. When the platoon moved in toward the trail about a hundred yards east of the river, it was met by intense machine-gun fire. Baker pulled off to the left and again moved east. Again the Japs withdrew along the trail and were ready for them when the platoon worked its way toward the trail to attack. Baker again pulled back from the trail. Gradually they were accomplishing their purpose, for each successive move forced the Jap gunners to pull back farther to the east. The pressure on B Company had already been relieved, but there was another danger: Baker knew that G Company had advanced to the east on the opposite side of the trail. The Japs, who seemed to be able to outmatch his fire power, would now be dangerously near the rear and left flank of the advancing G Company. If G Company had struck opposition, this rear and flank threat could be dangerous. The longer he could keep the Japs busy, the better for G Company.

He leapfrogged again. The Japs had pulled back, were again in position, and opened up with heavy fire. But this time Baker built up a base of fire in the jungle overlooking the trail. Then, leaving a small cadre of men to keep the Japs tied down, he cautiously withdrew the rest of his men. Before he started off again he instructed Sergeant Phillips to make his way as quickly as possible back to Le Guin to give him the platoon's location and future intentions. Then, while the men near the trail indulged in a spirited fire fight with the Jap machine-gunners, the rest of the platoon made a wide arc, moving as rapidly as possible through the swampy jungle, then worked their way toward the trail. Don knew his offsets but almost lost confidence in his compass. The trail had dissolved in the jungle. Finally he spotted it. He could hear a fire fight off to the other side of the trail, but that was all. Not a sign of a Jap. This time he had outflanked them and was in a position to ambush their next withdrawal. He ordered the machine-gun to set up and cover the trail. The brush was thick, and it was difficult to get an unexposed field of fire.

Quietly Baker and DeLamar set an ambush. The platoon was well hidden by the thick jungle growth. The green of the sweaty, mud-stained uniforms blended with the foliage. Don gently parted a bush. No sign of life. He glanced quickly at the various positions. The machine-gun was well placed, the B.A.R. man had a good position, the riflemen were O.K. He let the bush snap back, sat down, and started to make a terrain sketch to send back to his company commander.

He was interrupted by the sound of excited, squeaky chatter . . . Japs! Don threw the safety off his carbine and looked out toward the trail. There they were! A group of Japs were hot-footing it down the trail toward the east, chattering as they ran. One carried a heavy machine-gun, another carried a Nambu, the rest were burdened down with ammunition. Maderos lay behind the machine-gun. One eye was watching Don—the other on his sights pointing toward the trail. Don winked. Maderos held his fire. A few seconds passed . . . not a sound from the Marines. The Japs, noisier than ever and burdened with their heavy loads, waddled on up the trail. Don dropped his arm, and Maderos raked the trail. The Japs plunged forward on their faces. They were good Japs now . . . all dead.

But the platoon was still in for a rough time. In making the wide arc, they had advanced without knowing it to the edge of a Japanese strong point facing them from the east. Machine-guns from this sector opened up. They were in for a fight. DeLamar pulled his men into a skirmish line to counter this fire from the east. He worked his men forward. Creeping forward cautiously, DeLamar located a Jap machine-gun nest. With his left hand he signaled a man behind him to move into position. A bullet tore through his hand, nearly severing his left thumb. Don covered the wound with sulfa powder and suggested that DeLamar go back to the C.P. When DeLamar protested, Don ordered him back with the information about this new development and gave him a sketch of their location.

DeLamar, protesting, had no sooner left than flanking fire started to pour in from the other side of the trail. Thirty-caliber bullets tore through the trees from across the trail. During a pause in the firing Don heard an unmistakable Georgian voice shouting at them: "Come out, you son-of-a-bitch, and fight!" It was Billy Langdale..

"Hold your fire—it's Baker!" yelled Don.

But Langdale had already carried on a spirited debate with the Japs earlier in the day, and he wasn't going to be tricked by their ability to speak English.

The firing became heavier from the Jap positions to their east. The platoon was returning the fire.

"Say 'lollapalooza'!" shouted Billy Langdale, knowing that Japs can't pronounce the letter "l."

"Lol-la-pa-looza," shouted Don in his best pear-shaped-tone diction.

But it wasn't good enough for Langdale. "Come out and fight!" he repeated.

"Lol . . . la . . . pa . . . looza—it's Baker, Don Baker," shouted Don.

A burst of fire from one of Langdale's B.A.R. men sawed the limb above Baker's head. Suddenly Don had an inspiration. He didn't know Billy very well, and through the noise of rifle fire the other officer hadn't recognized his voice. But they had both been in New Zealand, and had experienced "Down Under" hangovers.

"Battle of Queen Street!" shouted Don.

"O.K.," drawled Billy. Don's reminder had worked.

There was the sound of more firing from across the trail. But the air didn't crack the way it does when bullets are coming toward you. Now that Billy had been convinced, he was devoting all his attention to the enemy in the other direction.

Things were getting rough from the east. Don decided to attack. Little did he know what was waiting for him. As they started to work themselves forward, Phillips crawled up to him: artillery was to be laid down. Joe, the battalion commander, had sent Phillips back with orders for Baker to withdraw.

Don started to pull the men back. Getting the wounded out was the big problem. Walkowiak, a B.A.R. man, was wounded in the leg. Gandi covered Sergeant Sibilian by fire as the sergeant went after Walkowiak. Gandi was killed in the performance of his mission.

Later that afternoon Baker got the wounded and the rest of his men back to the C.P. He felt bad about Gandi. The order to withdraw had arrived just in time. Later they discovered the size of the hornets' nest they had stumbled into. If they had gone through with the attack all of them would probably have been massacred.

Chapter 14

THAT SAME MORNING of November 21, on the ridge, Platoon Sergeant Kennedy took out a small patrol just before dawn, and reconnoitered more of this high ground. The ridge extended generally north and south. About 200 yards from the spot where Cibik's platoon had bivouacked for the night, the patrol found a deserted Japanese defense position with well-dug foxholes. As soon as Steve Cibik received the report he moved his outfit to the new position. While Kennedy placed the men in a perimeter defense, Steve placed the machine-guns. Two trails were discovered leading to the top of the ridge: one along the top running north, the other down over the side running generally east. Steve used two of the machine-guns to cover each of the two trails and placed the third to cover their own route of approach from the south. The Jap holes were deeply dug, but they all faced in the direction of our forces and were located on the top of the crest. Steve wanted his defensive position placed correctly on the military crest of the ridge, and in a position where they would have visibility and a field of fire toward the enemy. The one shovel had to be used for the construction of the machine-gun emplacements. The men went to work again on their own foxholes with bayonets and helmets.

Steve began to understand the picture. The ridge had been used by the Japs during the day as an observation post. It was a good one. Then, just before darkness, in order to escape the harassing fire which our artillery laid down in front of our lines each night, they would retire to the perfectly defiladed reverse area in the jungle on the east side of the ridge. The high ridge acted as a shield and masked their bivouac area.

About a half-hour after Steve's men were in position, one of the men opened fire from a position overlooking the eastern trail. The Japs were just on their way up to take their posts for the day. They must have been surprised. They attempted to retake the ridge again about noon, but were driven back. After the platoon had repulsed the attack, two of the boys crept down the east side of the ridge and discovered a cache of Jap hand grenades, which they promptly commandeered. The Japs had spotted the machine-guns and were making Japanese preparations to wipe them out. But up to this time not a machine-gun had been fired. The section had only eleven boxes of belted ammunition with them, and Steve had given the machine-gunners specific instructions not to fire until absolutely necessary.

The telephone had not worked since their arrival the night before. Steve sent Bush back to retrace their trail and to give a report to Buck Schmuck, his company commander.

The Fox arrived later that afternoon with some communicators, who had laid another line to the position. The ridge boys were sure glad to see him—now they would be in touch again with Battalion. Later that afternon they heard a medley of chopping, digging, and Nipponese jabbering over on the east side of the ridge. Steve got Buck Schmuck on the wire and requested mortars. At about 4:30 that afternoon they were there—Lieutenant Gibby Young, F Company's Weapons Platoon commander, and ten men. Gibby and Steve went to work. They shot accurate azimuths on each noisy location and worked out the ranges. The mortar crews dug into position.

There were now a total of 62 men up on the ridge, with three machine-guns and two 60-mm. mortars. This would be a tough little garrison to pry loose. But Steve had no illusions—he knew the Nips would try.

The rest of the day was quiet. The valuable respite was used to advantage in consolidating the position. The men were mighty tired as darkness set in. So were the Japs resting below. They had been doing considerable construction work all afternoon. They needed a lullaby to sing them to sleep. Gibby gave it to them in C Minor with a hundred rounds of 60-mm. mortar shells.

Both E Company, which had crossed the Piva River and turned toward the native village northeast of the Piva Forks, and G Company, which had crossed the Piva and moved up to make contact with the left flank of E Company, had run into considerable opposition. Both companies were in touch with Colonel "Joe" De-Zayas at the Second Battalion C.P.; all the information on the disposition and strength of the enemy had been relayed back through Joe to the Regimental C.P. Communication was excellent. Information got back and orders went forward rapidly. E and G Companies were developing the situation. It's the hard way to make a reconnaissance—to discover what's out there—but in the jungle it's the only way.

By the middle of the afternoon Regimental Headquarters had part of the enemy picture. E and G Companies were ordered to withdraw back across the river in order that an artillery concentration could be laid down to soften up the enemy positions. A withdrawal is a difficult operation, and when units engaged with the enemy have suffered casualties (which must, of course, be pulled out), when the jungle is so thick that one must cut his way through and fight at the same time, when the swamp is so deep it takes hours to negotiate a hundred yards, where it is necessary to fight a rear-guard action every foot of the way, then such an operation is a true test of skill and endurance. Both of these crack companies stood the test. The withdrawal was successfully executed. G Company went into a defensive position along the river, while E Company was brought back in reserve in the vicinity of the Second Battalion C.P. The two remaining platoons of F Company were already dispersed and providing security for the battalion headquarters. C Company of the First Battalion was brought up on the line and closed the gap between B Company and Cibik's platoon up on the ridge. The battalion of the Twenty-first Marines, which had formerly held part of the area to the rear of this new line, had reverted back to their own regiment's control and had moved to the south. Thus, on the night of the 21st, E Line had been reached and occupied. In the Third Marine sector—the only sector of the perimeter beachhead line receiving enemy opposition—A Company anchoring the right flank was tied into the Twenty-first Marines on the south. B Company (also of the First Battalion) held the sector of the line to the left of A Company, tying in with C Company and filling the gap between C Company and the platoon on the ridge. The perimeter line then curved and faced the northeast, running along the top of another ridge northwest of Cibik's Ridge. The occupation of this high ground facing the northeast had already been "penciled in" on the situation map. This completed the Third Marine sector of the beachhead line.

Since D-day, the occupation of each new forward line of the beachhead perimeter had been achieved without opposition. But the northeast sector—which included the new proposed bomber and fighter strip area—had been bitterly contested: O'Neil's Numa Numa trail action, the Messer-Railsback fracas. But E Line had been reached and occupied. The Third Battalion had fought every inch of its way, but it was there on the line on time in possession of the commanding ground facing the northeast. Here's how the Third Battalion got there.

On the morning of the 21st the Third Battalion prepared to occupy the center of their new Line, garrisoned by the platoon from K Company on the right and the platoon from I Company on the left. The battalion had quite a day ahead of it. Each unit must remain in contact with its commanding parent organization of the next higher echelon. Reports of the strength and condition of the unit are relayed back during all stages of an operation. When an outfit is in the midst of combat these reports are often delayed. The heckling that follows this delay in paper work often comes at an inopportune time. Captain Scott, the operation officer of the Third Battalion, describes a personal experience:

"It was November 21st. Our battalion had been fighting most

of the previous day. The Japs had attacked our rear. Now we were to reverse our direction, move back 300 yards through the battle area, cross the Piva River, then attack and seize a ridge to which the Japs had apparently withdrawn after their defeat of the previous day.

"My mission as operations officer was to take Lieutenant John O'Neil (who knew the ground) and an eight-man patrol with a wire team, move to the Piva River, and select a suitable site for the battalion to cross. We spliced our wire into the Regimental Battalion line and moved quietly to the bank of the Piva. As I crept to the river's edge, the men covered me, moving in perfect silence to the flanks. We could detect the smell of dead bodies mixed with the smoke of our previous night's artillery fire. Creeping and crawling along the river bank, I selected a likely spot to have the battalion cross at.

"As I moved to hook in my telephone to call Colonel King, my Battalion Commander, John O'Neil, gripped my arm and whispered in my ear 'Look, Scotty.' He was pointing across the river to the canebrake. A bush was moving. We were both sure that there was at least a Japanese division on the other side. A twig snapped on our right. Probably a regiment working around our flank. Pfc Curry, our ace Jap killer, tested his bolt. O'Neil warned him to be quiet.

"I tested my 'phone. 'Scotty calling Rex. Come in, Rex.' No answer. I was whispering, with my lips pressed against the receiver. O'Neil was crouched over me, covering me while I talked. Curry was smoothing his stock.

"Suddenly I heard the click on the wire that tells you someone's on the line. 'Hello, Scotty. Is that you, Scotty?'

"By this time, convinced that I was facing the greater part of the Japanese Imperial Army, I was becoming extremely cautious.

" 'Yeah. Scotty on. That you, Rex?'

"The exasperated voice shouted, 'No, this isn't Rex—it's Brannon.'

" 'Who?'

"'Brannon. Clyde Brannon, damn it—R-1.'

"'Yeah, Brannon, whadda ya want?'

"The bush on the other side moved again. Probably bringing up another regiment.

"'*What do I want!* Listen, Scotty—it's eleven o'clock and I still don't have your damn personnel report! What's the matter with you people, anyway? Where's Cromie? Jees—Division is on my neck. They want my report right away. It's urgent, Scotty—you *know* that stuff is, and . . .'

"The bush moved again. Japs bringing up tanks and artillery, probably. I asked Brannon whether I could call him back."

The Third Battalion moved out. The trail extending from the rear of its position went across the Piva River and up to the ridge that marked the center line. It was the logical route of approach. Obeying one rule of combat in the jungle—that the hardest way is usually the right way—the Battalion moved through the worst possible terrain. Before reaching the Piva, the men were forced to slide down a thirty-foot bluff to the river below. The Piva was waist-deep, with a mud bottom. On the other side of the river there was more cliff, a bamboo thicket, and then a steep ridge. The trail was now off to the Battalion's left crossing the river at a low point and winding easily up the ridge. The Battalion, in contact-imminent formation, moved straight up the side of the hill. Heavy rain made the climbing very difficult. As the forward scouts hit the crest of the ridge, Nambu machine-guns from two bunkers opened up on them. Lieutenant Smith flanked one from the left and knocked it out, and L Company blasted the other one out with grenades. The Battalion discovered 150 Jap foxholes arranged in a perimeter defense. But the Japs who had remained alive as the Battalion advanced steadily up the hill took off to the northeast. The principal Jap defense had been organized on and around the trail. He was dug in securely and was waiting patiently for the boys to come up the trail. Instead, they had come up the side of the hill to his rear and flanks, and his defense had been useless.

It had been a long pull through slippery, thick terrain. The men of the Third Battalion had reached their objective and had captured the hill. There was a feeling of elation, satisfaction over a job well done, and few casualties. But the day had not ended. They would still be called upon to "pay the piper." They started paying a short time later. The Japs in the hills beyond this ridge were working out the range and direction and were ready with their mortars. Suddenly a concentration of deadly Japanese 90-mm. mortar shells came in on top of the Third Battalion. Men scattered for cover. Control was difficult as the men tried to clear the hill and go underground.

A few moments before, two buddies of long standing had been talking joyously, examining a captured Japanese flag. One boy had left to try to match this coveted souvenir. When he returned, he found his buddy lying on the ground a bloody mess. Both legs had been sheared off above the knees, and he was screaming in agony. His buddy stood over him . . . helpless . . . tears pouring from his eyes. It was like a nightmare. Who could even imagine such suffering? A corpsman worked like mad to stem the flow of blood that poured from the ragged stumps of this young kid's legs. On a man in that condition, morphine has no effect. His buddy suffered the tortures of the damned . . . the damned. A clean-cut kid just off the sand lots! That wonderful kid, his best friend, the only guy he could talk to. He stood there and watched his buddy bleed to death—stood there . . . stunned . . . limp . . . weak . . . nauseous . . . faint. Then mounting anger drove the blood back into his head.

"Why didn't I shoot him? Why does *anybody* have to suffer like that? Why didn't I shoot him? If we'd been alone, I'd have shot him through the head."

A Marine grabbed him by the sleeve of his dirty dungaree jacket and pulled him away. The corpsman covered the dead Marine with a poncho. They left the other boy alone. He sat down and cried. Then he wiped his face on the sleeve of his jacket and stared blankly into the jungle.

He wiped his face again. He thought of his buddy's home and all he had heard about it. "If I ever get out of this alive I'll write his Mom. I'll tell her that I was there. I saw him get it. I'll tell her that he never knew what hit him." He got up and walked away . . . and dug some more on his foxhole.

Everybody liked the Karvelas twins—William and Robert. Robert is the elder, born thirty minutes ahead of William twenty-two years ago. They were our Regimental light heavyweight champions. Both the boys had reached the finals in the laddered tournament; but they were twins, and they refused to fight each other. It was a twin championship.

Sergeant William Reed, their squad leader, was the only man in the Regiment who could tell them apart. "There is a small scar on Robert's nose," Reed said; "but you have to get close." They were built exactly the same, the same height, the same actions, they talked just the same. When they went overseas they both grew mustaches, and the two mustaches were exactly alike. When both men were put on a working party, only one would have to go, because he could cover for both. Back in Samoa the two of them could always get an extra ration of beer. One of the brothers would get in the beer line. He'd collect his ration, give it to a buddy, and get back into the line some time later.

"I gave you your beer," said the clerk.

"Not me—I didn't get any beer," the same twin would answer.

"Musta been your brother."

"Yeah, that's right."

Then hours later the other brother would arrive back from unloading a ship. The clerk would see him get off the truck and join the new line at the Post Exchange.

"Didn't you get your beer?" the clerk would ask.

"Are you kiddin'? I just got off a working party."

Now what clerk could be so hard-hearted as not to give a man his beer when he'd just come off a working party? Something was all screwed up; he could have sworn he'd given beer to both

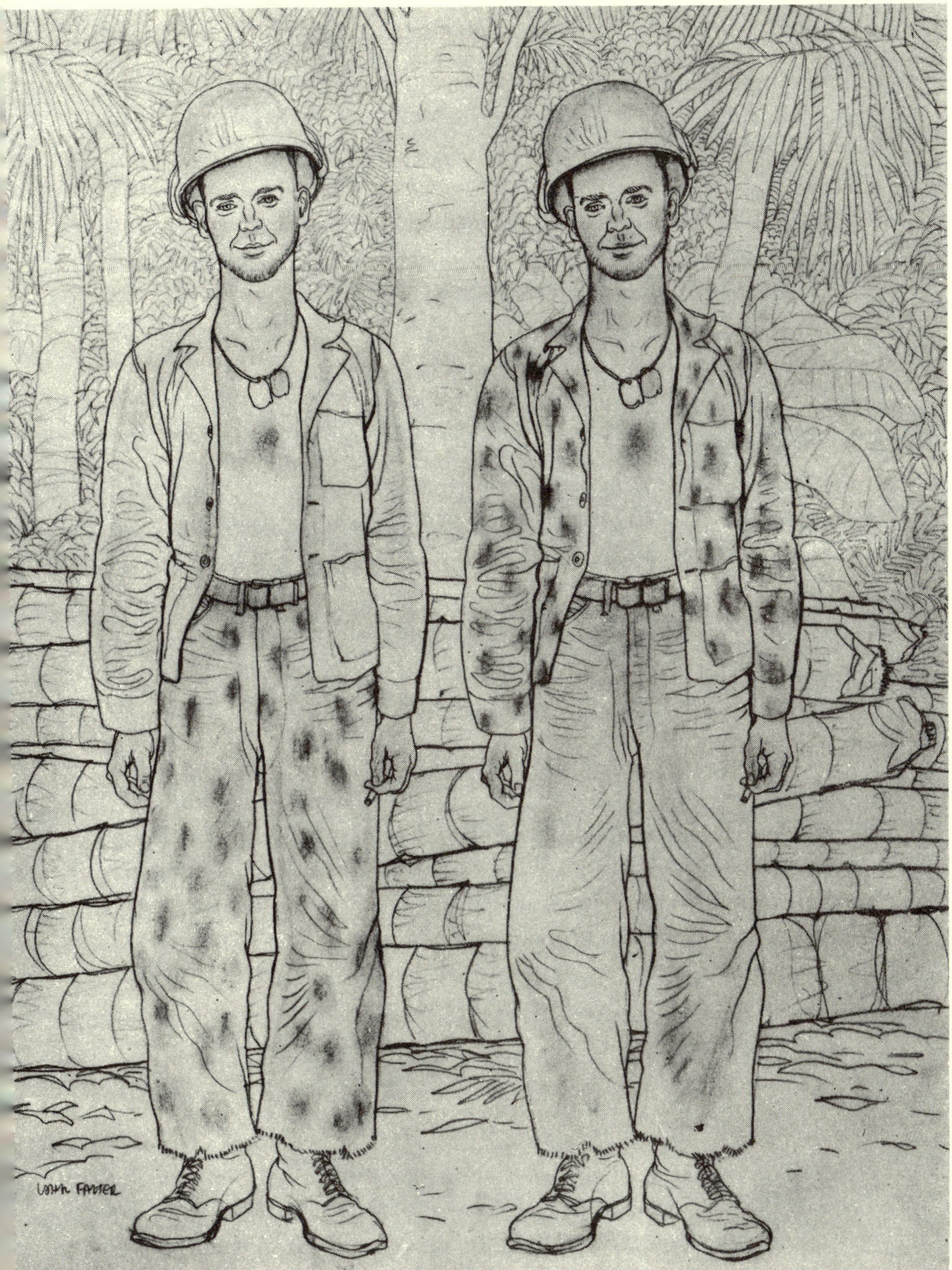

brothers—but how could you tell? They looked alike. Keeping all that stuff straight for the monthly inventory was tough enough, but those twins . . . too much for him. The other twin got his beer.

"They could do anything," said their squad leader. "I could use them as scouts, B.A.R. men—anything."

Reed's squad was part of a patrol sent out by the Third Battalion after they had reached the top of the ridge. They were to locate I Company somewhere down there in the jungle on the left flank. The jungle was very thick, the going was slow, and they had a tough time finding it. They were finally successful and had started back. Reed's squad ran smack into a concentration of Japs. The squad deployed quickly and tried to fight their way out. The Japs were set up in the gap between the ridge and I Company; it was impossible to get through. Their one chance was to pull back to I Company and get reinforcements. William and Robert had become separated. One by one the men tried to work themselves back. The Japs were crowding them. William had a B.A.R. with Tinsley. When the squad had pulled back, Robert was there, but Tinsley and William were missing. No one knew where they were. The men who had pulled out rushed back to I Company. Captain Frost had heard the fire fight and had readied his mortars. He didn't have enough men to cover the wide gap to the hill. By this time the two lost boys would be either dead or out of the area. Robert begged his company commander to let him lead a volunteer combat patrol back to look for his brother. The request couldn't be granted. Frost had to close that gap. Mortars were the quickest way. He would wait a while longer. Robert nearly went crazy. The minutes rushed by. Then he looked down the trail they had just made. In walked William and Tinsley. William was carrying a hand grenade. He had had the B.A.R. shot out of his hand while he was firing. Another Jap burst had torn away his B.A.R. belt. The two of them had fought it out together with hand grenades and one rifle. That's why they had taken a little longer.

"A few days after this William saved my life," said Reed. "A sniper put two bullets in a tree right next to my head. William grabbed the B.A.R. out of Robert's hand and sprung the sniper out of the tree."

One month later Robert and William both came down with attacks of dysentery, malaria, and filariasis, both of them at exactly the same time. They were evacuated together.

"You see," said Reed, "they were identical twins."

Chapter 15

REINFORCED with the information derived from the results of the exploratory probing tactics of the Second Battalion the day before, the size and disposition of the enemy's forces engaged by the Third Battalion since the 18th, data carefully examined and analyzed from the Japs already killed in the last three days' engagements, the men at the planning boards back at Regimental Headquarters educed that the enemy of a strength of two reinforced battalions were establishing a defensive position on the ground east of the east branch of the Piva River, with outposts on the high ground to the northeast and with the positions organized in depth to the foothills farther to the northeast near the Torokina River. Carefully co-ordinated plans were being drawn to attack and destroy the enemy on November 23.

Action for Cibik's men on the ridge started again at dawn on the 22nd. The outpost along the North Trail opened up on a party of Japs moving up toward the ridge. Steve Ryder was hit in the leg. The boys covered for him, and he managed to crawl back within the main defenses. Then he sat down on a log and looked down at his leg. A buddy came over and helped him make the examination. The sniper's bullet had entered his leg high on the thigh and had gone clean through. The bullet's exit was dangerously close to the groin. Steve whistled gratefully. "Almost got my tinker," he said.

The night before, Cibik and Gibby Young had cut away the tops of the trees masking the approach to the North Trail. This was clever foresight, for soon after the initial fracas of the day began Kennedy, crawling to the forward foxholes, spotted some Japs moving in behind a large banyan tree. The men on the ridge directed their fire in this direction, but the Japs had good cover. Kennedy called for mortars. A well-placed concentration of mortar fire from Young's boys drove the Japs away. Later an outpost on the east side of the ridge reported that the Japs who had taken cover behind the tree were the advance elements of a column of seventy Japs who were moving up to attack the hill. Toward the end of the fight Major Buck Schmuck arrived. He was pleased with the set-up, and drew terrain sketches of the ridge and surrounding country, took compass shots, and oriented the position accurately. The ridge, providing excellent observation of the entire Empress Augusta Bay area, as well as the high ground to the north and northeast, was a veritable gold mine for the Regiment. Buck realized its great value immediately, and coming events during which Cibik's Ridge featured so prominently were to substantiate his prophecy. It must be held at all costs . . . but these were his officers, his men . . . the Japs would have to be terribly strong and terribly good to dislodge them. Buck knew it was a hot spot, but he wasn't worried.

While Steve was extending his defenses north along the ridge to a point overlooking a saddle which formed a low gap between the ridge and the high ground to the northeast, the Japs opened up with a heavy mortar. He could see that the mortar was dropping shells into the Third Battalion area, and he ordered Gibby to pour it on again with his 60s. Gibby did. Nothing more was heard from this particular Nip mortar.

The saddle between these two hills was reconnoitered and found to contain a large concentration of bunkers. The surrounding area had been developed into a powerful defensive strong point. The Japs had done a thorough job of organizing the terrain—and not without reason, for through this gap between the high ground on the northeast and Cibik's Ridge (which they formerly held) passed their main supply route. between their forces to the east and their combat companies, two of which the Third Battalion had dislodged and were still battling, northwest of Cibik's Ridge.

Sergeant Henzi crawled out to the edge of the Japanese position and took a telephone with him. From this precarious perch he relayed fire data back to Gibby Young, directing the fire, and brought the shells down on the Jap positions—at times within twenty-five yards of himself. It was a remarkable piece of fire direction, and the boys back at the tubes responded to his inspiring courage and skill. The shells landed thick and fast—so fast and so accurately that a captured prisoner from this area later asked to see our automatic mortars.

A patrol worked its way down the west side of the ridge, then over to the north where the Japs had been first spotted, and found several dead Japs whom they promptly searched, machine-gun parts, and ammunition. The Nips had met death trying to get the machine-gun into the banyan tree. Another patrol working its way down the east side of the ridge gave the Jap positions a warm reception with two B.A.R.s and a shower of grenades.

That evening thirty-some men from Regimental Weapons Company pressed into service as riflemen came up to relieve the Cibik platoon; but, as the momentous event planned for the next morning was postponed one day, Steve and his boys remained for the night. Gibby and his boys were relieved by the mortar section from C Company.

Early that same morning Colonel King, commanding the Third Battalion, sent Lieutenant Messer's platoon as a combat reconnaissance patrol to move alongside the trail to the Battalion's front. Messer ran into a strong concentration of Japs and was pinned down by their intense machine-gun fire. He requested mortars. Railsback, the wizard of the tubes, kept them falling thirty yards ahead of the patrol. After knocking out several positions Messer rapidly withdrew while Railsback followed his withdrawal. In the meantime a concentration of 81-mm. mortars was being prepared. Lieutenant Smith stood by with another platoon ready to jump off as soon as the mortar barrage lifted. Railsback's mortars and the 81s had done a thorough job, and Smith's platoon was able to advance over 250 yards. They ran into another ridge loaded with

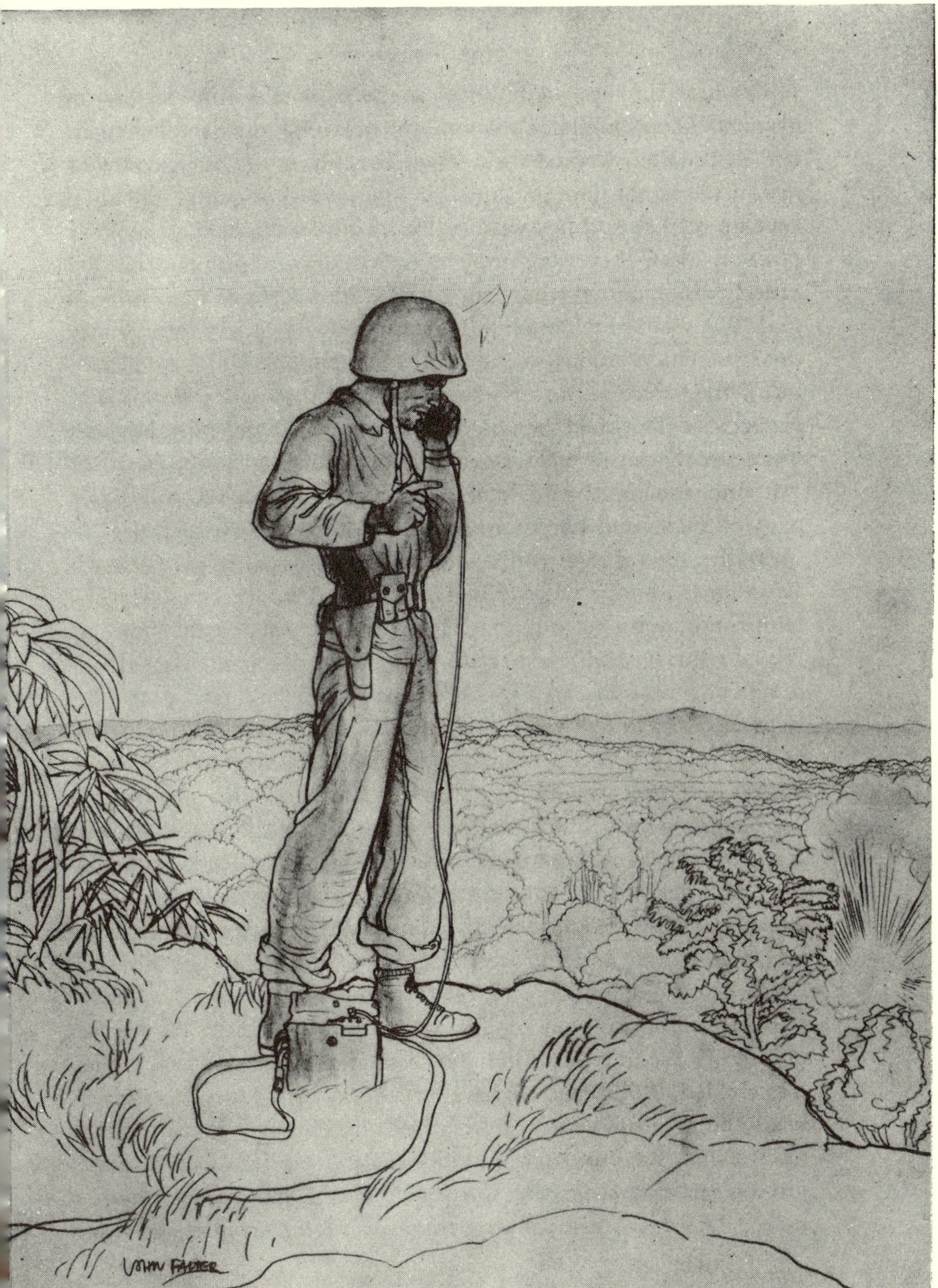

Japs, where they were greeted by grenades, and Smith lost one of his men. Then the platoon was plastered with Jap light "knee mortar" shells. They worked their way toward the top of the ridge. One man made it; the Japs got him. The platoon kept going. The fight kept up for hours. They were still working on this strong Japanese position when they were ordered to withdraw. The platoon were bitterly disappointed—they had gotten within sight of their difficult goal. But the Third Battalion had just received orders to turn over their present positions to the Raiders and proceed to another sector. Things were in the air; the men sensed the coming events with excitement. They had seen plenty of action since the 18th, but they suspected that even greater excitement lay ahead.

Lieutenant Frenchy Fogle describes a surprise received by E Company of the Second Battalion on this morning of November 22:

"Bullis, one of the scouts who had been left behind when the Battalion withdrew the day before, returned to our lines. He had lain in the mud and water and let Nips kick him around for dead. He had survived our own artillery barrage. He had dragged one of our own wounded to a sheltered spot where he might escape the Nips' notice. He had spent the night with enemy all around him, and he returned to the company the next morning looking quite healthy . . . for a man already believed to be missing in action.

"Bullis reported the wounded man and asked if he might lead a patrol back to where he had hidden him. As artillery was scheduled for that area in about an hour, the time was short. But a patrol was hastily formed with Gunnery Sergeant Evans in charge and sent out to find the wounded man. When they reached the spot where the boy had been left they found him gone. The patrol started back. Before they could reach their own lines artillery began registering around them and they scattered for cover. When they reassembled, Bullis and Evans were missing. A hasty search was made, but there was no trace of the two. The patrol started back toward their own line once more. You can't survive 105-mm. shells just by ignoring them. On the way back the patrol spotted what looked like a Jap company moving toward the river. These were not the typically runt-size Japs, either, but big 200-pounders carrying heavy loads of weapons and ammunition. The Nip patrol was reported to Battalion Headquarters as soon as the patrol got in. All hands were put on the alert."

At the extreme right flank of the Third Regimental sector, where A Company tied into the Twenty-first Marines who were holding the section of the line to the Third Regiment's right, there was a machine-gun position, and it was a honey. The stream, flowing from the north, suddenly turned at almost a right angle and wound on off to the east away from the front lines, which were along the west bank. On a mound about twenty feet above the river Sergeant Brown and his boys had set up their gun. They were able to cover the part of the stream flowing down from the north and that part of the stream and comparatively open area where it wound off to the east. If the Jap were to attempt a stream crossing anywhere within range to the left, they could smother him with enfilade fire. Any attempt to advance across the stream from their immediate front or to attack from along the banks of the stream from the west, their right front, would be met by direct fire from their gun. The crew had taken advantage of the terrain. The position had been skillfully prepared. They were ready for the Jap.

Sergeant Brown was thirty-one years old, six feet tall—plenty tough. For a long time he had had quite a problem on his mind: his wife had joined the WACs and had been made a corporal. But after *he* was made Sergeant he didn't care.

Lis, the gunner, was bathing his infected feet in the sun when Captain Pollard, acting as an artillery forward observer with a patrol from the Second Battalion, stopped by on his way back through the lines with word that a force of Japs was moving toward their position.

Logan, the squad leader, and Trott were with Lis. Barlow, another member of the crew, was on the gun. Brown had gone back to his company C.P. to arrange for their day's rations.

A Jap Nambu machine-gun opened up from across the stream. Lis, Trott, and Logan dove for the emplacement. Lis got back on the gun. Right in the middle of the open area where the stream bent toward the west, a Jap was sighting in with a rifle. Lis gave him a burst and the Jap went down. Then a group of Japs charged. Lis cut them down. It looked as if this rapidly developing situation might become a machine-gunner's dream. Logan sent Trott back for some more ammunition.

Another group of Japs coming right across that open stretch rushed toward the machine-gun. Again the gun spit out its deadly stream of 30-caliber steel-jacketed bullets. The Japs screamed and crumpled to the ground. Trott returned with another group of men he had met on the way rushing extra ammunition to the position. As he jumped into the emplacement, Lis was chopping up another fanatical bunch of charging Nipponese warriors. Trott yelled, "Let me get one of them!" Lis kept firing. Suddenly he paused. Trott was sighting in. He squeezed the trigger of his carbine. The ground was pulled out from under the feet of the leftover Nip, and he pitched forward on his face with a bullet through his head.

Brown rushed up just before the next charge. The men could hear a Jap officer shouting orders in the jungle on the other side of the stream. Then the Nips came at them again. One group tried to outflank the gun to the right. Lis shouted the target designation to Brown. Brown smothered them with grenades. A sniper off to the right front was beginning to give them trouble. Brown eliminated him a few seconds after he was located. By this time the boys were working as a team. Lis was still behind the gun, Barlow was feeding, and Logan was pulling the belt through as Lis fired. Brown was watching every quarter and protecting their flank with hand grenades. He loved grenades and could really toss them. Logan went back to get "Lightning" Jenkins and his mortars. Trott took his place at the gun.

The Japs couldn't seem to learn. More orders, and another fanatical shouting charge . . . right out in the open. The gun got so hot that Lis couldn't keep his finger on the trigger except to fire. After each burst he would stop to let it cool. The Japs would reorganize out of sight and charge again. The same fate . . . they never had a chance. Finally Jenkins came forward, estimated the range, and went back to his mortars. While the machine-gun squad cut down every Jap in sight, Jenkins poured in the mortar shells, creeping them up to within 50 yards of the machine-gun position. Two hours after they had received the first report of the advancing Japs, the fight came to an end. The man had fired eight full belts of machine-gun ammunition, and the mortars had added to the deadly toll. The Jap attack had been stopped cold. Seventy-four dead Nips lay out in front of the machine-gun position. The ones who got away never came back. Charging a machine-gun laid as well and manned as accurately as that one is a rugged affair—even for fanatics.

On the evening of the 22nd the Second and Third Battalions had moved back to assembly areas to the rear of the right and left flank of the First Battalion. The First Battalion remained on the line.

The Japs were pushing ahead their preparations also, and had moved 75-mm. guns and howitzers and more 90-mm. mortars into position. All during the day and night they threw in shells and harassed our positions.

Preparations stemming from the Regimental C.P. were being pushed to a rapidly mounting crescendo. General Cauldwell had been in constant touch with the Commanding General at Division. The Commanding General had given the Third an A-1 priority on supply. It had been raining on and off all during the time the Third Marines had been in this new sector. Every available amphibian tractor had been shifted to this quarter, and they were all churning up the impassable jeep roads with chow and ammunition. Communicators were working day and night to tie in all the outfits. Quartermasters were straining frantically to get badly needed shoes and clothes to the men. C Company Medical Field Hospital, which had moved up to the Regimental C.P., was making hurried preparations for the forthcoming casualties. Battalion operation officers were marking their lines of departure, Battalion commanders were issuing their attack orders, Company commanders were doing the same, checking their equipment and the condition of their men. The men were tired. Many were sick. They would push through to the last drop of their endurance, but they still needed shoes and clothes, a hot meal and a rest. They would carry on till they dropped, but the toughest test of courage, skill, and endurance was coming up. It was a daring enterprise; to fail meant more than humiliation—it might mean disaster. General Cauldwell and Big Mac asked for one more day of preparation. It was granted.

The Japs kept up their harassing fire with their mortars and artillery. More casualties streamed into the collecting station and field hospital. The men on the line remained steady and alert at their guns. The men in the Second and Third Battalions pulled into their assembly areas and ate their third hot meal since November 1.

On the 23rd The Traveler got up before dawn. It was going to be a busy day. Not that Major Sid McMath had had an easy one since the day he had closed the door of his law office in Hot Springs, Arkansas, and joined the Marine Corps to give his share to the defense of his country. Major McMath was the kind of operations officer a regimental commander dreams about: thoroughly trained, mentally and physically dynamic, humorous, courageous, dogged. The men knew The Traveler better than any other officer on the Regimental Staff—they saw him oftener. When Sid McMath planned an operation, he planned it for himself as well as for the men. He was always up there with them when they carried it out. Marines know their officers; they know them very well. When the men of the Third were given a tough assignment, that added wave of confidence which Mac inspired made the job easier. And the men like to remember that Sid McMath was never too busy to talk to a sweating private, struggling with a machine-gun through tangled vines and knee-deep mud. "How's it going, lad?" The smile of a thorough gentleman, that look of appreciation and understanding, the inspiration which makes a man glad he's giving the best that's in him.

The Traveler knew that this was going to be an exciting, dangerous day, so he drank his morning coffee a little earlier. And while he drank it he had a strange feeling of someone's being near—someone he couldn't see, speak to, or really understand . . . but definitely there, watching Mac caress his raider knife as he wiped away the mud from the razor-edged blade and jabbed it into its sheath on his side. The ghost of The Traveler's ancestor, Sidney of the clan of Math, follower of Bruce, guerrilla fighter against the English for years afterwards, watched his descendant with the pride of a fighting Scotsman. Guerrilla fighting had changed somewhat since his day, but the intention was the same. The beacons had been lit, the clans were gathering in the hills, he could see the love of the dirk on his descendant's face, and he knew that the younger Sid could hear the sound of bagpipes ringing in his ears. This was one day the old warrior wanted to be around.

And so when The Traveler moved cautiously through the jungle on his way to the exposed top of Cibik's Ridge he was probably followed by the happy, curious ghost of his ancestor. And the ghost hung around patiently all day while the skillful Major, together with Major Bob Armstrong and Captain Tom Jolly, directed the registration of seven battalions of artillery on every probable Japanese position. Then he undoubtedly followed The Traveler back down the hill and down the trail towards the Regimental C.P. where there was still much to be done.

Gibby Young was lying near the edge of the trail trying to locate a sniper who had been harassing his patrol. He watched The Traveler approach. Then he saw him glance down calmly as a Japanese bullet kicked up the mud at The Traveler's feet.

"Take cover, Mac!" shouted Gibby.

"Haven't got time," yelled The Traveler.

"There's a sniper shooting at you!"

"Can't help it, Gibby. When you gotta go you gotta go." The Traveler and the ghost kept right on walking.

The ghost of Sidney the elder knew he didn't have to hang around any longer, but perhaps he didn't want to miss the big scrap which would rise to a mounting crescendo the next day. He probably stayed around a month longer—just long enough to see The Traveler awarded the Silver Star and spot-promoted on the field of battle to Lieutenant Colonel.

Jungle fighting is pretty rugged for an old ghost. So when The Traveler left the island, the ghost probably shoved off too—back to a cooler bivouac in the Highlands.

The men were given shoes and clothes; some of them didn't fit, but it didn't matter very much—tomorrow wouldn't be formal. More ammunition was brought up to dumps established near the assembly areas, and hot meals were cooked on the hastily erected field kitchens. All newly arrived mail was rushed to the men in the front lines and in the assembly areas. Ammunition, rations, and clothes took precedence. Mail was next. The amphibian boys got it up there. Men sat on logs or in their foxholes in the rain and devoured the latest news from home. The letters were passed around. Every man "got a letter." It may not have been addressed to him, but it sounded as if it were when he read it—his buddy didn't care.

By evening the Second and Third Battalions had completed their reconnaissance. The First Battalion, Regimental Weapons, and the Raiders had brought up every available machine-gun and every captured Jap Nambu, and put them on the line. Corpsmen drew their extra cans of blood plasma, morphine, bandages. Extra kits were filled to overflowing. Except for Steve Cibik's boys up on the ridge, it was a day of vigorous preparation rather than of strenuous combat.

Early in the morning of this same day the mortar platoon from the Raiders relieved C Company mortars on the ridge. At about 9:30 Steve received orders from his battalion commander to attack down the east side of the ridge following a five-minute mortar concentration by the Raiders and the mortar platoon of B Company. If the attack was successful, he was to have his platoon move south in a reconnaissance by force and join B Company of the First Battalion on the line. The platoon started moving down the hill about ten o'clock. The mortar concentration was scheduled for 10 o'clock, to be lifted at 10:05. The mortars from the ridge started and lifted on time. At 10:08 the other mortar platoon had still failed to fire and Steve gave Mitchum, who was leading the forward squad, orders to move out. Seventy-five yards farther down the ridge the Japs opened fire. Steve ordered Mitchum to build up a firing line and pick out definite targets while he moved forward to locate the scouts and see what they were up against. But it was impossible to build up a firing line of more than four men, as the ground dropped off on the right side to an almost vertical cliff and on the left also it was very steep and wide open.

"As I moved by Mitchum," said Steve, "he was placing Levesque into position. A burst got Levesque in the leg. Mitchum told Levesque to try to make his way back to the ridge; he started across the trail, and a burst killed him instantly. I was about five yards below Mitchum when he called to me that he was hit. I couldn't find either one of my scouts. The Japs were pouring the lead to us.

"As I started back up toward Mitchum's squad, I ran into a man sitting on the trail. I told him for Christ's sake to get off the trail or they would get him. Just as he stood up a burst got him in the chest. He fell against me and rolled down the hill. I yelled at him, but he never answered.

"Then I ran into Skinner. I put him in position and told him to stay there with his B.A.R. and fire only at definite targets that he knew were Japs. Then I moved up a few yards farther and told Kennedy to get two B.A.R.s into play against two large trees which I knew had machine-guns in them. My orders had given me the alternative of pulling back if things got too hot, and it looked as if I might lose too many men. I had already decided to pull back to the top of the ridge. I needed some fire power so I could get the wounded out. So I called for my light machine-gun under Corporal Davis. He set up behind a large tree and I pointed out the area to fire into while we got the wounded out. I told Jacob Solomon, who was in Mitchum's squad and knew the general positions, to work his way down and get out everyone he could.

"The light machine-gun fired bursts of 20 and 30 rounds and

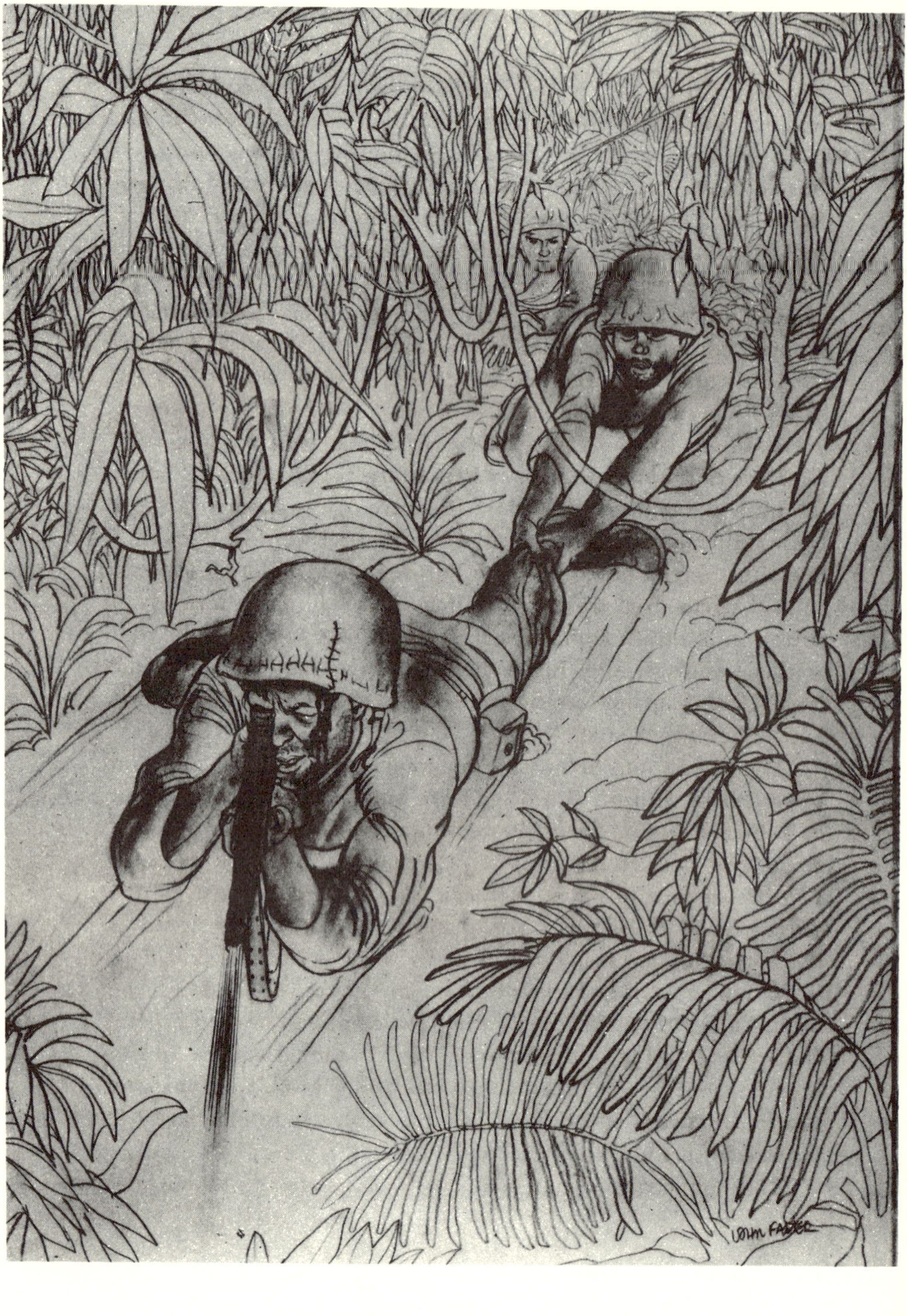

attracted most of the fire. This gave Solomon a break. He got Mitchum first, who was shot through the arm. He couldn't touch either Levesque or the other man who had rolled down the hill; apparently they were lying in an exposed open spot. When he got to Skinner, the B.A.R. man had a bullet in his leg and a bad crease in his hand. But Skinner kept right on firing even while they were helping him out. We still couldn't locate the scouts. But very shortly they worked themselves back up the ridge. Neither of them was hurt. Kennedy pulled the other two B.A.R. men out, and I went after Davis, the machine-gunner.

"By the time I got back on the ridge Skinner was bleeding badly. I called the C.P. to get some plasma. Old McHugh made record time up to the top and fixed Skinner.

"That ended the final round, with two killed and two more wounded. We left the ridge that afternoon and returned to the company area, where we got some clean clothes and chow and got squared away for the next day."

So ends the tale of the capture and defense of Cibik's Ridge.

E Line had been reached as scheduled on the 21st. It would be impossible to hold the new line with an enemy force the size of the one in front of the lines securely entrenched, rapidly building up its offensive strength, and intending to attack and break through the beachhead. The men at the helm had decided to beat the Japs to it. By darkness of the 23rd we were ready. The next morning at H-hour the Third Marines, attacking with two battalions, were going to drive out or destroy the 23rd Japanese Infantry.

The plan of attack was as follows: The First Battalion, in position along the bank of the east branch of the Piva River, was to form a base of fire astride the East-West trail subdividing the position; 44 machine-guns, captured Nambus, twelve 81-mm. mortars, and nine 60-mm. mortars being included in its fire plan. At H-hour the Second and Third Battalions, advancing abreast from their assembly areas on either side of the East-West trail, were to pass the lines of the First Battalion, attack to the east, destroy the enemy, and organize a battle position 500 yards east of the line of departure. From H-minus-25 to H-minus-5-minutes, four battalions of artillery were to fire 5600 rounds into the area to be attacked by the Second and Third Battalions, Third Marines, and three battalions were to fire 1000 rounds of 105-mm. and 155-mm. on Japanese supporting positions. From H-minus-5 to H-hour, the First Battalion was to traverse and search the front with all available weapons. H-hour was at 9 o'clock.

The night of the 23rd of November was dark, wet, and—except for the artillery passing overhead—ominously silent. It was a time for grabbing every last minute of rest—sleep, if possible. It was also a time for thinking. Private thoughts . . . personal inventories . . . chopping up your life into a simple synopsis. Reviewing it carefully before you attempt that critical chapter—perhaps the final chapter of the book. It was a time for prayer. Not that most of them thought of being killed. Almost everyone felt the same as Captain John—Captain John Winford, the Will Rogers of the Third Regiment, who in the last war had survived seven battles with the Marines, had had his machine-gun shot out from under him, had been blown off an ammunition wagon, had gone to France with the first contingent of Marines as a private and returned as a commissioned officer—without a scratch. "I never thought I would be killed," Captain John told them. "Now don't misunderstand me. That doesn't mean I haven't been scared. Hell, I'm a living example of a man who *can't* be scared to death—if I could, I'd have been dead twenty-five years ago!"

Very few thought that they were going to die. It was just that that night for the first time in everyone's life he knew more clearly what was ahead. He knew what was out in front. He knew the Japs had artillery and mortars and had been registering on our sector for days. He knew the quantity of shells to be fired by our own supporting artillery. He knew that a certain percentage of those shells would have to fall short into our own advancing men— this was just cold-blooded, accurate statistics. War is no longer a question of two men matching their courage and skill against each other. The development of explosives has gone far beyond the development of the mind and endurance of man. That started with the invention of gunpowder. War has changed as far as the little man with the rifle who must always take the dirty end of the rap is concerned. No longer is it merely a question of the survival of the fittest—it is just as much a question of luck. You made it or you got it. So many heads . . . so many tails. No one expected that he would be killed. But each man knew—as well as he knew his weapons, his individual tactics, his own name—that tomorrow he would face death. That didn't make him very happy, but it didn't make him sad either. No one had kept anything from him. He knew there was a Jap force out there planning to attack. It had to be destroyed. There was only one way to do it. It would be done. Funny how your outlook changed. You looked forward to a day at the beach . . . a new suit . . . seeing the girl friend . . . fried eggs and bacon . . . clean sheets . . . any place where it was dry . . . a poncho . . . just being alive tomorrow night. Try to get some sleep.

Chapter 16

DAY CAME. November 24th. Thanksgiving Day.

The officers and men had committed to memory their parts in the show. Breakfast, ordinary field rations, were eaten in silence. At eight o'clock the word was passed to move out.

Big Mac, The Traveler, a man to keep the journal, two communicators, and two or three men from the intelligence section moved up to a forward Regimental C.P. in the First Battalion Headquarters area just behind the line of departure. Chuck Bailey was all set for them. Telephones were in. Everything was ready. Speed was at the other end of one of the 'phones at the Regimental C.P.—up there with us just as he said he would be. He had worked with Big Mac and The Traveler far into the last five nights. He had a direct line to the Commanding General at Division. The chain of communication was complete. Careful planning, thorough reconnaissance, properly placed fire support, perfect co-ordination from all supporting units and the higher echelon. The preparation had been complete. On stage! Places! A few minutes more—and then the artillery would open up with the overture.

The two attacking battalions—the Second on the right, the Third on the left—moved up toward the line of departure in columns of companies. Tanks, amphibian tractors, trucks, and jeeps moved down the East-West trail in the same direction. Through the jungle on both sides of the trail the men of the Third Marines moved silently forward . . . lines of rugged, seasoned, jungle-fighting men, armed to the teeth, staring straight ahead, jaws set, determined, ruthless, iron in their blood, figuring the odds.

The columns halted about fifty yards behind the front-line companies of the First Battalion to wait for the start of the barrage. Before the barrage lifted, these men would be on their feet and moving toward the lines of the First Battalion. They would cross the line of departure at H-hour, nine o'clock. There could be no time gaps between the artillery preparation, the succeeding small-arms and mortar preparation, and the crossing of the line. One must blend into the other with expert timing.

At twenty-five minutes to nine—H-minus-25—right on the second, the seven battalions of artillery opened up. The roar was deafening. The men on the line crouched low over their guns, gritted their teeth, and gasped for breath through the concussion of hundreds of shells landing out in front. The men waiting to move up to the line of departure lay in the open, their eyes on their leader, his eyes on his watch. Noise you can take—it's a jarring surprise, that amount of noise, but you soon get used to it and for the first ten minutes we had things pretty much our own way.

At H-minus-15, our own artillery was firing in a mounting crescendo. Then the Jap batteries opened up with their counterbarrage. No one was exempt. Shells poured into the first lines, into the attacking battalions' areas, the forward Regimental C.P. area, the rear C.P., the trail. The noise was much greater now—not only the deafening roar, but, added to it, the sharp terrifying sound of a shell exploding close by . . . cracking the air . . . then the tearing rip of a tree splitting down the middle . . . the terrible screams of the mangled . . . the agonizing moans of men shouting for corpsmen, for help, for relief from burning torture . . . the maniacal screams and sobs of a man whose blood vessels in his head have burst from the blast concussions of high explosive devised by the clever brain of civilized man. The Third Battalion took it. The C.P. area took it to the tune of fourteen men killed and scores wounded in a period of five minutes. But the men of the First Battalion on the line—men who had already fought two major engagements—and G Company, the leading assault company of the Second Battalion, took the worst dose the Nip could administer. Some men took it with their teeth clenched praying for the enemy to run out of shells. Some took it in the silent confidence of knowing nothing could hit them; some men took it laughing; some made jokes.

One man huddled under a log, hurriedly thumbing through a small Bible, yelled laughingly at a neighboring buddy, "Now let's see—where was I?"

Captain Bert Simpson and Billy Langdale were lying in the roots of a large banyan tree. Bert called nervously to Billy to give him a cigarette.

"Hell, skipper—you've got two already," laughed Billy.

"That's all right, Bill—give me another one."

It's a favorite trick of the Japs to pour mortars and artillery into the lines while your own barrage is still going on. The impression on anyone at the receiving end is that your own artillery is falling short. They use the trick to confuse a company commander and cause him to call back, report this fact, and request that the artillery be lifted. But these company commanders weren't fooled. They knew some of our shells were falling short, but not that many—they knew where the shells were coming from.

At 8:50 it was time to move. No matter what happened, whatever the consequences, whatever the loss, the line of departure must be crossed on time.

Amidst the groans and screams of the wounded, and within sight of the mangled dead, the officers called the men to their feet. Both battalions moved forward.

Simpson, though his company had been hit worse than any other save the men on the line, expressed the feeling of every company commander.

"That was the most difficult single sentence of my life," said he later. "I took a deep breath and stood up. 'On your feet, men!' I shouted. We had started out with 190 men. Every one that was left—to a man—rose and went forward. There were fewer than 100. Death, wounds, and blast concussion will do that to a unit."

The leading companies of both battalions reached the front line

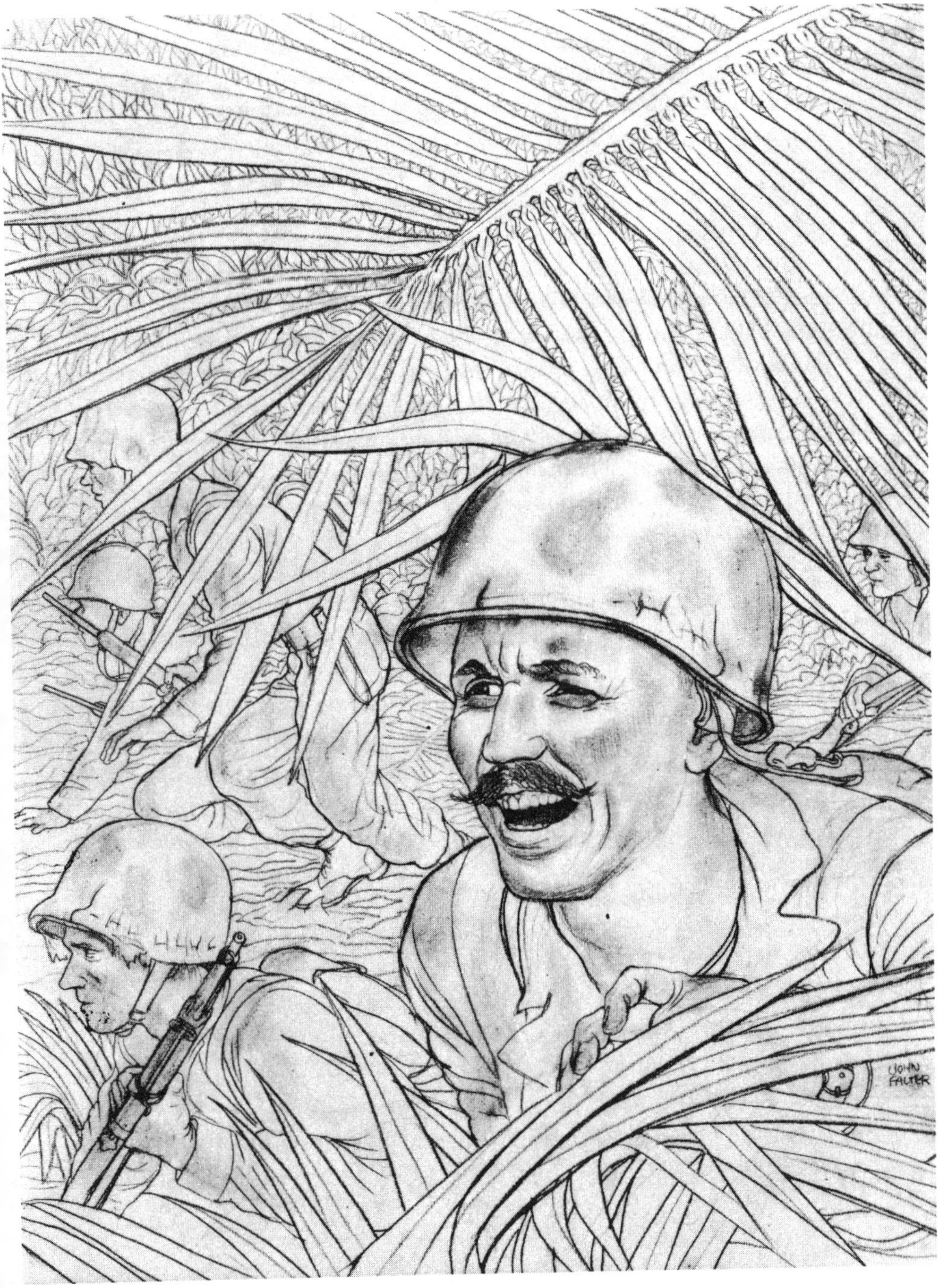
JOHN FALTER

companies in the middle of the H-minus-5-minute machine-gun, small-arms, and mortar preparation. The trees on the other side of the river were being sawed apart. The ground rocked and shuddered with the mortar blasts.

Bert Simpson, lying on the edge of the river bank waiting for the last few deafening minutes to end, had already sent word back to his executive officer, Stets Holmes, to bring up his 16-man company C.P. Stets had been everywhere—back and forth from one platoon to another. A shell would burst and four men would go down. The rest of the men would halt momentarily. "What's the matter? You going to let the Japs make a Christian out of you?" he shouted. "Well, they're not making a Christian out of *me*—I'm going after them." The men followed him forward.

Holmes came up to his company commander with three men. "Where the hell is the C.P.?" yelled Simpson. "This is it," said Stets.

The artillery forward observer assigned to his company, and everyone else but the first sergeant and two other men, had been killed or wounded by the enemy barrage.

Then Stets called back to one of the platoon leaders, Lieutenant Sawyer. The time was getting short. "Where the hell is your platoon?" yelled Stets.

"Here they are—what's left of them." Sawyer had 14 men left out of a platoon of over 40 men. "But we're moving up, so don't worry," yelled Sawyer.

Simpson turned again to Holmes. "That's an awful narrow place to cross. When we hit the other side we've got to spread the men we have left into a contact-imminent formation. Do you think it will work?"

"Sure it will work. You know why—because it's got to work!" answered Stets.

"That's right," said Bert.

Bert gave his executive officer last-minute instructions, then moved to another spot on the bank where he would lead the company across the river. He came up to Billy Langdale, who was waiting to take the plunge. Both men were kneeling next to a B Company machine-gunner who was pouring steel into the jungle beyond. Suddenly the gunner clutched his chest and pitched forward on his face. No movement—not a sound. Langdale looked down at the gunner, then turned to his company commander and remarked casually, "Dead."

On the dot of nine the roar of the mortars and machine-guns suddenly ceased. Both battalions started across the river. They were crossing the line of departure on time.

The Third Battalion crossed in a column of companies, then moved into a contact-imminent formation on the other side, two companies forward, expanding to a 400-yard front. L Company changed direction, moved off to the left, and came abreast of I Company. The command group moved up to the center of the two leading companies. K Company echeloned to the left. At the first phase-line check, the formation was correct and the battalion moved forward.

The Second Battalion also crossed the river in a column of companies. Tributary streams and deep swamp on the other side made the going exceedingly difficult. Water ranged in depth from ankle-deep to waist-deep. At the first phase-line E Company, the next in order, pushed up to G Company's right flank.

For the first hundred yards both battalions advanced abreast through a weird, stinking, plowed-up jungle of shattered trees and butchered Japs. Some hung out of trees, some lay crumpled and twisted beside their shattered weapons, some were covered by chunks of jagged logs and jungle earth, a blasted bunker, their self-made tomb. The Marines pressed forward on their destructive mission toward their clearly defined day's objective.

The Second Battalion never became pinned down and was able to advance unimpeded for 500 yards to the proposed Regimental phase-line.

But the area through which the Third Regiment must pass had been partially masked by the ridge to the Jap front. The Nip defenses close to our front lines had been severely blasted by our mortars, and the snipers near our lines were raked out of the trees by the tremendous concentration of machine-gun and small-arms fire. Less than 300 yards past the line of departure, the Third Battalion ran into a complexity of machine-gun bunkers and tree snipers. The Battalion C.P. was 75 yards behind the Third Battalion's front. Casualties began pouring in, and the Battalion aid station was moved up to the C.P. Snipers were working over the C.P., potting away at all of the headquarters personnel. The forward companies were having trouble with the Jap bunkers up ahead. The Third Battalion requested artillery support and marked their front with smoke. Captain Jolly on Cibik's Ridge spotted the smoke and directed the support. Then the Japs opened up with another counterbarrage.

Four high-ranking officers from the higher echelons had come up to the forward C.P. to see how the battle was coming on. They spent a hot ten minutes of regret. The Japs smothered all approaches as well as the forward C.P. area. One man was severely wounded outside the open dugout in which the officers were lying. All communication lines went out. The communicators rushed out during the fire to restore the lines.

Then Tom Jolly, perched on the ridge, located the Jap battery off to the northeast. He spent a bad few minutes anxiously waiting for the communication lines to be repaired. Finally he reached Captain Smith back at the fire-control center.

"Are you sure you saw it?" yelled Smitty over the 'phone. The Jap battery was still firing with deadly accuracy.

"Hell, Smitty, I can count the lands and grooves," shouted Jolly.

Shells were landing dangerously close to the crest of the ridge. Jolly was on his feet directing the fire mission.

"You'd better take cover!" shouted another officer.

"I've been waiting all my life for this," yelled Jolly. "I'm not going to miss it now." He went on with the fire mission. Smitty gave him fire from a battalion of 75s and a battalion of 105s. The remnants of the Jap battery were found some days later; it would never fire again.

A short time later, Jolly located a Jap 90-mm. mortar by sound. He started calling a fire mission. Lieutenant Doveton, an artillery forward observer with the Third Battalion, spotted a Jap mortar a few minutes later. He reached Smitty on the 'phone.

"Hold on," said Smitty. "We're in the middle of a fire mission. We'll take yours next."

Doveton heard Jolly yell over the 'phone.

"Fire for effect!"

"On the way!" yelled Smith.

Then Doveton saw his target blown to bits. Both he and Jolly had spotted the same mortar.

What would we have done without the artillery? And *what* artillery! Lieutenant Colonel Fairbaurn, the artillery regiment's operation officer, and Lieutenant Colonel Jack Taber, the commander of the Third Battalion, Twelfth, who had been straining every moment to give us support since the day we landed, now co-operating in every detail. Smitty, Jolly, Pollard, West, Bob Armstrong—each and every one of the forward observation teams—the men back at the guns: all of them. We had been together on Samoa—we were used to each other. What a team!

Slug Marvin's men from Captain Woodward's Company of Engineers were handling the flame-throwers with the front-line troops of the Second Battalion. Slug and his boys had accomplished every possible kind of chore for the Third Marines since D-day. They had fought and unloaded ships on the Cape; built roads; dug large emplacements and dug-outs in various C.P.s; buried the dead; thrown a bridge across the east branch of the Piva River out ahead of the front lines in 16 hours—a bridge containing four 16-foot stringers weighing 14 tons apiece, which they had moved by hand; and built the bridge without a single piece of machinery—nothing but hand axes. Now they were back in combat with the flame-throwers. As a Marine commented, "A man ought to get a Silver Star just for carrying one." But one of Slug's operators was wounded before the Battalion's line of departure. Slug told him to turn over the flame-thrower to another man and go back to the aid station. The man kept begging: "I gotta go . . . I gotta go . . . they're my life's work . . . I gotta see how these things work." The man was past the draft age and had a wife and two children back in Pittsburgh.

When the second Jap barrage hit, Slug was lying next to one of his men with the tank of the flame-thrower strapped to his back. These tanks contain highly inflammable liquid. Slug, trying to get the tank below the surface of the ground, kept shoving the man farther and farther down in the mud. The struggling man finally forced his head above the surface. "Slug, you wanna drown me?" he gurgled.

"The tank—the tank—how about the tank?" yelled Slug.

"To hell with the tank! We'll have to take a chance."

"O.K.," said Slug, who had been taking chances for years. "I was only trying to save your life."

Things were getting tougher and tougher on the left flank of the Third Battalion. The 'phone lines kept going out, and Big Mac and The Traveler in the forward Regimental C.P. had a difficult time getting the real picture. The attack was bogging down on the left. It mustn't bog down—not now. Once the Japs stopped this push, they could organize, throw everything they had at this flank, push behind the Third Battalion, advance beyond, encircle the Second Battalion making good progress on the right, and cut this salient being thrust out ahead of our lines off from the rest of the Regiment. It all added up to one stark, definite decision: Keep pushing forward. The artillery would give all possible support. What the artillery couldn't reach would have to be cleaned out by hand. And, in this area, that was some assignment.

The Japs had organized a brilliant defense. Taking advantage of the thick jungle swamp through which men had to cut their way a few feet at a time, waist-deep mud, and many streams winding and flowing in every conceivable direction, the Japs had constructed earth-covered log bunkers, each containing multiple machine-guns, protected by interlocking slit trenches and foxholes. Cleverly cut fire lanes, low to the ground, carefully concealed from the front, covered all approaches from any quarter. Surrounding each small defensive strong point was an intricate network of snipers—fanatical killers—with no place to go once they were discovered, but not afraid to die. Many of these snipers were rigged on platforms with plenty of ammunition and rapid-firing Nambu machine-guns which cut like a buzz-saw. This is what was facing the Third Battalion. L Company on the left flank was busily engaged. It is impossible to lay a light machine-gun effectively in waist-deep mud; yet somehow they had to gain fire superiority, while other men would worm their way through the web of snipers and fire lanes to attack the bunkers on their weakest side and clean them out by hand. This was the hottest sector on the front—and it was a bloody, desperate, hand-to-hand scrap.

The snipers were doing their worst. One man was wounded in the arm. Sergeant Val put him up against a tree. Doc Cardin, the popular fighting corpsman with L Company, started to patch the wounded man's arm. While he was still working, a sniper put a slug in the wounded man's other arm. The man looked indignantly at Cardin. This was overdoing it. "Guess they're gunning for me, Doc!" he said.

Cardin helped the man to some cover, hurriedly bandaged up his arms, then dashed to the relief of another wounded Marine. But he never came back. A Jap shot him while he was aiding another injured buddy. Doc Cardin was buried the next day.

Captain John "Hunky" Kovacs, skipper of L Company, had two officers left. Marbaugh had been pulled out of the swamp with a bad attack of filariasis on the 17th, and Hendershaw had been badly wounded on the 20th. Morris stopped a bullet with his knee earlier in the day. Just two other officers—tough, wiry, popular Captain Bones Turnbull, and 1st Lieutenant John "Irish" O'Neil, who had already honored the pages of fighting Marine history. John was on the telephone up front near his two assault platoons, talking to his battalion commander, when the word came back about Bones. His platoon had been pinned down. Bones had led them in a charge toward a Jap bunker that was inflicting a heavy

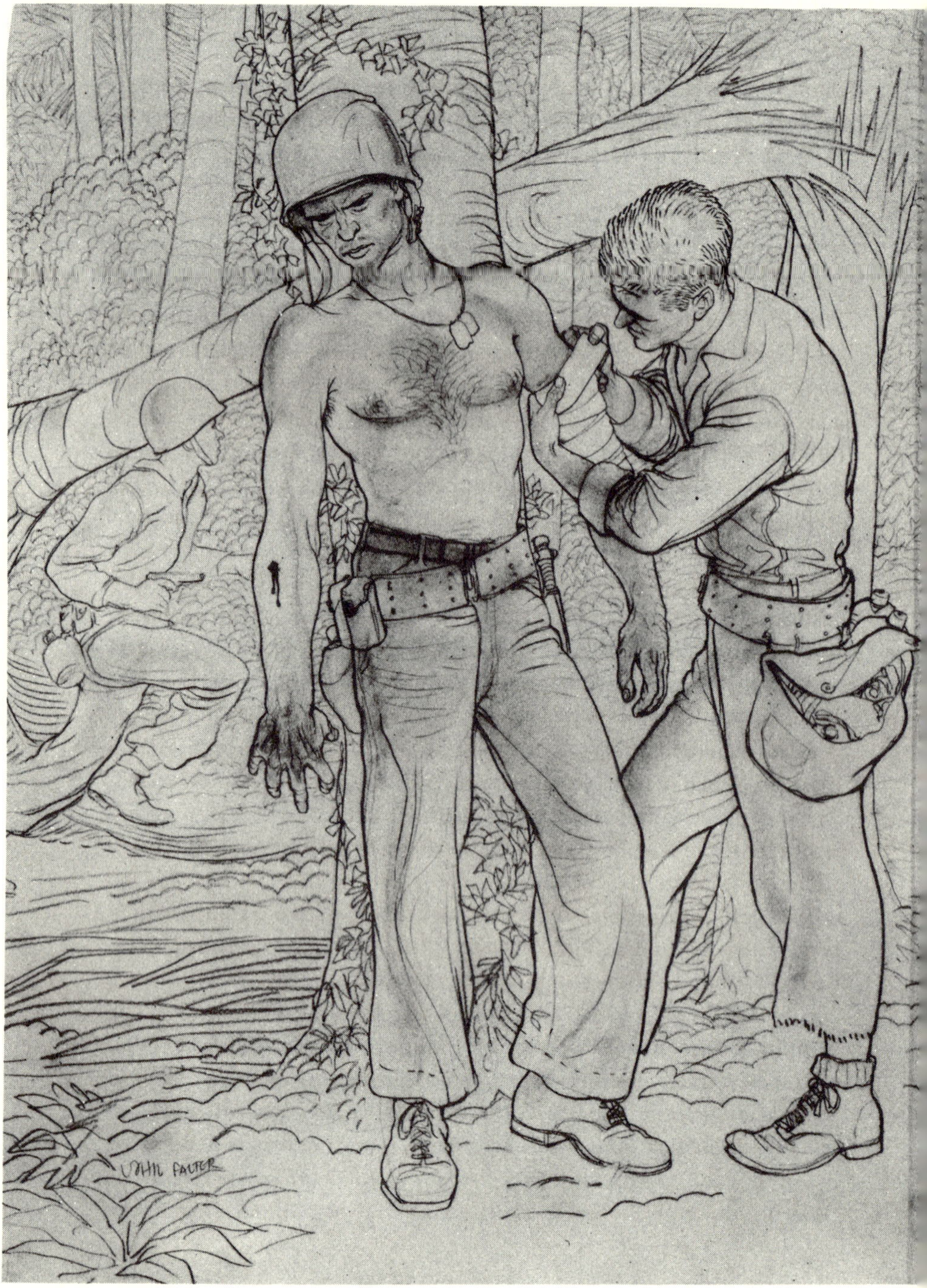
JOHN FALTER

toll. Bones was a great woodsman, a great patroller, a great Marine. His men admired him. He made them work, he taught them everything he knew, he never asked them to do one thing that he wouldn't do himself. The men knew that. And they saw him prove it. Bones went down trying to save his men—trying to silence forever a ruthless enemy which he recognized as a dangerous foe but still held in utter contempt. Bones led the charge that finally silenced forever that devastating bunker. But he never knew it, for a few seconds later a stream of machine-gun bullets ripped across his chest. And Bones was dead. That fateful afternoon the Third Marines lost a great officer. Every buddy—and Bones Turnbull had them all—every man who knew him lost a great friend.

When "the Hunky" heard the news he was trying desperately to work out a plan to flank and knock out the machine-guns that had him pinned down. He was ordered to advance. He called John O'Neil back to the 'phone and gave him the situation. Kovacs took over the platoon on the right, O'Neil the one on the left. Just the two of them left—they'd work it out together. Kovacs started off; the platoon made about twenty yards; then a bullet hit him in the back. Johnny kept going. "Let's go, L Company!" he yelled. They kept on. Then he fell on his face in the mud. Two men tried to pull him out, but he had fallen in a fire lane. Finally a man grabbed his feet. John pushed with what strength he had left and they dragged him out of the lane. Two men rolled him in a poncho and struggled through the deep mud to get him to the advance dressing station.

Dr. Harring and Dr. Bell were swamped. Hard though it was to get the wounded out of the mire, they were coming in thick and fast. It had been like that all day. When John's turn came, a doctor went to work on him. Out there in the swamp there wasn't very much one could do beyond easing the pain and getting the wounded back to the rear dressing station and the Field Hospital as quickly as possible.

As John was being carried out of the advance dressing station, in walked John O'Neil. Sergeant Ray Martin had been the only man near him when he was hit. O'Neil was wounded badly in the head, and Martin felt he had to get this last officer back as quickly as possible. He was dying, and Martin didn't want "Irish" to die. Sergeants Val and Moman had rallied what was left of the company. Martin and O'Neil dodged snipers all the way back. How he ever made it no one will ever know—except Martin; they *had* to make it. The Sergeant left O'Neil at the dressing station and started back to rejoin his hard-pressed company.

"I'll never forget you, Martin," O'Neil called weakly.

The doctors tried desperately to save O'Neil. Kovacs and O'Neil had a few moments together. Then they carried Kovacs away.

"Be seeing you, John," said his company commander.

"Yeah—see you at Paddy Clark's for a drink," said O'Neil. "Irish" was carried out a few minutes later. But they never had that drink at Paddy Clark's. John O'Neil, the brilliant young officer who had come to the Marines soon after college, great story-teller, writer, poet, student of the classics, inspiring troop leader—this courteous, considerate, skillful fighting Marine lies in the cemetery on Bougainville; for "Irish" died on the way to the Field Hospital.

Word came into the advance C.P. The Third Battalion was still fighting desperately, but making headway. The Japs were covering the wounded in the L Company sector. The Traveler was unable to reach the Battalion on the 'phone, but he got Captain Bob Keith, executive officer of K Company, and ordered him to take a platoon and fight his way through that area, reinforce what was left of L Company, and get the wounded out before dark. Keith got in touch with Captain Torian, his company commander, then started off with Lieutenant Peck's platoon. They fought their way through. Meantime I Company, on the right, had reached its objective. The left flank was still hard-pressed and the swamp was full of wounded.

Even back near the East-West trail, Jap snipers had infiltrated and were peppering away at the tractor and jeep ambulance drivers. The wounded were piling up in a bad bottle-neck. Back near the First Battalion C.P., Doctor Etheridge, assisted by Dr. Sam Elmore and Dr. Willets, was working desperately to save dying men who had been carried in ponchos through the hundreds of yards of deep swamp. Lieutenant "Honker" Swenson was rushing ammunition up to the Second and Third Battalion front lines. An officer dashed down to him and asked him to get a truck up to the wounded. Honker told him he'd get it there. Corporal Berry jumped on a truck. Honker told him to be careful—the wounded depot up ahead was covered with snipers.

"If they value their lives they'll keep away from me. I'll shoot their friggin' heads off," yelled Berry, pointing to a B.A.R. lying on the front seat of the truck. Then he churned up the road and helped bring back the injured men to the dressing station.

Since the opening barrage, this day had been a nightmare. It had been the toughest, most desperate, exhausting, agonizing day the men in the Third Marines had ever gone through. But they were Marines. They had learned that tough going makes tough men. With death all around them, they still had the grins.

Father Kempker had been up near the front lines all day. He was always where the men needed him. He had always been there since the day we landed. In the middle of the afternoon the Father, who walked unhesitatingly in amongst the snipers, who had been through the barrage, who was always in the heat of battle, was laying out eleven dead Marines. He was busy writing down their names and serial numbers from their dog-tags and covering them over with ponchos. They would be brought back to the cemetery and given an honored burial.

Two men carrying a poncho with a man in it out of sight plodded past him.

"Wait a minute," called Father Kempker. "Is that a body there?" He pointed to the poncho.

Slowly the head of a boy appeared above the edge of the poncho. "Yes, it is, Father," he grinned. "But you ain't going to bury it!"

Father Kempker smiled. The carriers plodded on through the swamp.

The Second Battalion passed the 500-yard phase-line before they struck tough opposition. All the territory through which they had prowled for two days in their reconnaissance by force had been devastated by the artillery and mortars. At this point they started to hit the Japs, who had retired rather abruptly when the artillery had started to land and had moved back into the area. The two forward companies, G and E, followed by F in reserve, plowed right on through. The Second had already suffered heavy casualties from the Jap artillery, and they suffered more from snipers and machine-gunners. Their casualties were equally difficult to remove. There were many long, back-breaking hauls—but they got the wounded back.

Two Marines carried a man into the Second Battalion aid station. It had been a long haul. He'd been dropped, jostled, and—on several occasions when the carriers had sunk up to their waists in the mud of the swamp—he had been spilled. But they got him there. He was now waiting his turn. Finally Dr. Etheridge, sweaty, tired, and dirty from the long day's grind, bent over the Marine. The boy had two slugs in one leg and one in the other.

"How you doing, son?" said the doctor kindly.

"Gosh, Doc, I feel awful. Have you got any vitamin pills?"

You've got to have the grins.

All night long the night before, Lieutenant Breen had had the cooks from Regimental Headquarters Company cook turkey. Breen was the Regimental commissary officer, and he really did a job. Though most of the time it had been cold rations, the men had never gone hungry. The real honest-to-goodness turkeys which had been brought in that day were down at Division waiting for us. It just happened that they arrived on the 23rd. It was draw them then or never, our refrigeration facilities on this South Sea island being slightly inadequate. So Breen had drawn the turkeys. Late in the afternoon, carrying parties tried to get the birds, cut into large chunks, up to the front lines. Some of the meat got there, some didn't. But it was a good stunt, and a necessity; no one would have been forgiven if it had been left to rot down at the Division Commissary just because we had a battle!

The men sat on logs eating their turkey. Near by a Jap lay rotting in the swamp. Heads and arms of dead Japs floated in the near-by jungle streams. Not a very enjoyable setting, but these were tired, ravenously hungry men who had been fighting all day. And it was Thanksgiving. Those who were able to get it enjoyed their turkey.

The Second Battalion drove on beyond the day's objective and never stopped till they had gone 1100 yards through the swamp beyond the line of departure. They had killed everything in their path. Here resistance ended, and they went into a hasty defense. It was impossible to dig in. The men set up their machine-guns and lay down beside them in the water.

Over on the left flank the Third Battalion was still bearing the brunt of the Jap resistance. Captain Torian was ordered to execute a passage of lines through what still remained of L Company. Meantime, Captain Bob Keith was fighting his way forward and getting out the wounded. Berry, a corpsman, was leading group after group down through the fighting and pulling others out. Every one of the corpsmen kept pushing forward to a wounded man. There was no thought of personal safety—there wasn't time. There have never been a more courageous bunch of men. Before that day ended, thirty-five per cent of the Third Battalion corpsmen were casualties.

Bob Keith and his men kept at it. A Nambu lashed across Keith's legs and he went down. Torian came up with the rest of K Company. He reorganized and added the remnants of L Company to his own. There was a 250-yard gap in the battalion. Torian was ordered to make contact with I Company on the right, and at the same time to protect the wounded who were still out there. It was almost dark. Torian took L Company's Weapons Platoon and all of Val's men and organized a strong point protecting Keith and the rest of the wounded. He sent Railsback with K Company up to I Company. Torian closed the gap. The Third Battalion made contact with the Second Battalion on the right.

Shortly after dark, Keith heard a man working his way out toward him, and thought it was a Jap. "Man Mountain" Bob had

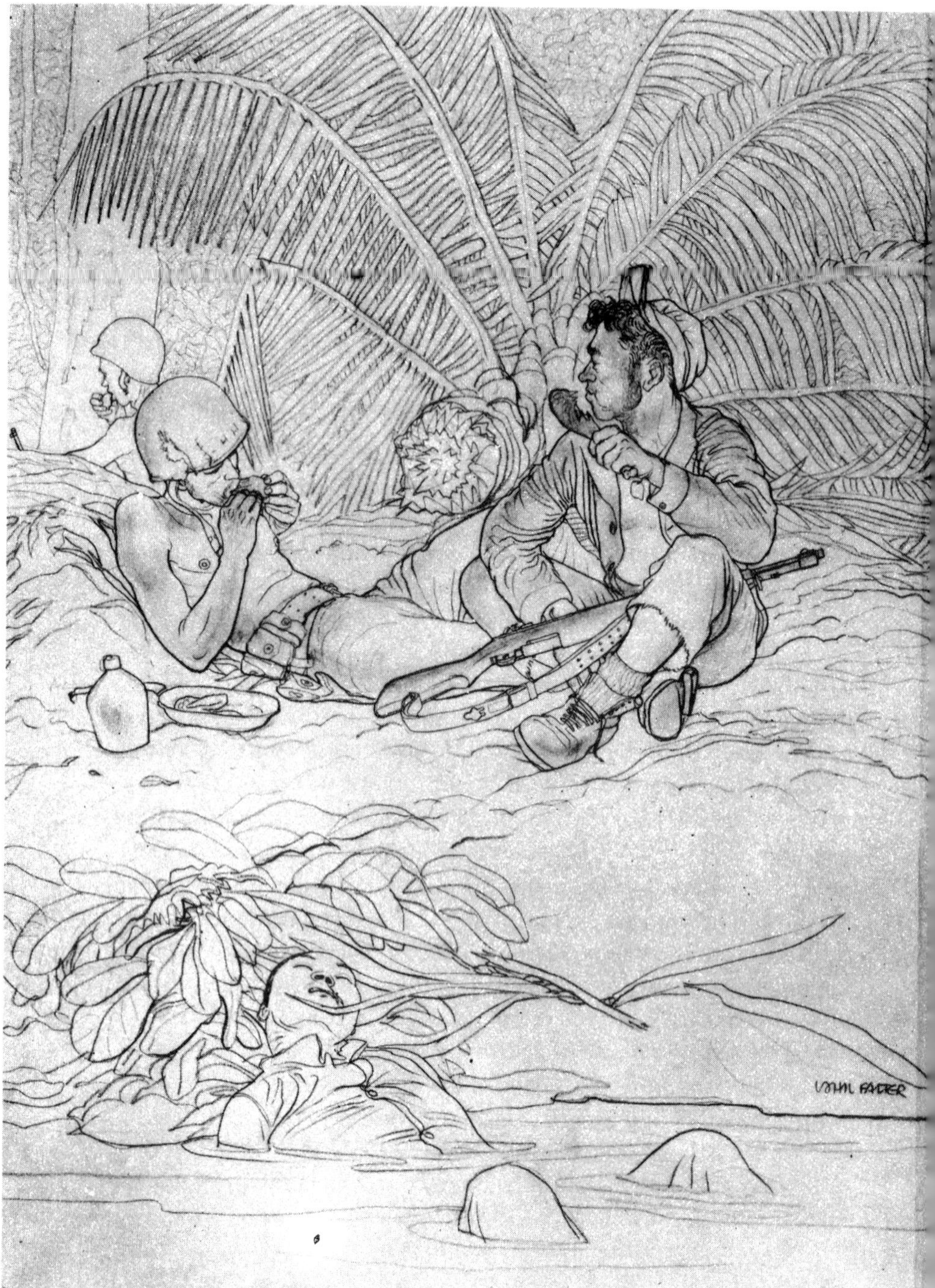

a wound in his leg, but he wasn't going to be taken alive. So he threw a hand grenade. It just missed Oswald, a corpsman, buried itself in the mud, and exploded harmlessly. Oswald reached Keith, gave him morphine, and patched him up. Then he went after the other wounded. Oswald's shuttle trips from one man to another all during the night saved many a valuable life.

After the Third Battalion tied in with the Second, it organized a tight defensive position for the night.

Big Mac left the forward C.P. The Traveler was about to follow. He leaned up against the side of the dug-out. An officer who had been there all during the day looked into the Regimental Operations Officer's weary face.

"We've been in this C.P. about six months," said The Traveler. Then he followed Big Mac down to the East-West trail. There were a few weary Marines trying to make their way back to their outfits. They had brought back casualties. There was one big, tired, black-bearded Marine who said he was from L Company. He was about to drop in his tracks. When asked what had happened, he was almost too tired to speak; but he answered, in weary, confused gasps:

"There were machine-guns out in front of us, Rex say go forward. Bones gets up . . . Bones dead. The Hunky say we got to go forward . . . the Hunky go down. Irish get up . . . try to go forward . . . Irish dead. All officers gone. Whole company split up . . . I bring Hunky home."

"Join your outfit in the morning," said The Traveler gently.

"Yes, sir."

The Traveler called to an officer from the Regimental Weapons Company: "O'Connell, organize these men for the night. Get them back to their outfits in the morning."

"Come over here," yelled O'Connell, gathering the few together and leading them inside his platoon's area.

Big Mac and The Traveler headed back toward the Regimental C.P. The salient out in front of the lines was securely fixed for the night. Plans now had to be rechecked for tomorrow. It was

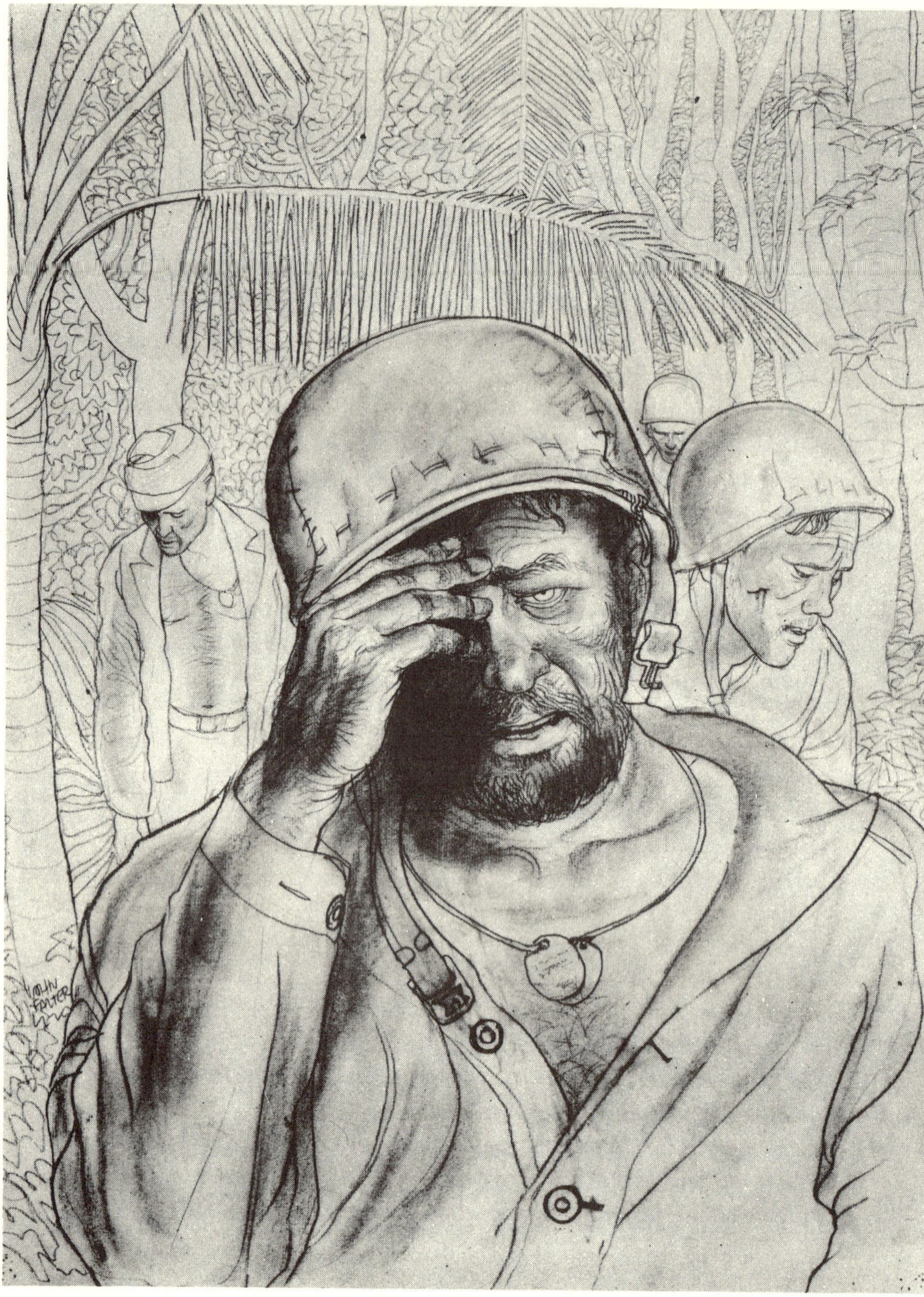

only the fighting end of the day. But what a day! The reports of the casualties were very heavy. The mission had been accomplished. Two battalions of the Third Marines—under strength and weary, but still fighting like hungry tigers—had pushed through the organized defense and broken the back of a Japanese regiment.

As the Colonel's party walked into the C.P. area, a small group of communicators were gathered around a jeep radio. One man on the earphones was writing down the news as it came over the air in code. The rest were taking turns reading what had already been decoded.

"Any news on the South Pacific?" asked one of the men as they passed.

A communicator read aloud:

"*The Marines have enlarged their beachhead on Bougainville and have encountered only minor enemy patrol action.*"

Chapter 17

ALL DURING THE DAY of the 24th trucks, jeeps, and amphibian tractors had jammed the road leading into the C Medical Company Field Hospital located in the C.P. area. Every available officer and man was on the job disentangling the traffic snarls, getting stalled vehicles out of the mud, lifting stretchers out of amphibian tractors, carrying wounded to the hospital, and lifting more stretchers back into the vehicles which would haul the wounded down the muddy bumpy jungle road to the evacuation hospital near the beach.

Dr. Lu Fisher, the Regimental Surgeon, his assistant Dr. McGeorge, and Dr. Smith, the Regimental Dentist—all of their corpsmen were busy with evacuation—were taking down the personnel data from the tags of the casualties, directing the walking wounded, comforting the starry-eyed and shaking blast cases, cheering up the injured who were waiting their turn outside the surgical tent, and segregating the dead.

The premise on which medical science is based—the saving of life, direct antithesis of combat—helps to make all doctors in a combat zone look like wonderful guys. Whatever the reason, they are wonderful guys. No one works harder. No one is more sincere. No one contributes as much to the little man. Most combat outfits have good doctors. The Third Marines were twice blessed: every doctor throughout the Regiment was not only an expert in his profession but also the friend and counselor to every man, officer or private. Every doctor—there were no exceptions. And in addition we had an outfit, attached to the Regiment as far back as Samoa, which will live forever in the hearts of the Third Marines: C Medical Company. What an outfit!

During the training days the medical company accompanied us on all of our problems. Sometimes the company would set up a full-scale field hospital just for practice. Casualties would be declared and rushed back exactly as it would be done in combat. Every doctor, every chief, and every corpsman took the rugged training.

C Medical was more than just attached to the Third. It was part of the Regiment. We worked together, we drank together, we went out on dates together, we traveled together, we landed together, we fought together. Officially they were part of the Navy, but as far as we were concerned each and every one of them was a Third Marine. Dr. Glystine, the boss, with a beard like a pirate and the eyes of a saint, Dr. Leo "Boondocker" Koscinski, Dr. "Gordy Baby" Grant, Dr. "Chucky-Wucky" Goodwin, Dr. "Wizard-with-the-Knife" Sheppard . . . every one a character.

C Medical had made the long push with all of its equipment across the jungle on the 20th. A platoon of engineers had been detailed to help on the construction of the new Regimental C.P. Digging-in part of the new field hospital had the highest priority, but for some reason someone got his signals crossed and used the platoon for a less important project, and by dusk on the 20th nothing had been done. Just at this time arrived twelve stretchers bearing casualties severely wounded by Jap 90-mm. mortar fire. Twelve badly injured men . . . nothing set up . . . mortars still dropping in the area . . . no place to put the wounded. Captain John Winford made the rounds. The men at headquarters, exhausted from a grueling day, were in their foxholes.

"I know it's been a tough day, and you're all tired," said Captain John; "but anyone who wants to, grab a shovel. Let's dig the wounded in."

Anyone who wants to. These wounded were our boys. Officers, doctors, communicators, cooks, intelligence men—everyone in the area grabbed a shovel, pick, bayonet, and helmet. Tree trunks began to fly out of the new dug-out.

"You've been in there long enough. Gimme that shovel!"

"Here, Doctor, you need your hands. I'll do the digging," said a headquarters man, taking a shovel away from Lu Fisher.

Twenty minutes later the dug-out was finished, a tent rigged overhead, an operating table set up, and the wounded underground. That was the beginning of a long, weary stretch of working as fast as every man could work to save the lives of Third Marines.

When Jap mortar shells were falling dangerously close to the tent in which he was performing an operation, Dr. Sheppard paused for a moment, pointed the instrument he held at the doctor who was assisting, and commented: "I don't mind the bombing as much as the mortar fire. That mortar fire seems too personal." But on the 24th there wasn't time for comments. By dark he had performed over a dozen major operations. He never left that hole in the ground all during the night—and by dawn of the 25th his score had climbed to more than twenty.

There were some bad times for the doctors of C Medical that night, because many of the officers and men who lay on the operating table were their personal friends. Dr. Sheppard and two other doctors worked on Captain Johnny Kovacs for over an hour. The surgeon went into his back but couldn't find the bullet; then he turned him over and went into his belly. In the middle of the operation Kovacs stopped breathing. The doctors worked frantically for five minutes. Johnny had some unfinished dame business to take care of in this world, and he came back to life. The doctor who had been administering the anesthesia told an officer the next morning: "That damn Hunky! I'll never forgive him—he took ten years off my life."

Probably the most pitiful of all the casualties were the blast cases. Every time our own artillery went off during the night these men would jump, cry, and then scream for hours.

The plans for the following day were completed. Artillery barked intermittently all through the night. The Japs made their nightly bomb runs. But sleep, that precious luxury, was hungrily enjoyed. The two battalions out in the forward salient waited for a night counterattack. No sleep for the weariest; instead, long anxious hours of watchful waiting. But there was no attack. The Jap was a little tired too.

The next morning a man sat out on a log enjoying the privilege of knowing he was still alive. Another man walked past him. Both of them were getting wet.

"Damn it—it's raining again."

The boy on the log looked up and smiled. "I don't care," he said.

Early in the morning of the 25th an officer hurried over to the field hospital of C Medical Company. Dr. Glystine, red-eyed from lack of sleep, was coming out of one of the ward tents.

"How's the Hunky doing, Doctor?" asked the officer.

"I think he's going to make it," said the doctor. "You want to see him?"

"If it's all right."

The officer followed Dr. Glystine into a tent-covered dugout. Eight wounded men were sleeping on stretchers. All of them had been operated on the night before. All were sleeping . . . the forced, painless sleep of drugs, but sleep nevertheless. And each moment of respiration added one more tiny erg of precious energy; mixed with the conscious will to live, it would take them that much farther away from the "Never-Never Land."

The officer looked down at the sleeping Hunky. Not the swashbuckling, joking, gesturing Hunky. A silent, motionless, pale, cadaverous form lay on his back on a stretcher breathing heavily, fighting his way back to the land of laughs.

"God . . . he looks sick!" said the officer.

"He is. It took over an hour to find the bullet."

"When will he be evacuated?" asked the officer.

"Probably tomorrow. He'll sleep most of today."

"I'll be around early in the morning. Like to see him before he goes."

The next day the officer came around again. He talked to the other doctors. They were tired and still very busy; but the same good-natured enthusiasm, the same optimism, prevailed. And they were proud. They had a right to be. Out of all the wounded who had streamed into the Field Hospital since the morning of the 24th, they had lost but one man.

The officer went in to see the Hunky. He lay in the same position on the stretcher, but he was awake and gazing up at the roof of the tent.

"Hi ya, Hunky!"

The wounded officer tried to shift his position, but he was girdled in bandages and it was difficult. The officer moved nearer to the stretcher, looked down at his buddy, and smiled. The Hunky recognized him. He spoke quietly. "I lost half my company and every officer," he said.

"No," the officer told him. "A lot of them got separated, but most of them got back. The company's in pretty good shape."

"Bones and John were killed."

"Yes."

"That's rough."

"One of those things, Hunky."

The wounded officer looked up at the tent. For a moment the two friends were silent. Then the visitor spoke again:

"They're going to ship you out in a couple of days, Hunky. Anything I can do for you?"

"If you see any of my boys, tell 'em I'm all right. Tell 'em to keep punching."

"Sure I will. I'll tell 'em. Well . . . take it easy, Hunky. See you back in the States."

The Hunky smiled. Then suddenly he grew serious again. "My pistol," he said. "Do something for me, will ya?"

"Sure."

"Check and see who's got it."

"Leo's got it. He told me."

"Did he get it cleaned?" asked the Hunky.

"He had a corpsman clean it."

"Tell Leo I want to take that pistol with me. Sentimental reasons. I don't want to go without it."

"Sentimental reasons, hell," kidded the officer. "You just want it to help you keep those blonde nurses away from you."

The wounded man smiled. "I don't want to keep 'em away from me. I want to crowd them into a corner."

The Hunky was going to make it.

The Third Marines were to be relieved in this northeast sector of the perimeter by the Ninth Marines, starting on the 25th, with the relief to be completed on the 27th. The Third Marines were to occupy the sector on the right flank of the beachhead perimeter bounded by the sea on the right and the right flank of the Twenty-first Marines on our left.

The First Battalion was relieved on the morning of the 25th. The men came out of the line and started down the trail toward the south.

The company columns moved down the trail toward an assembly area to the rear of the present Ninth Marine lines. Some platoons were being commanded by sergeants; Gunner McAlexander was in command of a company; a former platoon leader, Captain Rouse, was now a company commander. There had been many other changes. Major Steve Brody had been evacuated because of illness, and Major Chuck Bailey had been in command of the Battalion for the last five days. The Battalion was considerably under strength. Most of these men had been in three major battles in the last twenty-five days. But it was still a battalion. The men were tired, but they weren't beaten—they were proud, defiant, still riding one another, still having the grins. They hiked down the trail with their heads in the air. They still looked tough. They still looked **dange**rous. They looked like Marines.

Both the Second and the Third Battalions were holding the salient out in front of the beachhead line. The latest plan called for expanding the Division perimeter line out to the forward edge of this salient. Until this could be accomplished, the two Battalions must hold what they had.

Captain Jolly moved down off the ridge and joined the Third Battalion, which had extended and strengthened its lines. Torian had got the rest of the wounded out and had rejoined his parent organization. Barbed wire was sent up to the Battalion and it was told to prepare for enemy counteraction. About noon a Jap 90-mm. mortar started to work on their area. Jolly registered a battalion of artillery on it and the mortar was silenced. Patrols located more Japanese bunkers out to their left front. The Battalion's mortars went to work on them. There were still many left.

A battalion of the Ninth Marines was expected to move up on the Third Battalion's left flank, so the troops in this area were told to hold their fire. They got most of their barbed wire laid before the Japs spotted them and opened up on the wire details. About 4 o'clock in the afternoon Captain Torian called the Battalion C.P. The Nips were outside his position and were organizing for an attack. He requested permission to fire. He was refused permission and told to wait. He called five minutes later and said there was a full squad in front of one of his platoons and more were moving in toward his flank; and he again requested permission to fire. But the Battalion was short on ammunition—there was no supply route through the swamp; and again permission was denied. Two minutes later he called again. The Japs were coming in and had already dropped a "knee" mortar shell inside his lines. He recommended that he open fire. Permission was now granted. His machine-guns opened up. Railsback went to work again with his mortars and dropped shells within 35 yards of the front lines. The mortars and the machine-guns drove the Japs back. They started to reorganize for another attack. Captain Jolly registered artillery 200 yards to the front. The men in the Third Battalion could hear the piercing screams and moans of the Jap wounded. They had been trapped in between the mortars and the artillery concentration. A patrol later found the mangled bodies and abandoned equipment. The best part of a Jap company had been massacred.

Over on the right flank of the salient the Second Battalion were also standing by for a ram. They were still unable to dig foxholes because of the deep swamp, but the lines had been tightened and the men were ready. The counterattack came at about the time when the Japs were hitting the Third Battalion—around 4 o'clock. Ammunition was low but spirits were high. Not a Jap broke through and the attack was repulsed.

During the day each company had sent back carrying parties for chow and ammunition. Corporal Josephs had been detailed for supply work in the rear but had begged to be taken along on the attack the day before. Now he was in one of these carrying parties and was making his way back through the swamp. He spotted a Jap ground sniper in the roots of a tree. Whipping his Tommy-gun around, he squeezed the trigger twice but nothing happened. The Jap just looked at him. Josephs kept pointing the gun at him—then yelled: "Stay there! I've got you covered. Hey, Delaney . . . come here quick!"

Delaney came plowing through the swamp, a .45 pistol in his hand. He saw the Jap, aimed, and fired. Josephs looked at his Tommy-gun with disgust: "How d'ya like that? I been carrying this damned weapon for *one solid year.*"

The two Battalions spent another long wet night out in front of the lines. But they weren't bothered by Japs. The men shivered in their mud- and rain-soaked clothes, listening to the beautiful music of friendly artillery blanket their front with harassing fire, and waited out the night.

Early on the morning of the 26th the Second Battalion was notified that they were to be relieved by a battalion of the Ninth Marines. The companies prepared to turn over their sectors. A company commander from the Ninth brought his men up to relieve a company of the Second Battalion, Third. Then he turned to the skipper of the company in the Second Battalion.

"Is this it?" asked the new skipper.
"Yeah, this is it," answered the old skipper.
"No dry spots?"
"No dry spots."
"No foxholes?"
"No foxholes."
"Just get behind the guns and wait?"
"Yeah . . . that's right."
"Have you been hit up here?"
"Yes. Yesterday afternoon. But we held."
"Hmmmm . . . This is not a bad set-up!"

It couldn't have been worse, but the Ninth Marine Captain was a good Marine.

Lieutenant Colonel "Joe" DeZayas, commander of the Second Battalion, stood watching his men as they pulled out of the lines and filed past him.

"Hi, Joe!"
"How they goin', Red?" smiled the Colonel.
"O.K."
"Hello, Shorty. You need a shave," called the Colonel.
Shorty grinned.

The men had been told they were moving to a position farther south along the Piva River. All of them were looking forward to a bath. A tired, ragged Marine beamed through his scrub-growth beard as he passed his battalion commander.

"Hi, Joe. We're goin' down to Piva on a seventy-two!"
The Colonel laughed. He was very proud.

The column moved toward the trail. The men were anxious to get out of the swamp and were jamming up. Lieutenant Barber turned around and addressed his nearest squad leader:

"Huntoon, disperse your squad more."
"O.K.," said Corporal Huntoon. He faced the rear. "Smith, take your interval."

This company had entered the battle on the 24th at full strength

—about 190 men. There were 72 left. "But," their company commander declared, "I'd take those seventy-two anywhere."

As the Second Battalion trudged down the trail on the way to their new position, Lieutenant Stets Holmes started to laugh.

"What are you laughing at?" asked Lieutenant Sawyer.

"During part of the barrage I was lying on the ground," Holmes related. "Bert was on one side, and another Marine was on the other. I asked Bert whether he was a Christian yet, and Bert said, 'Yes, sir!' Then I asked him how he'd like to be in New York.

" 'What do *you* think?' Bert asked. A shell exploded near by. The Marine lying next to me brushed part of a limb off of him, turned to me, and said: 'I'd just as soon stay here—I'm wanted for white slavery back in the States!' "

"Nice people you meet in foxholes," said Stets, laughing.

Twenty-five days in the swamp and Stets Holmes was still laughing. What an officer!

The Third Battalion was relieved the following afternoon. Captain Tony Akstin, M Company commander, had insisted that Muslin's piano accordion be brought up to the front lines. After ammunition and chow, the accordion had the highest priority. Corporal Muslin had already given the Third Marines many happy hours. During the dull waiting periods, whenever we were stuck for entertainment, Muslin could always be counted on to squeeze out the tunes. The rain and mud had given the instrument a vicious beating, but it still worked. The weary Third Battalion hiked down the muddy tractor trail toward their assembly area on the right flank of the beachhead perimeter with Muslin coaxing out notes from the battered accordion and the men singing "Roll Out the Barrel."

Then they noticed considerable construction work off to the right of the trail.

"What the hell is that?" asked one.

"Looks like a road."

"A *road?*"

They had been in the swamp so long that they had almost for-

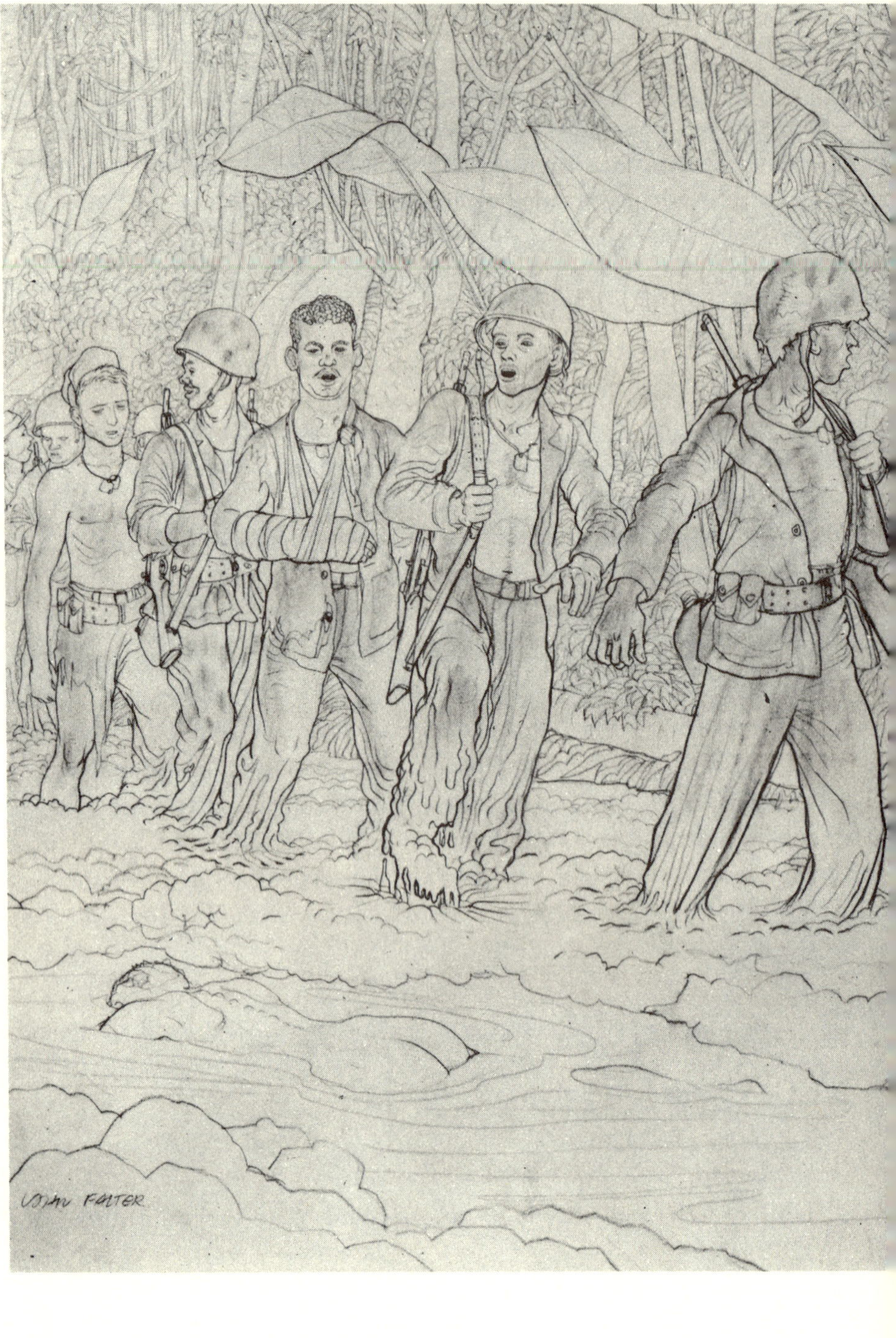

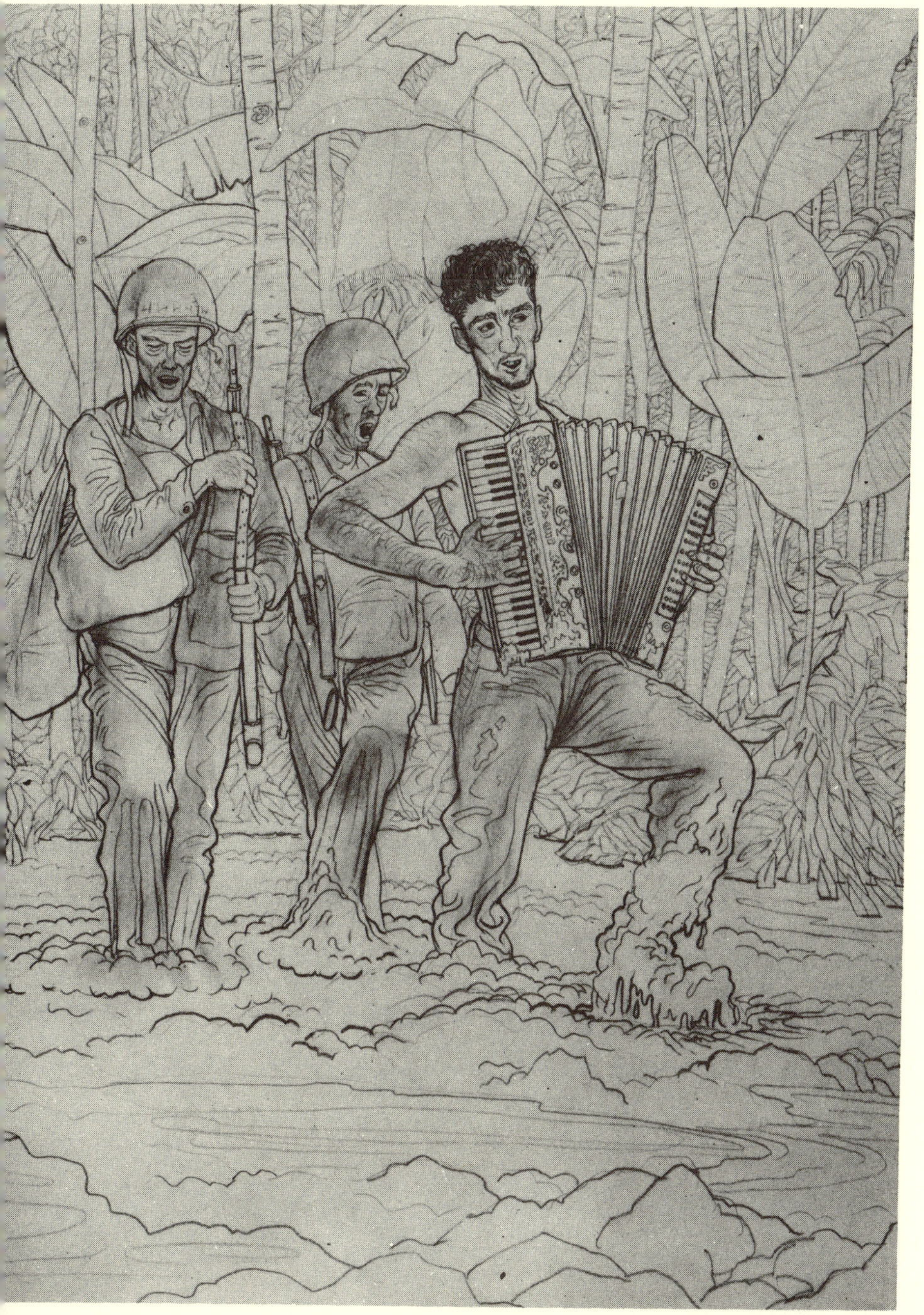

gotten what a real road looked like. But now they saw one—about 2000 yards farther on, immediately ahead of them where it crossed the tractor trail: a beautiful four-truck highway made out of coral with large, deep drainage ditches on both sides. They thought they must be dreaming. But they weren't. It was the lower part of an excellently constructed road over which the heavy equipment of a newly arrived Seabee Battalion was rolling on its way up to the new bomber-strip site. This new battalion was already clearing away the jungle.

And then they saw the sign. A large sign set up by the Seabees on heavy pipe to let everyone know what branch of the armed forces had fought this campaign—what branch had captured this terrain—what branch the road was named for. The sign read:

MARINE DRIVE HI-WAY

TO OUR VERY GOOD FRIENDS AND ABLE PROTECTORS THE FIGHTING MARINES WE DEDICATE THIS HI-WAY-MARINE DRIVE

BUILT BY 53RD N.C.B. 1ST M.A.C.

WE GRATEFULLY ACKNOWLEDGE THE HELP OF THE 75TH C.B.

BOUGAINVILLE, B.S.I.

Chapter 18

A THOUSAND YARDS farther on, the Battalion left the road and moved east to an assembly area near the First Battalion. They were heading toward rest, a bath, dry clothes, and some hot chow.

"That night was the most perfect night of our lives," Captain Scott relates. "Everyone was completely worn out. To lie down was the best feeling in the world.

"The chatter of the evening was about everybody. About Railsback, now called 'King of the 60-mm. mortars.' About Torian, protecting Bob Keith. About Gray, holding his machine-gun platoon together through the hell of the 90-mm. mortar incident. The L Company fight. The final defensive fight. About O'Neil and the dozens of things he did before they got him. About Peck's charging the ridge. About those unbelievable corpsmen. About all the private little deeds of heroism in the last week. About the incomparable Val, recommended for everything in the books. About Logan, who knocked out one machine-gun, was wounded, then went after another and was killed. About the innumerable incidents that tomorrow will be legends of the Marine Corps. It didn't rain at all that night. They didn't bomb us, either. Good for sacking."

Not only in the Third Battalion, but in every unit in the Regiment men were talking. In the First Battalion area some who had been with him were talking about Jim Feltman—Sergeant Jim, the cocky, loquacious extravert, popular with the officers, popular with the men. His feats ranged from being one of the best intelligence noncoms in the regiment to making C-ration coffee taste good. His features didn't reveal his part-Indian heritage, but his jungle attitude caused men, when describing him, to mention Jim Bowie or Davy Crockett.

On the morning of the 24th Feltman went up to the front line to man a light machine-gun with his friend Poweley, during the five-minute small-arms barrage. A fragment from one of the shells which the Japs were throwing in with great intensity tore through their shelter and wounded Poweley in the leg. Feltman administered first-aid while Poweley continued to man the gun. But when there were only a few minutes left, the anxious Jim hollered: "Here, Poweley, hold your own tourniquet. I want to get in a few more bursts before we're relieved." Feltman fired the rest of the belt, then carried Poweley back to the dressing station. And while the counterbarrage was still taking a heavy toll, he picked up a can of coffee he had left brewing on a home-made heater at the First Battalion C.P., walked calmly up the side of a hill dotted with moaning wounded, strolled into an open dug-out where two generals, three colonels, and a few lower-ranking officers were huddled together anxiously waiting for the Jap gunners to run out of shells, and remarked casually: "Thought somebody might like some coffee." Nor will it detract from the credit to be given to this courageous sergeant—who by this time is probably a first lieutenant and may wind up a major—to mention that there were other "Feltmans" equally brave, reckless, and efficient.

In the Second Battalion some of the men were laughing about Stinky Davis. While Davis was on his way to the Piva River to enjoy his first bath after twenty-five days in the jungle swamp, a husky replacement on his way to the front lines, heavily burdened with new equipment, unavoidably blocked Davis's path. Stinky shoved him out of the way. When the replacement protested, Stinky shoved him again.

"You keep that up and you'll get your friggin' head knocked off!" snapped the husky Marine.

Davis looked daggers at him and shoved again.

"O.K., Mac—you asked for it," said the replacement, laboriously extricating himself from his full pack harness.

Davis drew the toe of his boondocker through the mud. "Just cross that line, you eight-ball. Just cross that line," growled Stinky, drawing himself up to a fighting pose and looking more vicious than the "Wild Bull of the Pampas."

The husky replacement, ever anxious to oblige, walked quickly across the line, and was about to bring up a right uppercut from deep left field when Stinky burst into a broad grin, extended his right hand in a gracious gesture of long-lost friendship, and remarked, "Now you're on my side."

Every man had a story; every story was a good one; most of them will never be recorded. Some will be told softly in the privacy of one's favorite gin mill; some to a listening wife who has waited anxiously for that special moment in the dead of night, not for the plot, but just to hear the sound of her man's voice. Some stories will never be told. Time will smother the past in a wave of forgetfulness. Potent problems of the future will blot out the bitter, and the sweet will disappear in the urgency of a new objective. But the first night in a quiet sector, after days on the move, fighting off a jungle fever, plowing on, tapping that last reserve of energy so as not to let the skipper down, jungle discipline in the front lines at night, silence, alertness, patience, fighting as part of a fire team the next day, fighting with and for your buddies, fighting to keep alive. Day after day, night after night. Then the let-down. You've got to talk. It's got to come out.

And so men in little groups talk privately and frankly about their officers and about other men. Tomorrow, as far as the outside world is concerned, all would be forgotten. They'd keep it in the family. Fighting men belong to a very close family. A unique fraternity of practical idealists. Those on the outside who fight their wars vicariously through books and honest queries will learn only a part of this great world story. Those who bury their heads in the sand and try to escape the unpleasant, and those who refuse to help, won't learn much about the war. Nor will the selfish few who work the angles, scorn the idealist, avoid the unfortunate, snub the more honest; who burn their fingers in a frenzied effort to snatch up the torch of patriotism when danger is imminent, and then crawl back smugly into their sheltered castles to nurse their power complex; who closet themselves away from the annoyance created by the idealist who returns and humbles himself to ask not for the world with a fence around it, not for the world, but just for a broken-down picket. Those selfish few—and there are only a few— will learn nothing about the war, nothing about men, nothing about courage, nothing about tempered steel friendships. They'll keep right on knowing nothing about the exciting world upheaval through which they think they have been living. This group will be exposed to only a few of the stark realities. The vicarious strategist will voice an opinion and become a critic. The curious onlooker who saw the picture from a sheltered observation post will understand only the little that he is professionally equipped to understand. Only the man who is a member of that special fraternity which is always open for new members, yet remains a small distinctive organization, only the fighting man, though he may never tell—only he will know the truth.

The Second Battalion moved back into the front lines as soon as it reached the new Regimental sector. The First and Third Battalions spent two days in an assembly area. All the men in the Regiment were in bad physical shape, and practically all of them had filariasis. Many had not yet developed the symptoms; others had hidden their red streaks and swollen arms and legs and testicles for over two months . . . ever since the last island staging base. They had refused to turn in to the doctors for fear of losing the chance to prove themselves in battle. They dreaded the idea of having endured the many months of hard training and then of losing the chance to go into actual combat. They lied to their platoon leaders, waited patiently in actual pain for the day to shove off, then limped aboard the transports. Yet these same men had traversed the entire beachhead semicircle and had fought on both flanks and in the northeast sector of the perimeter. They had patrolled the jungle hunting out the Jap for twenty-six days, and returned each night to sleep in mud, to stand four-hour watches, to eat cold chow. Some had been evacuated; most of them had fought on through and were suffering now and would be carried out soon; some would be struck down later.

When the Third Marines were relieved after this last battle of the Piva Forks, 1107 dead Japs had been counted. The enemy's anchor on the Piva River, from which he could attack the beachhead, had been destroyed. His defensive position, which stood in the way of our advance to the northeast, had been eliminated. We had broken the back of a Regular Army Japanese regiment—had taken the high ground from which observation of the entire Empress Augusta Bay area had been established—and had advanced the Division's lines nearly 2000 yards. So stands the record of these Third Marines.

On the second day in the new sector the First Battalion was called upon to furnish a company patrol for a two-day scouting mission into enemy territory along the Torokina River. The Battalion sent a composite company of 150 men. Out of all who were left, approximately 400 in the battalion, this was all who were able to walk. All the rest were suffering from one or more of various tropical disorders: dysentery, jungle ulcers, malaria, and filariasis. The jungle swamp had won its battle, but too late for the Japs to break through the beachhead and prevent the Marines and Seabees from accomplishing their mission.

This last stop turned out to be a quiet sector. Replacements arrived to relieve the growing list of evacuations. Again the old routine of teaching these new men the jungle. They were trained in the front lines. When they were good enough, a few at a time, mixed in with the veterans, were taken on patrols. They learned fast. They had to. They were in a hot league and they felt it. They were proud. They were Marines.

The First and Third Battalions went back into the lines after their two-day respite. During this period the front line was again moved forward, and the Third Regiment garrisoned all the high ground in its sector between the Piva and the Torokina rivers. Large gaps of swamp made the supply problem an acute one, but again the amphibian tractors came to our rescue. The Regiment remained in this sector for the remainder of its stay on Bougainville. We returned to active patrolling, but no evidence could be discovered of an imminent Japanese attack. Nevertheless a permanent defense was set up in each company sector. It involved intricate fences of barbed wire, mine fields, and covered bunkers. A short time after the Regiment had established its final line, everyone was ready and waiting. If the Japs had attempted to breach that defense they would have been slaughtered.

When Father Kempker's lists had been completed, we learned for the first time the names of all the men who had been killed. There was one mistake. Here's how it happened.

Herbert L. Desimone had dropped this pack with his name on it soon after he hit the swamp after crossing the line of departure. Another man passing through the same area a short time later saw the pack, picked it up, and put it on his back. Later in the day the man was killed. When Father Kempker found the dead boy he was wearing no identification. The Father found the name on the pack. Herbert L. Desimone was recorded as killed in action. A friend of Desimone told him about it, and Desimone rushed down to Father Kempker.

"Father, my name is Desimone. Have you got me on the dead list?" asked the worried Marine.

The Father looked in his book. "That's right, Desimone. Dead and buried."

"Well—well—if it's all right with you, Father, knock it off."

The man who had been killed was finally identified and the mistake corrected.

Numerous events occurred to brighten up the scene while the Regiment remained in this sector. Twenty-one days after the start of construction of the fighter strip, a Marine fighter squadron landed on Cape Torokina. We boast with pride of the 75th Seabees. They had fed thousands of Marines in their galleys. They had never turned a Marine down. A helmet, a part for a rifle, a pair of shoes, or anything else they could give us—a good word, or a piece of equipment—was given voluntarily. We knew that this Seabee outfit had set some kind of record. But most of all they were our buddies, as are all Seabees and all Marines. The two units have an unshakable confidence in each other. A Marine will tell you, "The Seabees are winning the war." Ask the Seabees about Marines and the answer is apt to be: "Marines are the greatest fighters in the world." It's a great combination, and an encouraging sight to see these two branches of the service work together.

Before the last echelon of Marines had left the island, both the new bomber strip and the new fighter strip had been completed. Mighty discouraging for Mr. Tojo. Bougainville started to spell disaster for the Japs' powerful base at Rabaul. November 1st, our D-day, was the start. Subsequent landings on New Britain had further contributed. The Navy would soon ring this port with steel. Rabaul was doomed.

Another important event took place while we were still in this right flank sector. Details from each company were selected and gathered together to hear our former skipper and loyal friend, Brigadier General Speed Cauldwell, dedicate the picturesque Marine Cemetery and honor our buddies who had fallen. Buddies we must leave behind. It was a time of great reverence. But it was a time of great sadness, too. For the men of the Third had been through adversity together for over eighteen months. It would be hard to leave the brave, honorable men behind. We would never see them. We could never talk to them. We could never laugh together or fight by their side again. We could only honor them with thoughts of pride, and some day ask the world to listen to their saga. For these heroes were men of great character, unselfish men who gave their lives for their country, as many others had before and as many others will have to again. We had only one comfort: we would always love them. We of the Third can never forget them. And we will miss them . . . forever.

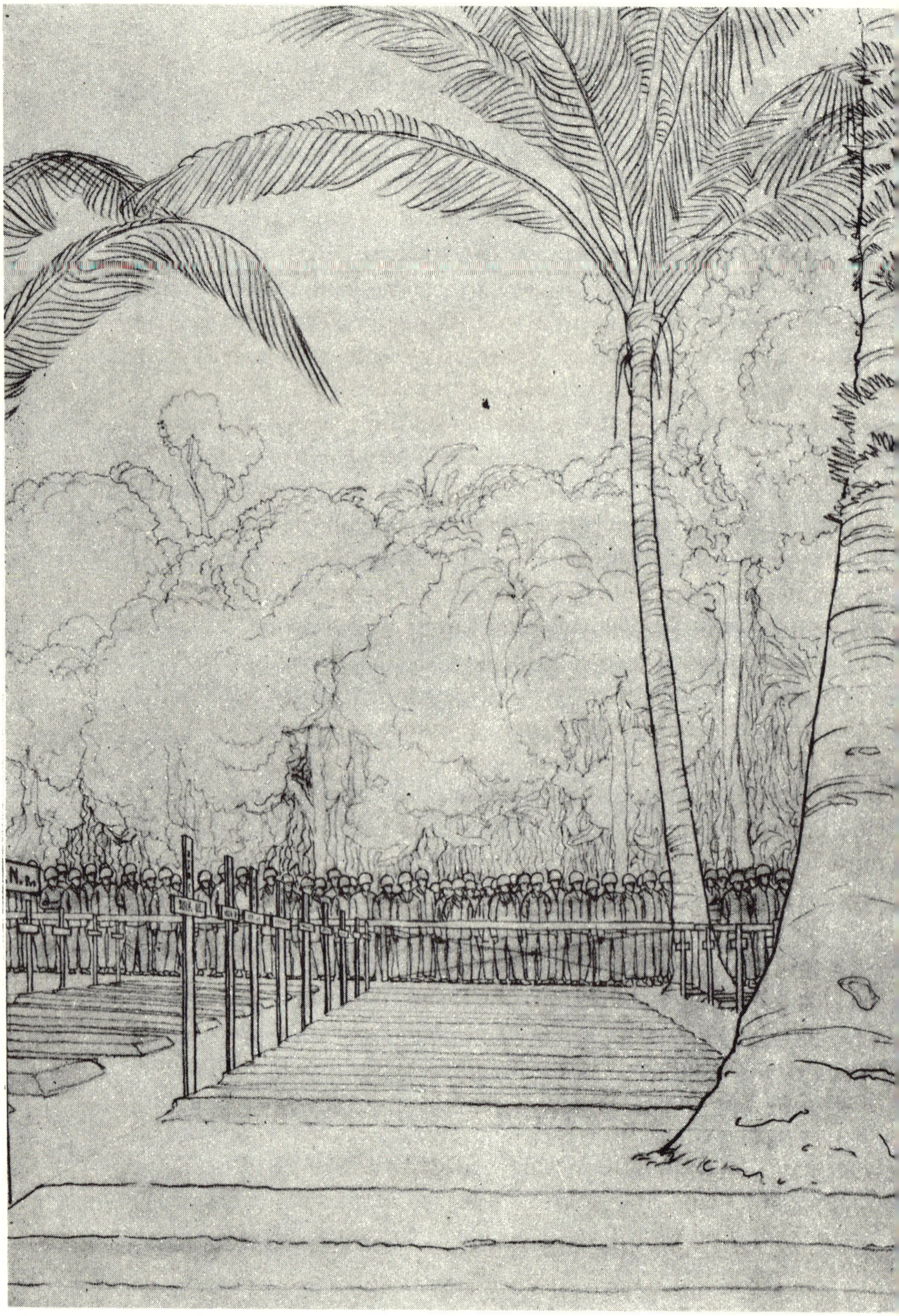

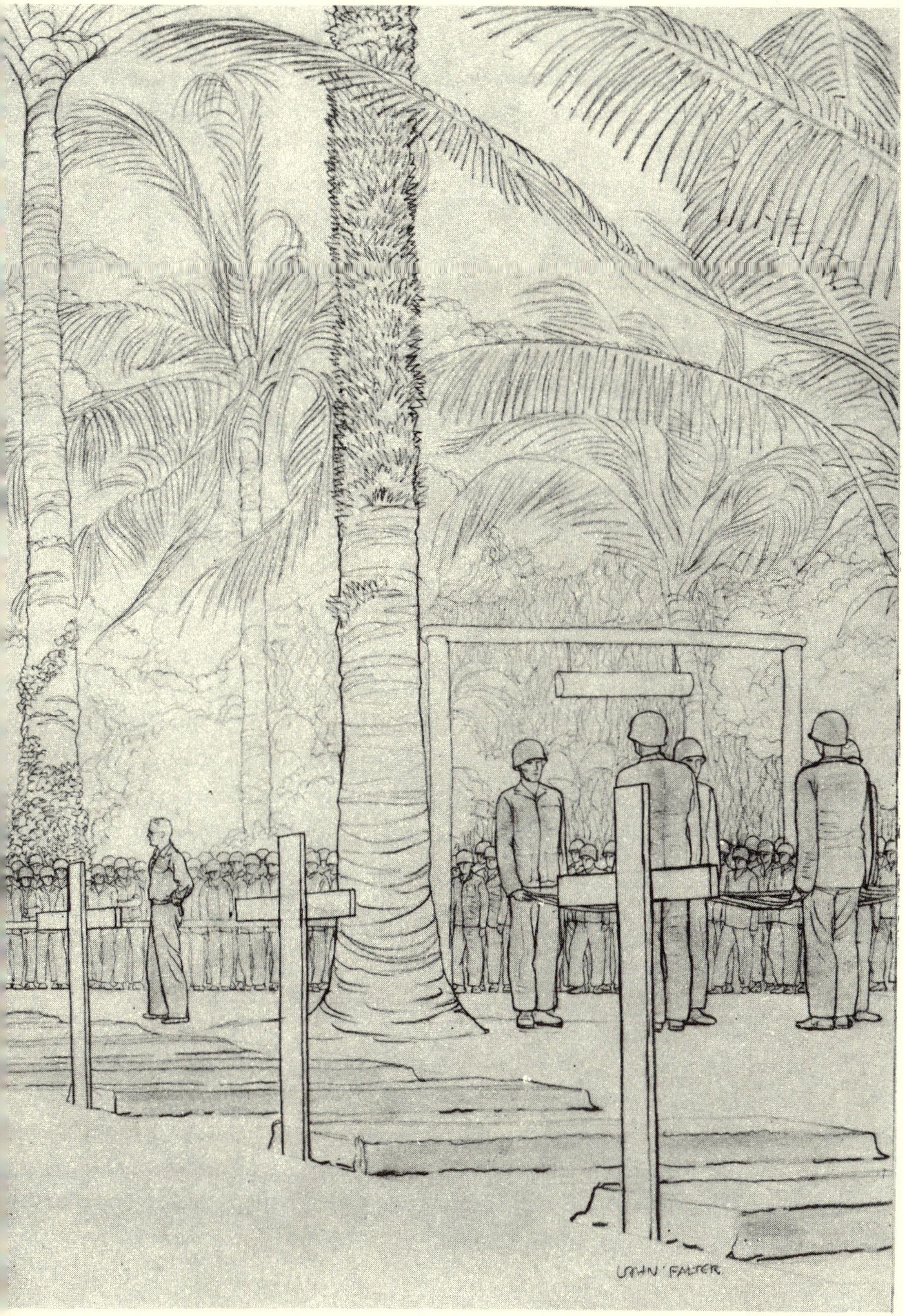
JOHN FALTER

The word was passed that we were soon to be relieved by the Raiders; and they would be relieved a short time later by the Army. We were to go back to the staging base which we had left, to rest, reorganize, and prepare for the next campaign. Christmas was approaching. Our packages were being held back at the base. It wouldn't be long now.

A week before we left, General Cauldwell was talking to one of the men. Speed likes to talk to the men.

"Well," laughed the General, "I guess everything has happened to us but an earthquake."

On the morning of December 24 the Third Marines were in another assembly area. It was a great day, the day that they were to hike back to the beach and embark on transports. They were leaving Bougainville. Back to the coconut grove, back to cots and tents and hand-made showers. Christmas packages waiting. Outdoor movies. Rest, better chow, more training. They were awakened just before dawn—awakened violently, for the ground shook as it had never shaken before; but there were no explosions. The men of the Third Marines were experiencing their first earthquake.

The men were lined up on the beach waiting for their turn at the landing boats which would take them out to the welcome transports. This was one sea voyage they were really going to enjoy. The wait gave them time to talk—about the campaign, about their buddies, about the best of all subjects: home. They were moving on, rest, then more rugged days ahead. But the drama would have to end some time. The curtain had to come down. Then they would be going home.

"I wonder if the people back in the States will really get the scoop," said one Marine.

"Hell, no. They won't," said another. "Wait till you try to get a job."

"I'll get a job."

"Maybe . . . if there's one to get."

"I don't know," said the more optimistic man. "They gotta make jobs. There's a lot of guys fighting this war."

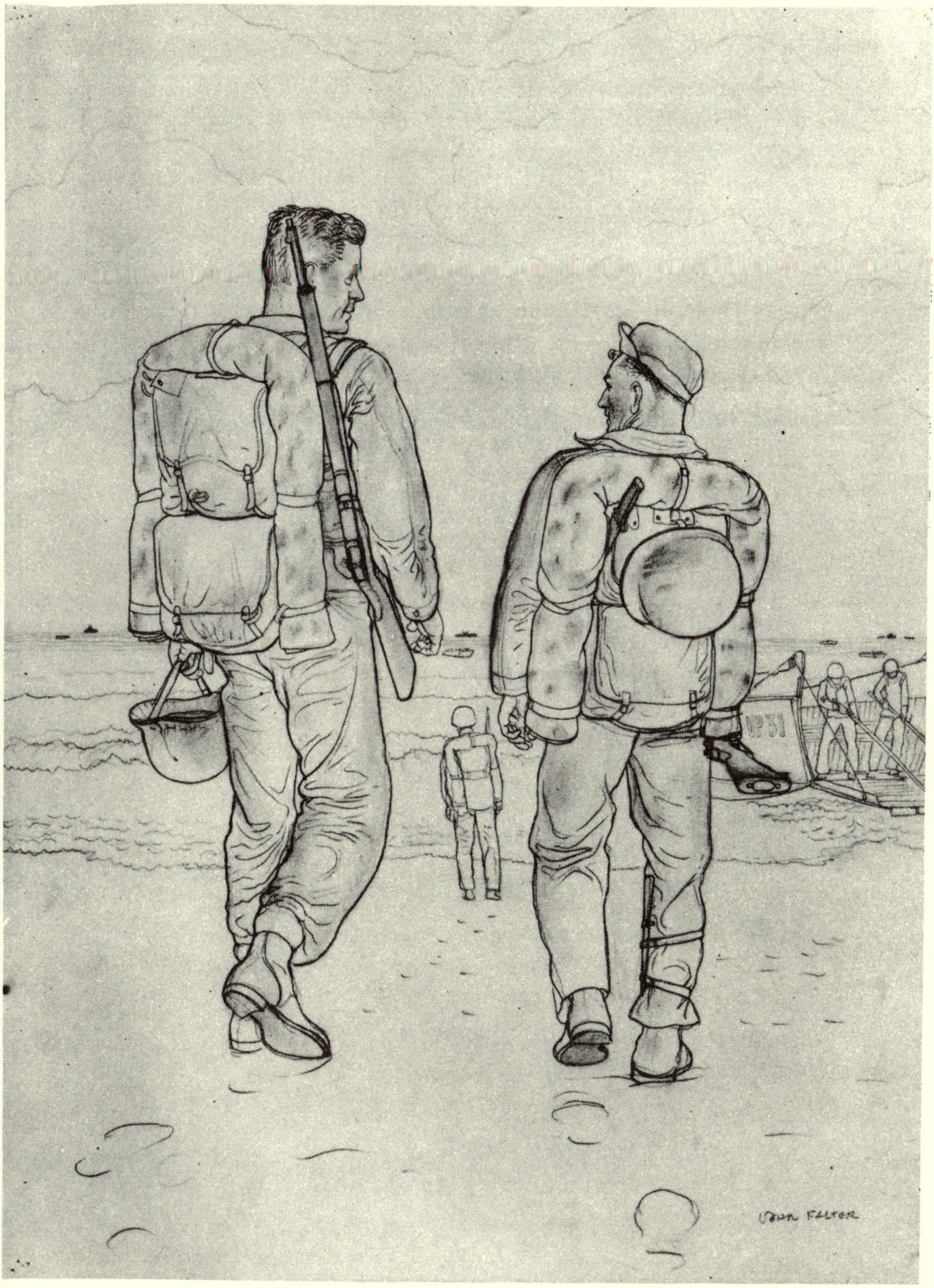
JOHN FALTER

"So what? As long as the guys back there are making money, do you think they're goin' to worry about the guys who did the fightin'?"

"This time I think so," said another Marine. "This time they're going to get hurt."

"Who?"

"Everybody. Everybody's got a brother or a kid or a fella in the war. This time I think they're goin' to appreciate what the fighting man's been through."

"Are you kiddin'?" asked the realist. "The other day I got a letter from my sister. There's a guy next door with two kids in the Army in Africa. Gas is short back in the States, but *he* can always get gas. Do you know where he gets it?"

"Where?"

"He knows the right people. From a bootlegger . . . black market."

"Tell me something, will ya?" asked the optimist. "Why do people do that?"

"Semper Fidelis, Mac . . . Semper Fidelis."

"Yeah . . . *Semper Fidelis!*"